# Reflective Practice for Elevating Higher Education

# HIGHER EDUCATION RESEARCH AND POLICY

VOL. 12



The *Higher Education Research and Policy* (HERP) series is intended to present both research-oriented studies of higher education systems in transition, especially for comparative international perspectives. Higher education systems worldwide are currently under multi-layered pressures to transform their funding and governance structures in rapidly changing environments. The series intends to explore the impact of such wider social and economic processes as globalization, internationalization and Europeanization on higher education institutions, and is focused on such issues as the changing relationships between the university and the state, the changing academic profession, changes in public funding and university governance, the emergent public/private dynamics in higher education, the consequences of educational expansion, education as public/private goods, and the impact of changing demographics on national systems. Its audience includes higher education researchers and higher education policy analysts, university managers and administrators, as well as national policymakers and the staff of international organizations involved in higher education policymaking.

Peter Mitchell and Saleh Al-Busaidi (eds.)

# Reflective Practice for Elevating Higher Education: Voices from Oman

PETER LANG
Berlin · Bruxelles · Chennai · Lausanne · New York · Oxford

**Bibliographic Information published by the Deutsche Nationalbibliothek**
The Deutsche Nationalbibliothek lists this publication in the Deutsche Nationalbibliografie; detailed bibliographic data is available online at http://dnb.d-nb.de.

**Library of Congress Cataloging-in-Publication Data**
Names: Mitchell, Peter J. (College teacher) editor | Al-Busaidi, Saleh editor
Title: Reflective practice for elevating higher education : voices from Oman / [edited by] Peter Mitchell, Saleh Al-Busaidi.
Description: Berlin ; New York : Peter Lang, [2026] |
Series: Higher education research and policy, 2193-7613 ; vol. 12 | Includes bibliographical references and index.
Identifiers: LCCN 2025032685 (print) | LCCN 2025032686 (ebook) | ISBN 9783631926413 hardback | ISBN 9783631926420 pdf | ISBN 9783631943106 epub
Subjects: LCSH: Education, Higher--Oman | Reflective teaching | Artificial intelligence--Educational applications--Oman | College teachers--Training of--Oman
Classification: LCC LA1434 .R44 2026 (print) | LCC LA1434 (ebook)
LC record available at https://lccn.loc.gov/2025032685
LC ebook record available at https://lccn.loc.gov/2025032686

This edited volume is based on papers presented at the Reflective Practice symposium hosted by Majan University College on February 5, 2024, sponsored by the Sultanate of Oman's Ministry of Higher Education, Research & Innovation and co-sponsored by the United Kingdom's Advance HE.

This edited volume is based on papers presented at the Reflective Practice symposium hosted by Majan University College on February 5, 2024, sponsored by the Sultanate of Oman's Ministry of Higher Education, Research & Innovation and co-sponsored by the United Kingdom's Advance HE.

ISSN 2193-7613
ISBN 978-3-631-92641-3 (Print)
ISBN 978-3-631-92642-0 (E-PDF)
ISBN 978-3-631-94310-6 (E-PUB)
DOI 10.3726/b23183


Published by Peter Lang GmbH, Berlin (Germany)

info@peterlang.com



This publication has been peer reviewed.

**www.peterlang.com**

# Table of Contents

# List of Figures

# List of Tables

# Foreword

*Her Excellency Prof. Rahma Al Mahrooqi*
Minister of Higher Education, Research & Innovation, Sultanate of Oman

I am inspired to write the foreword to this important edited volume because of the profound effect reflection has had on my personal, educational, academic, and professional life. At the personal level, reflection has helped me navigate my way through ambiguous situations. As a child, I grew up in the care of my grandmother who had lost her eyesight before I was born. I understood early on that she was unlike me or any other members of my family who had no visual impairment. As I grew older, I became the closest person to my grandmother, and because I was so attached to her, I wanted to help her see through my eyes, feel what I felt, and perceive the world with the same clarity with which I was able to perceive it. That is why I always had to reflect on our exchanges and communication to avoid ambiguity and to demystify what was unclear to her. When I accompanied her on family visits, I had to count every step of the stairs we had to descend or climb to protect her from missing one and falling. I would spend time thinking and reflecting on what could make things easy for her and what could make her happy. That incredible journey of reflection has given me much insight into individual differences and led me into introspective thinking, which became a mark of my character until I became an adult.

Reading has been another factor that instilled and ingrained reflection in me. I have always engaged in reflection while reading, after reading and between reading new books or articles. Reflection enables me to read between the lines, to understand themes, characters, and the motives driving them. It gives me insight into different cultures and different types of personalities. And when reading academic books, such as books on developmental psychology or psychological challenges, such as depression and personality disorders, reflection helps me understand vividly the personality types of the people I read about in literary pieces. Reflection helps me connect the dots and understand the complexity of relationships. This helped me mature and develop resilience in my own life, and it also shaped me as a young educator once I started teaching at Sultan Qaboos University soon after graduating. As a beginning teacher, and due to the small difference in age between me and my students, I could understand them well, but to explain English lessons to them, I had to ponder on how I could make the lessons crystal clear to them and how to make the classroom active and alive. Things did not always go the way I had planned for them because the dynamics of every classroom are different, and sometimes the same classroom of students is different from day to day. Reflection after delivering every lesson or when preparing for a new one demystified dilemmas for me and afforded me a stronger stance upon which I built new lessons. All of that helped me emerge as a confident and well-grounded educator.

As a professional who has served in various administrative positions, reflection was a lifesaver for me. Having assumed administrative roles very early on in my career, reflection was my way to piece things together, to present ideas in a convincing manner to the group of professionals I worked with, most of whom were much older than me. Coupled with hard work, reflection made me well prepared to negotiate new ideas, innovative projects, and unconventional solutions to existing challenges with the senior administration of the university, often achieving excellent results.

When my journey as a researcher started, I found reflection an important tool to build connection between new knowledge and my background knowledge and to cultivate my schemata on various research topics. Because I was interested in a wide array of research topics, spanning from brain research and how we, as people, master language, reading and writing; to language as a communicative medium; to linguistics, applied linguistics and sociolinguistics; and to language arts and literature; reflection was a very important tool enabling me to create links between the disciplines to demonstrate their connection and to give depth to any analysis I did when engaging in writing. Here, the reservoir of background knowledge I gained from reading was a true aid for me.

My life experience, love for reading, my engagement in research and my varied professional experience have shaped and been shaped by reflection. Reflection is indeed a powerful tool from which insight, wisdom and the ability to influence others in positive and impactful ways can emerge. It can help educators form and re-form student experience, improve curricula, rethink assessment, and reimagine classroom environments. Through reflection, the educator, researcher and professional can gain self-worth and confidence and fulfill her/his duty in the best way possible. This edited volume showcases valuable insights from leaders, educators and researchers in the Sultanate of Oman's vibrant higher education community for whom reflective practice is both a foundation and a means for continuous enhancement of educational provision. As such, I hope that educators around the world will find inspiration in it as we seek to share experiences and elevate our practices collaboratively.

# Editors' Introduction

*Peter Mitchell and Saleh Al-Busaidi*

We are witnesses to perhaps the fastest changing environment in the history of higher education, where policy and technology are in a constant state of flux. It is no surprise, then, that the temptation to pause and reflect is overshadowed by mountainous workloads and a sense that we in the academy need to respond instantaneously to new trends or risk being left behind in what is unarguably an extremely competitive market.

The Sultanate of Oman is home to a relatively young higher education sector, albeit significantly influenced by the quite older Anglo-American higher education tradition. The founding of Sultan Qaboos University, Oman's first higher education institution, in 1986 marked the birth of higher education in the Sultanate. The year 1995 saw the establishment of Majan University College as Oman's first private higher education institution. Only three decades hence, Oman now has around 30 public and private higher education institutions with new degree programs being approved every year. There is, indeed, much to reflect on.

The idea for this edited volume emerged from the Reflective Practice symposium held at Majan University College on February 5, 2024, under the patronage of Her Excellency Prof. Rahma bint Ibrahim Al Mahrooqi, Oman's visionary Minister of Higher Education, Research & Innovation. We are indebted to Her Excellency for gracing this publication with her Foreword.

This publication brings together scholars from across Oman, both Omani and expatriates, whose diverse perspectives on reflective practice is grounded in a common context and with the united aim of further elevating higher education in the Sultanate. There are ten chapters contributed by fourteen authors. These comprise four senior academic leaders, two administrators and seven academics ranging from senior lecturer to senior professor, representing five Omani higher education institutions, and one policymaker from the Sultanate of Oman's Ministry of Education.

We make no pretensions to universal applicability, though we do believe that our experiences may be of interest to a worldwide audience facing many of the same issues in our global higher education community. We hope that the various case studies and approaches shared here will contribute to professional development and pedagogy in tertiary education.

The first part of the book sets the scene by exploring the concept of reflective practice through the lens of teacher education.

In the first chapter, *Reflections on Reflective Practice for Teacher Education*, Peter Mitchell examines, based on an extensive literature review, how reflection can be operationalised and the ways in which reflective practice can be enhanced to scaffold teachers' development as reflective practitioners.

Sharifa S. Al-Rawahi and Sulaiman M. Al-Balushi, in the second chapter, *Reflective Practices in the InTASC Standards*, probes the reflective practices emphasized in the Interstate Teacher Assessment and Support Consortium (InTASC) standards, widely utilized by teacher education programs worldwide, including Sultan Qaboos University. The chapter explores such themes as the concept of reflection, its significance, practical application, integration into teaching, and assessment methods.

The third chapter, *Reflective Teaching Practices of Omani Pre-service Teachers: The Status-quo and Enhancement Mechanisms* by Mohamed Abdelraouf Attia Elsayed, reports on a study that aims to identify the level to which pre-service teachers at Sultan Qaboos University use reflective teaching practices (RTPs), and if the level of these RTPs differ according to the variable of their academic major. The study proposes some mechanisms to enhance RTPs for pre-service teachers.

The second part of the volume delves into reflective practice for continuing professional development and quality assurance from the perspectives of academic staff, higher education management, and administrators.

Chapter four, *Reshaping Teacher Beliefs*, by Brian Poole, is based on data collected from lecturers at an Omani higher education institution during teaching-related staff development sessions over a 4-year period, which are used to illustrate and discuss how beliefs about what constitutes effective teaching can be influenced and shaped by professional development initiatives.

Sulaiman Al Hasani, in the fifth chapter, *Observation of Teaching and Reflective Practices for Sustainable Enhancement of Teaching Quality in Higher Education*, addresses teaching observation practices, emphasizing their developmental and reflective nature, and examines their methodologies, objectives, and impact on professional growth and the quality of education, sharing best practices and discussing policy frameworks and forms of infrastructure essential to support teaching observations.

In the sixth chapter, *A Reflective Journey to Professional Development: Advance HE Fellowship Experience*, Mohammed Siddique shares his personal reflection on professional development as a senior administrator in an Omani higher education institution. The chapter explores his experience of self-reflection as part of the process of applying for Senior Fellowship of the UK's Advance HE.

The third part of the book addresses reflective practice in the context of new challenges and opportunities connected with Artificial Intelligence.

Chapter seven, *Human Minds, AI Hands: Reflections on Using AI in Academic Research*, by Mohamed Salah El Din, provides a reflection on the ethical and responsible use of Generative AI in enhancing the quality and productivity of academic research. The chapter sheds light on the focal areas where AI could be harnessed as a valuable tool in academic research, providing practical examples from international as well as personal experiences, and promotes greater comprehension of AI's capabilities and constraints as a research assistant by encouraging academics to reflect on their use of this transformative technology.

Shams Salim Al Zakwani, in the eighth chapter, *The Impact of a Reflective Professional Development Program on Omani Teachers' Utilisation and Attitude Towards Artificial Intelligence Tools*, reports on an empirical study that aims to design, develop, and implement a professional development program for teachers on AI tools for education, and also seeks to determine the program's impact on participant teachers' utilization and attitudes towards AI tools.

The fourth part of the volume focuses on student support, grounded in the context of English Language Teaching.

In the ninth chapter, *Integrating Technology in English Language Teaching: Challenges and Opportunities*, Ahmed Al Rahbi, Iman Al-Khalidi, Salwa Al Anqoodi and Iman Al Hajri share their reflections on how technology can enhance student academic support through the example of English language teaching at an Omani university.

In the tenth and final chapter, *Enhancing L2 Learners' Awareness of Teacher's Corrective Feedback in Language Classrooms through Reflective Journal Writing*, Ehsan Rassaei examines how reflective journal writing can enhance English as a Foreign Language learners' perceptions of an implicit form of Corrective

Feedback known as recasts. His study, conducted at an Omani university college, captures the impact that student reflection can have on learning.

Finally, we are grateful to Peter De Costa for contributing the Afterword, in which he masterfully sums up our scholars' collective efforts with the objective eye of an external observer.

Our ultimate hope is that, in sharing diverse examples of reflective practice, readers may perceive opportunities to enhance their own practice and elevate their particular contexts. This book may prove useful as a resource for educators and students, academics and administrators, and researchers and policymakers, in Oman, the Middle East, and the wider world.

PART I

# Reflective Practice Through the Lens of Teacher Education

# Reflections on Reflective Practice for Teacher Education

*Peter Mitchell*

**ABSTRACT**
There is no universally accepted understanding of what reflective practice is or can be. This chapter attempts to answer questions as to why we reflect, what we reflect on, and how we can reflect for the purposes of teacher education. The chapter reviews relevant literature and explores how reflection can be operationalised and the ways in which reflective practice can be enhanced to scaffold teachers' development as reflective practitioners. The author advocates grounding reflection in teachers' own experience; examining the relationship between teachers' beliefs, knowledge and actions; and ensuring a holistic approach to reflection, i.e. reflection for action, reflection in action, and reflection on action.

## Introduction

Reflection forms an integral part of teacher education, where novice teachers are expected to self-evaluate their lesson plans and lessons conducted, under the guidance of a mentor. This reflection typically concentrates on the extent to which aims – dictated via a 'prescriptive' prism – were achieved. Such a limited idea of reflection inevitably leads to 'tunnel vision' in an early-career teacher's concept of what self-evaluation can be. This is amplified by the dearth of professional development opportunities available to support teachers' reflection, in contrast to myriad courses on, for instance, methods and technology. This is a situation that the author is currently seeking to change in his capacity as Chair of the Professional Development Committee at Majan University College, a medium-sized higher education institution in Oman. This reflection comes from a literature review conducted by the author for a master's dissertation in teacher education at the University of Oxford (Mitchell, 2023).

Teachers in any subject specialism face common problems at the beginning of their careers as they navigate the chasm that can exist between 'theoretical' lesson planning and 'practical' classroom teaching. At the turn of the century, Freeman (2001) commented on the irony that teacher education in English Language Teaching (ELT), for instance, "has concerned itself little with how individuals actually learn to teach" (p. 73). More recently, Farrell (2022, p. 8) maintains the criticism that many ELT "teacher education programs focus their course content heavily on theory (such as second language acquisition theory or linguistic theory)" as opposed to real-life classroom practice. This assertion is supported by empirical research (e.g., Faez & Valeo, 2012; Macknish et al., 2017). Faez and Valeo (2012) and Freeman (2016) advocate for a redesign of teacher education courses to align them more closely with the needs of practising teachers. It follows that this requires awareness of what those needs are (Farrell, 2022). Teacher educators must be able to identify the skills needed by novice teachers (Tarone, 2007) and novice teachers themselves must be given opportunities to share their opinions and experiences (Gándara et al., 2005).

In many national contexts, and Oman is no exception, an absence of contact between initial teacher education (ITE) providers and their graduates means that early-career teachers' needs are often overlooked (see Baecher, 2012). For early-career teachers, the lack of post-ITE support also concerns provision for professional development. This is illustrated by Higginbotham's (2019) survey of 115 beginning ELT teachers' experiences in 25 countries, where approximately half of the teachers felt that their ITE insufficiently prepared them for their first teaching jobs and over 50% reported receiving insufficient support in their first teaching posts. A common theme arising from the survey was a lack of opportunities for continuing professional development (CPD). There is evidence that this is causing some early-career EFL teachers to leave the profession (Laats, 2020), but more in-depth and larger-scale investigation is required. Nevertheless, the desirability for provision of support for early-career teachers is perhaps axiomatic. We shall now turn to a deeper examination of the issues faced by early-career teachers in their professional practice.

## Issues in Practice

Entering the classroom can be a daunting prospect for any teacher, let alone a teacher with limited experience. A typical problem for early-career teachers is over-reliance on pre-existing teaching materials and similar resources when planning and teaching lessons (Lee & Bathmaker, 2007; Atkinson, 2021). Even in the 21st century, textbooks are still perhaps the most obvious resource on which teachers rely, as they are perceived to be authoritative, composed by experts and endorsed by major publishers (Cortazzi & Jin, 1999).

Baker (2015) writes of a need to move away from 'prescriptive approaches to teaching' (p. 244). This requires reflection on the part of the teacher since teaching materials, for example, cannot take account of the local contexts in which they are used and so "a teacher's responsibility goes beyond that of the textbook's author, as only the teacher can mediate between the text and the specific culture within the classroom" (Alptekin, 1993). The crucial role of the teacher in ensuring that materials are accessible to learners is supported by empirical research (see Douidi, 2021). Teacher knowledge relating to the use of methods and materials can be insufficient among beginning teachers. Teaching materials are too often created for generic users and can be ill-fitted to local realities (Gimenez et al., 2015; Nguyen, 2021). It follows that pedagogical decisions about the use of materials must be based on teachers' understanding of their learners and the relevance of the materials to their context (Ellis, 2008). As Lee and Bathmaker (2007) point out, it is the teacher and not the materials that should determine the pedagogical approach to be used in the classroom. This necessitates a consideration of teacher beliefs and, subsequently, teacher knowledge in greater detail.

## Teacher Beliefs

All teachers hold beliefs about education, although they might differ with regard to the terms they use (Pajares, 1992). There is, however, no consensus on a definition of teacher beliefs in spite of, or perhaps owing to, the not inconsiderable body of literature on the topic. The problem of a definition is compounded since beliefs cannot be directly observed or measured (Pajares, 1992), but can only be inferred (Rokeach, 1968), for example, from what teachers say and do. The utility of understanding teachers' beliefs is illustrated by Ernest's (1989) study of teachers' knowledge; it was found that teachers with similar knowledge may teach in different ways and, therefore, understanding teachers' beliefs would be more useful to make sense of their classroom practice.

It is, however, no easy task to neatly separate beliefs and knowledge (see Pajares, 1992, p. 309) and some researchers argue against attempting to distinguish between them (e.g., Beswick, 2012). Nespor (1987) considers beliefs to have stronger affective and evaluative components than knowledge and emphasises their crucial role in that "the contexts and environments within which teachers work, and many of the problems they encounter, are ill-defined and deeply entangled, and that beliefs are peculiarly suited for making sense of such contexts" (p. 324). In Pajares' (1992, 1993) surveys of the literature on teacher beliefs, she notes the variety of terms used in defining beliefs and attempts to identify commonalities. Pajares (1993) provides a definition of pre-service teacher's beliefs that the author has previously adapted to refer to in-service teachers' beliefs as "the attitudes and values about teaching, students, and the education process that teachers bring to their classrooms – attitudes and values that can be inferred by teacher educators not only from what teachers say but from what they do" (see Mitchell, 2023, adapted from Pajares, 1993, p. 46).

Calderhead (1996) notes that much of the research on classroom interaction and teachers' thinking focuses on the managerial aspects of teaching such as classroom organisation and lesson planning. This is a problem because of the "central role played by [student teachers'] pre-existing beliefs/images and prior experience in filtering the content of education course work" (Kagan, 1992, p. 140). It is therefore advisable to address teachers' prior beliefs in the course of teacher education programmes (Joram & Gabriele, 1998). Some research indicates that teachers' pre-existing beliefs are inflexible (Zuzovsky, 1995), although Kagan's (1992) review of the teacher education literature, examining 27 empirical studies, indicates that this could be due to teacher education programmes being ill-designed to tackle issues of teacher beliefs.

Empirical research in diverse contexts (e.g., Cabaroglu & Roberts, 2000; Stuart & Thurlow, 2000; Long & Stuart, 2004; Lü & Lavadenz, 2014) throws further doubt on claims about the inflexibility of teacher beliefs. For example, Cabaroglu and Roberts (2000) found that the beliefs of 19 out of 20 student teachers developed during a reflective teacher education programme, with only one teacher's beliefs being 'inflexible'. Research by Stuart and Thurlow (2000) and by Long and Stuart (2004) lends support to the transformative capacity of higher reflection on teacher beliefs in the course of teacher education programmes, although the latter investigation focused on three participants from an initial sample of 26, who were selected for their "high levels of reflection and notable change in their beliefs about teaching and learning" (p. 278) over a 13-week period. Moreover, the results of a planned three-year longitudinal study of the initial 26 participants (see Stuart & Thurlow, 2000, p. 120) remain unpublished, so any lasting impact on professional practice is questionable. Mattheoudakis (2007), in her longitudinal study of EFL teachers on a 3-year ITE programme, observed changes in teacher beliefs, but failed to identify how precisely courses/teacher educators impacted on these changes. It is also important to note that teacher education programmes in ELT can vary in length and depth from introductory/refresher courses lasting a few hours, to 4-week intensive ITE courses, to bachelor's and master's degrees (Farrell, 2022), which presumably have inherently differing influences on teachers' beliefs. This underscores the need to explore further the interaction between teacher beliefs and classroom practice in teacher education programmes.

Teachers' beliefs are operationalised – or not – in the classroom. It follows that their beliefs about learning and teaching might be inferred from their classroom practice and generally fall into two categories. The first relates to a more traditional, teacher-centred, knowledge-transmission approach where the learners' role is passive and involves remembering transmitted information. The second category is more constructivist and student-centred, with the teacher's role seen as guiding the learners to actively generate knowledge. As previously discussed, however, whatever a teacher's espoused belief, questions remain as to whether this belief is actually manifested in practice. Borg (2003) doubts whether teacher cognition can be meaningfully studied without reference to classroom practice since what actually matters is "understanding teachers' professional actions rather than what or how they think in isolation of what they do" (p. 105).

Discrepancies often exist between teacher beliefs and classroom practice. Fang's (1996) review of research on language teachers' beliefs indicates that many teachers' actual teaching is inconsistent with their espoused beliefs. It seems that teachers' prior learning experiences – when they were learners themselves – play a formative role in influencing future professional practice. Nagatomo (2012), in a small-scale study of Japanese university EFL teachers, observed that while the teachers did not always teach in the same way as they were taught, their prior learning experiences, as represented in their beliefs and knowledge about language learning and teaching, impacted considerably on their classroom practice. Moodie's (2016) findings lend support to this finding in that early-career teachers' negative prior experiences as learners were found to have influenced their beliefs and practices in terms of how *not* to teach.

Teachers whose espoused beliefs align with the literature that validates a communicative approach do not necessarily exhibit practice consistent with these beliefs. For example, a large-scale study of 60 language teachers at eight US universities revealed a mismatch between their stated beliefs, which were consistent with the literature, and their classroom practice (Emerick, 2019). The influence of external factors, too, cannot be ignored (Coombe & Burridge, 2020). For example, teachers who claimed to believe in an intercultural approach, did not employ it in the classroom owing to "(a perceived but untested) lack of learner interest, a lack of curricular support, a lack of suitable textbook material, a lack of ICC [intercultural communicative competence] testing, and concern about engaging with controversy" (Johnstone Young & Sachdev, 2011, p. 95). Additional factors such as class size, learner motivation and resistance to experimentation with new approaches, rigid curriculum, pressure to conform, and heavy workload, can all lead teachers to adopt a more teacher-centred approach, as demonstrated by Richards and Pennington (1998). In a review of 17 studies, Basturkmen (2012) identified context and constraints, such as curriculum requirements and time allotted, as mediating the relationship between teachers' beliefs and practices. Finally, even if a teacher is amenable to experimentation, pragmatism can lead them to quickly to abandon a technique if they do not perceive it as working (Carter & Doyle, 1995; Sercu et al., 2005, p. 164). Having explored teacher beliefs, we shall consider teacher knowledge as it is their combination that directs teacher activity.

## Teacher Knowledge

Much has been written about the knowledge that teachers need in their professional activity, yet there is still no consensus on what teacher knowledge means (OECD, 2019). Seminal works by Shulman (1986, 1987) have proven influential in establishing complementary categories of teacher knowledge, namely: content knowledge (also known as 'subject matter knowledge' or 'SMK'; general pedagogical knowledge; curriculum knowledge; pedagogical content knowledge (PCK); knowledge of learners and their characteristics; knowledge of educational contexts; and knowledge of educational ends, purposes, and values. It could be argued that SMK is fundamental in teaching, but it is insufficient for teaching effectively (Childs & McNicholl, 2015) since SMK is essentially foundational in nature (OECD, 2019). Rather, a teacher operationalises PCK together with SMK in order to enhance the effectiveness of teaching and learning. Furthermore, development of SMK seems to be most effective in combination with PCK (Mikeska et al., 2017). Additionally, teachers' knowledge of their context plays a significant role in the teaching and learning process through its influence on how teachers articulate and define learners' needs (Sharkey, 2004).

Depending on the context, the extent of any teacher's autonomy might differ widely and will inevitably impact on their approach to planning and teaching lessons. It follows that this, too, will affect their processes of reflection in terms of what they can realistically do in the course of their work and whether it meets the expectations upon them. This might depend on the national context, for example, culture (Lü & Lavadenz, 2014; Le Gal, 2018; Nguyen et al., 2021) or the classroom context where SMK and PCK interact to influence the planning and teaching of lessons (Emerick, 2019; Chan, 2021; Lou, 2021).

Shulman (1986) defines PCK as consisting of "the ways of representing and formulating the subject which make it comprehensible to others (...) includ[ing] an understanding of what makes the learning of specific topics easy or difficult" (p. 9). Shulman (1986) identifies the two main components of PCK, as comprising the most useful forms of representing topics (e.g., grammatical constructions such as use of the present perfect tense) and a teacher's understanding of what students find easy or difficult in learning a particular topic. As already mentioned, teachers' pedagogical approaches to planning and teaching lessons are influenced by PCK and SMK together.

The significant influence of teachers' SMK on their pedagogical approaches is noted in the literature (see, for example, Loewenberg Ball et al., 2008). As with teacher beliefs, gaining insight into the knowledge that teachers possess is inherently somewhat problematic. The literature suggests that since teacher knowledge is operationalised in professional practice (i.e., the teacher's actions), analysis of one may allow inferences to be made about the other (Ben-Peretz, 2011; Rowland, 2013).

Teacher educators need to be well aware of the knowledge needed by teachers. This not only involves the mentor's understanding of the context in which the mentee operates (Sharkey, 2004), but also the teacher educator making explicit the knowledge required by teachers (Crowe & Berry, 2007).

## Teacher Education

Guiding principles that teacher educators could employ in teacher education have been developed in recent decades – see, for instance, the influential works by Loughran (2005), Korthagen et al. (2006) and Crowe and Berry (2007). A common thread is the aim of "broaden[ing] the knowledge, skills and perspectives" of beginning teachers (Burn et al., 2022, p. 442). Korthagen et al. (2006) conducted a meta-analysis of teacher education programmes from which they developed principles focusing on reflective practice based on learning from experience. For the purposes of exploring reflective practice, certain principles are especially relevant.

The principle that knowledge is a subject to be created rather than a created subject is promoted by Korthagen et al. (2006), who espouse the idea that teacher educators should "actively create situations that elicit the wish for self-directed theory building in their students" (p. 1027). This tallies well with the idea of reflection (see, inter alia, Cabaroglu and Roberts, 2000, Van-Velzen, 2013, and Mulryan-Kyne, 2021), which is explored in greater detail below.

Additionally, Korthagen et al. (2006) advocate the principle that learning about teaching requires a shift in focus from the curriculum to the student. Segall (2002) notes that this can be supported by enabling student teachers to experience the construction and deconstruction of teaching practice. Moreover, mentors can create opportunities for novice teachers to "articulate and explore… different learner perspectives" (Crowe & Berry, 2007, p. 37).

The value of explicit discussion of pedagogical thought-processes is noted widely in the literature – see, for instance, Loughran (2005), Crowe and Berry (2007). Barnes (1998) relates how novice teachers can reframe their view of teaching via talking about their thought-processes. There are also benefits to novice teachers "gaining access to the thoughts of experienced teachers as they engage in the process of thinking like a teacher" (Crowe & Berry, 2007, p. 38), which can involve "thinking aloud" to make the pedagogical process more accessible (Loughran, 2005, p. 49).

An important factor in the effectiveness of teacher education is the quality of the relationship between the teacher educator and mentee where mutual understanding of needs and concerns is vital (Loughran, 2005). One aspect of this is the utility of scaffolding by teacher educators in supporting mentees through asking questions that guide them on *what* things to think about and *how* to think about them (Crowe & Berry, 2007, p. 39, italics in original).

Another aspect is the trust that needs to be established whereby both parties understand that challenges are not personal attacks, but "a genuine search for clarification and the development of understanding aimed at enhancing learning" (Loughran, 2005, p. 88). Discussing the mentoring of student teachers, Wang and Odell (2002) identify three important aspects as being the provision of social emotional support and development of self-esteem, the sharing of practical knowledge, and the performance of practical inquiries. Mentoring early-career teachers has long been considered to play an important role in professional development (Furlong & Maynard, 1995; Loughran, 2010; Van Velzen & Timmermans, 2014). In such a context, teacher educators can act as "reflective colleagues" for early-career teachers as they are socialised into a new community of practice (Lave & Wenger, 1991). Empirically, reflective practice and critical interaction with a mentor has generated positive results for early-career teachers (Hopper & Snyder, 2017).

## Reflection in Teacher Education

The literature on reflection in teacher education has been heavily influenced by seminal works on teacher reflection – Dewey (1920, 1933) and Schön (1983, 1987). Farrell (2022) laments the insufficient attention often paid to reflection in teacher education programmes. Yalcin Arslan's (2019) longitudinal study of four pre-service teachers found that their reflection became less superficial over the course of their teacher education, but did not investigate the precise ways in which the teachers were supported in becoming more reflective practitioners as per Schön (1987). Research indicates that development of reflective practice is more effective when teacher educators ensure that reflection is not hidden, but rather made explicit to mentees (Loughran, 2005). Opportunities for reflection can be provided in different ways such as via collaborative lesson planning (see Mutton et al., 2011) and post-lesson discussions (see Van Velzen, 2013). Where support for developing teachers' reflective skills is provided, a positive influence has been identified (Körkkö et al., 2016). Additionally, whereas a theory-into-practice or deductive approach to teacher education might make more sense in ITE because teachers' classroom experience is more limited, for early-career teachers a practice-into-theory or inductive approach allows the teachers to explore theory through the lens of their classroom experience (Farrell, 2022).

As detailed above, it is crucial for teacher educators to give due consideration to how their mentees reflect (see Loughran, 2005). Without guidance, early-career teachers can embark upon what Dewey called "blind experimentation" (1933, p. vii) as opposed to becoming "students of teaching" (Dewey, 1920, p. viii) through engaging in reflection. As Cirocki et al. (2019, p. 2) point out, "Teacher learning is an ongoing, reflective and constructive process… and continues in and outside the classroom throughout teachers' careers." It is not always clear, however, how reflection can be achieved – see, for example, Farrell's (2022) extensive exploration of reflection in ELT. Yost (2006) notes that early-career teachers require reflective tools for coping with challenges in order to become successful. Importantly, structured reflective opportunities in supportive environment can enable teachers' professional growth (Howe, 2006). Reflection is "operationalized by encouraging learner teachers to reflect on their *philosophy, principles, theory, and practice*, and *beyond practice*" (Farrell, 2022, p. 13, italics in original). Reflection, therefore, might start with teacher beliefs.

Kagan (1992) and Richards (1998) comment on teachers' prior beliefs serving as a filter through which novice teachers interpret the content of teacher education programmes and the new content is often used by the teachers to reinforce rather than challenge their prior beliefs (Kagan, 1992). This can lead to a clash in that any new content "will have to compete with, replace or otherwise modify the folk theories that already guide" both teacher educators and their mentees (Joram & Gabriele, 1998, p. 176). It is worth noting, however, that the issue is not necessarily that prior beliefs are "inherently wrong but [that] they are tacit", which "imprisons the teacher in a single frame of reference, which may be inappropriate" to a given context (Roberts, 2016, p. 67). It follows that teacher educators should seek "to free [mentees] from tacit images of teaching" (Roberts, 2016, p. 70). As Farrell (2022) discusses, "teacher educators can encourage their [mentees] to articulate their tacitly held prior experiences/beliefs… by making their prior beliefs more explicit, [mentees] can raise critically reflective questions so that they can discover whatever dogma, if any, may underlie such beliefs" (p. 23).

Farrell (2022) emphasises the importance of developing awareness of "what we actually do when we teach (as opposed to what we *think* we do)" (p. 34, italics in original) in order to reduce the discrepancy between "what we do and what we think we do" (Knezedivc, 2001, p. 10). Dewey (1933) viewed reflection as an ends-based model initiated by a problem in practice, or what Farrell (2022) calls "reflection-*on*-action" (p. 36, italics in original). Schön (1983) considered the question of what teachers do when problems arise and they need to react spontaneously, which can be called "reflection-*in*-action [which] also eventually leads to retrospective reflection-*on*-action moments as the practitioner considers the meaning in a distancing after the event" (Farrell, 2022, p. 37, italics in original).

In teacher education programmes, a shift is needed away from reflection as a reductive post-observation examination of what problems occurred in the classroom and how things could have been done differently (Akbari, 2007), which Freeman (2016, p. 217) refers to as "post-mortem reflection". Although valuable insight and growth can result from such reflection (Moran et al., 2019), Farrell (2022, p. 38) counters that "[t]his sole focus of reflection as an intellectual endeavour of solving classroom problems limits its implementation to 'reflection-as-repair' to fix those problems." A more balanced approach, including reflection on "teacher highs", would also benefit teachers (Farrell, 2008). Farrell (2007) also advocates a shift from concern with language teaching methods to development of skills of anticipatory reflection. In this connection, reflection on approaches to lesson planning could be particularly advantageous (see Ashcraft, 2014). Reflection on lesson planning could initially be carried out collaboratively, which would help the mentee gain "better understanding of the links between their own theories and practices" (Shi & Yang, 2014, p. 138).

## Conclusion

It is lamentable that reflective practice is often under-utilized in teacher education since it is clear from the literature that a greater emphasis on reflective practice could be beneficial in addressing common discrepancies between teachers' beliefs, knowledge and practices that can hinder their effectiveness in the classroom. It is the author's conviction, based by the literature, that teacher education programs could support more effective teaching by exploring the ways in which reflection can be operationalised and by scaffolding teachers' development as reflective practitioners. The key premises for reflective practice in teachers' professional development are as follows: reflective practice would be grounded in the mentees' own experience; reflection would examine the relationship between mentees' beliefs, knowledge and actions, and this reflection would be explicit; reflection would come from the mentee rather than be imposed by the mentor, and this would be underpinned by a trusting relationship between mentee and mentor; and a holistic approach to reflective practice would involve reflection prior to teaching (reflection-for-action), during teaching (reflection-in-action) and after teaching (reflection-on-action). It remains to be seen what impact such measures, if implemented, could have on teaching at the individual and institutional level. Majan University College, as a leader in Oman's higher education community, is well placed to serve as a platform for assessing how reflective practice can influence teachers' professional development.

## References


Akbari, R. (2007). Reflections on reflection: A critical appraisal of reflective practices in L2 teacher education. *System, 35*(2), 192–207.

Alptekin, C. (1993). Target-language culture in EFL materials. *ELT Journal, 47*(2), 136–143.

Ashcraft, N. (2014). *Lesson Planning.* TESOL Press.

Atkinson, D. (2021). The Adaptive Expertise of Expert ELT Textbook Writers. *RELC Journal, 52*(3), 603–617.

Baecher, L. (2012). Feedback from the field: What novice preK-12 ESL teachers want to tell TESOL teacher educators. *TESOL Quarterly, 46*(3), 578–588.

Baker, W. (2015). *Culture and identity through English as a Lingua Franca: Rethinking concepts and goals in intercultural communication*. De Gruyter Mouton.

Barnes, D. (1998). Foreword: Looking forward: The concluding remarks at the castle conference. In M. L. Hamilton (Ed.), *Reconceptualizing teaching practice: Self-identity in teacher education.* (pp. ix-xiv). Falmer Press.

Basturkmen, H. (2012). Review of research into the correspondence between language teachers' stated beliefs and practices. *System, 40*(2), 282–295.

Ben-Peretz, M. (2011). Teacher knowledge: What is it? How do we uncover it? What are its implications for schooling? *Teaching and Teacher Education, 27*(1), 3–9.

Beswick, K. (2012). Teachers' beliefs about school mathematics and mathematicians' mathematics and their relationship to practice. *Educational Studies in Mathematics, 79*(1), 127–147.

Borg, S. (2003). Teacher cognition in language teaching: A review of research on what language teachers think, know, believe, and do. *Language Teaching, 36*(2), 81–109.

Burn, K., Ingram, J., Molway, L., & Mutton, T. (2022). Beyond reactive responses to enduring growth: The transformation of principles and practices within initial teacher education. *Journal of Education for Teaching, 48*(4), 441–458.

Cabaroglu, N., & Roberts, J. (2000). Development in student teachers' pre-existing beliefs during a 1-year PGCE programme. *System, 28*(3), 387–402.

Calderhead, J. (1996). Teachers: Beliefs and knowledge. In D. C. Berliner & R. C. Calfee (Eds.), *Handbook of Educational Psychology* (pp. 709–725). Macmillan.

Carter, K., & Doyle, W. (1995). Preconceptions in learning to teach. *The Educational Forum, 59*, 186–195.

Chan, J. Y. H. (2021). Four decades of ELT development in Hong Kong: Impact of global theories on the changing curricula and textbooks. *Language Teaching Research, 25*(5), 729–753.

Childs, A., & McNicholl, J. (2015). Practical theorising. Designing tasks for science explanations. In I. Thompson (Ed.), *Designing Tasks in Secondary Education: Enhancing subject understanding and student engagement* (pp. 107–128). Routledge.

Cirocki, A., Madyarov, I., & Baecher, L. (2019). Contemporary perspectives on student teacher learning and the TESOL practicum. In A. Cirocki, I. Madyarov, & L. Baecher (Eds.), *Current Perspectives on the TESOL Practicum: Cases from around the Globe* (pp. 1–20). Springer.

Coombe, C., & Burridge, C. (2020). What it means to be a TESOL professional. In C. Coombe, N. J. Anderson & L. Stephenson (Eds.), *Professionalizing Your English Language Teaching*. Springer.

Cortazzi, M., & Jin, L. (1999). Cultural mirrors: materials and methods in the EFL classroom. In E. Hinkel (Ed.), *Culture in Second Language Teaching and Learning* (pp. 196–219). Cambridge University Press.

Crowe, A. R., & Berry, A. (2007). Teaching prospective teachers about learning to think like a teacher. In T. Russell & J. Loughran (Eds.), *Enacting a pedagogy of teacher education: Values, relationships and practices* (pp. 31–44). Taylor & Francis Group.

Dewey, J. (1920, reprint 1962). *Reconstruction and Philosophy*. Beacon.

Dewey, J. (1933). *How We Think: A Restatement of the Relation of Reflective Thinking to the Educative Process*. Prometheus.

Douidi, A. (2021). *Interculturality and Dialogic Pedagogy in ELT: An Investigation of Algerian Secondary School English Textbooks and Their Use in the Classroom* [Doctoral thesis]. University of Southampton.

Ellis, R. (2008). *The Study of Second Language Acquisition* (2nd Edition). Oxford University Press.

Emerick, M. R. (2019). Explicit teaching and authenticity in L2 listening instruction: University language teachers' beliefs. *System, 80*, 107–119.

Ernest, P. (1989). The knowledge, beliefs and attitudes of the mathematics teacher: A model. *Journal of Education for Teaching, 15*, 13–34.

Faez, F., & Valeo, A. (2012). TESOL teacher education: Novice teacher perceptions of their preparedness and efficacy in the classroom. *TESOL Quarterly, 46*(3), 450–471.

Fang, Z. (1996). A review of research on teacher beliefs and practices, *Educational Research, 38*(1), 47–65.

Farrell, T. S. C. (2007). Promoting reflection in language teacher education through case-based teaching. *The New English Teacher, 1*, 61–70.

Farrell, T. S. C. (2008). Critical incidents in ELT initial teacher training. *ELT Journal, 62*(1), 3–10.

Farrell, T. S. C. (2022). *TESOL Teacher Education: A Reflective Approach*. Edinburgh University Press.

Freeman, D. (2001). Second language teacher education. In R. Carter & D. Nunan (Eds.), *The Cambridge Guide to Teaching English to Speakers of Other Languages* (pp. 72–80). Cambridge University Press.

Freeman, D. (2016). *Educating Second Language Teachers*. Oxford University Press.

Furlong, J., & Maynard, T. (1995). *Mentoring student teachers: The growth of professional knowledge*. Routledge.

Gándara, P., Maxwell-Jolly, J., & Driscoll, A. (2005). *Listening to Teachers of English Language Learners: A Survey of California Teachers' Challenges, Experiences, and Professional Development Needs*. Policy Analysis for California Education.

Gimenez, T., Simões Calvo, L. C., & Salles El Kadri, M. (2015). Beyond Madonna: Teaching materials as windows into pre-service teachers' understandings of ELF. In S. Akcan & Y. Bayyurt (Eds.), *Current Perspectives on Pedagogy for English as a Lingua Franca* (pp. 225–237). De Gruyter Mouton.

Hopper, D., & Snyder, W. (2017). Becoming a "real" teacher: A case study of professional development in *eikaiwa*. *The European Journal of Applied Linguistics and TEFL*, *6*(2), 183–201.

Howe, E. R. (2006). Exemplary teacher induction: An international review. *Educational Philosophy and Theory, 38*(3), 287–297.

Johnstone Young, T., & Sachdev, I. (2011). Intercultural communicative competence: Exploring English language teachers' beliefs and practices. *Language Awareness, 20*(2), 81–98.

Joram, E., & Gabriele, A. J. (1998). Preservice teachers' prior beliefs: Transforming obstacles into opportunities. *Teaching and Teacher Education, 14*(2), 175–191.

Kagan, D. M. (1992). Professional growth among preservice and beginning teachers. *Review of Educational Research, 62*(2), 129–169.

Knezedivc, B. (2001). Action research. *IATEFL Teacher Development SIG Newsletter, 1*, 10–12.

Körkkö, M., Kyrö-Ämmälä, O., & Turunen, T. (2016). Professional development through reflection in teacher education. *Teaching and Teacher Education, 55*, 198–206.

Korthagen, F., Loughran, J., & Russell, T. (2006). Developing fundamental principles for teacher education programs and practices. *Teaching and Teacher Education, 22*, 1020–1041.

Laats, E. (2020). Novice teachers' satisfaction with teacher preparation and recommendations for improving teacher training. In *Proceedings of the 3rd International Conference on Research in Education, Teaching and Learning*, (pp. 1–12). https://www.dpublication. com/wp-content/uploads/2020/02/33-488.pdf

Lave, J., & Wenger, E. (1991). *Situated Learning*. Cambridge University Press.

Le Gal, D. (2018). Pedagogical shortcomings of global EFL textbooks and Spanish speaking learners. *Lenguas Modernas (Santiago), 2018*(51), 9–28.

Lee, R. N. F., & Bathmaker, A.-M. (2007). The Use of English Textbooks for Teaching English to 'Vocational' Students in Singapore Secondary Schools. *RELC Journal, 38*(3), 350–374.

Loewenberg Ball, D., Thames, M. H., & Phelps, G. (2008). Content Knowledge for Teaching. *Journal of Teacher Education, 59*(5), 389–407.

Long, D. T., & Stuart, C. (2004). Supporting higher levels of reflection among teacher candidates: A pedagogical framework. *Teachers and Teaching, Theory and Practice, 10*(3), 275–290.

Lou, M. (2021). Classroom activities in Chinese secondary EFL classes: Teachers' uptake of the learner-centred curriculum reform. *International Journal of TESOL Studies, 3*(2), 168–186.

Loughran, J. (2005). *Developing a pedagogy of teacher education: Understanding teaching and learning about teaching*. Taylor & Francis Group.

Loughran, J. 2010. *What expert teachers do: Enhancing professional knowledge for classroom practice*. Routledge.

Lü, C., & Lavadenz, M. (2014). Native Chinese-speaking K–12 language teachers' beliefs and practices. *Foreign Language Annals, 47*(4), 630–652.

Macknish, C., Porter-Szucs, I., Tomaš, Z., Scholze, A., Slucter, C., & Kavetsky, A. (2017). Voices from an MA-TESOL program: Bridging theory and practice from the ground up. In T. S. C. Farrell (Ed.), *Voices from the TESOL Classroom: Participant Inquiries in Pre-Service Teacher Education Classes* (pp. 29–36). TESOL Press.

Mattheoudakis, M. (2007). Tracking changes in pre-service EFL teacher beliefs in Greece: A longitudinal study. *Teaching and Teacher Education, 23*(8), 1272–1288.

Mikeska, J. N., Phelps, G., & Croft, A. J. (2017). Practice-Based Measures of Elementary Science Teachers' Content Knowledge for Teaching: Initial Item Development and Validity Evidence. *ETS Research Report Series, 1*, 1–72.

Mitchell, P. (2023). *Use of the Knowledge Quartet as a reflective tool in early-career EFL teachers' professional development* [Unpublished master's dissertation, University of Oxford].

Moodie, I. (2016). The anti-apprenticeship of observation: How negative prior language learning experience influences English language teachers' beliefs and practices. *System, 60*, 29–41.

Moran, W., Brandenburg, R., & McDonough, S. M. (2019). Pedagogical Confrontations as a Lens for Reflective Practice in Teacher Education. In J. Mena, A. García-Valcárcel & F. García Peñalvo (Eds.), *Teachers' professional development in global contexts: Insights from teacher education*. Brill.

Mulryan-Kyne, C. (2021). Supporting reflection and reflective practice in an initial teacher education programme: An exploratory study. *European Journal of Teacher Education, 44*(4), 502–519.

Mutton, T., Hagger, H., & Burn, K. (2011). Learning to plan, planning to learn: The developing expertise of beginning teachers. *Teachers and Teaching, Theory and Practice, 17*(4), 399–416.

Nagatomo, D. H. (2012). *Exploring Japanese University English Teachers' Professional Identity*. Multilingual Matters.

Nespor, J. (1987). The role of beliefs in the practice of teaching. *Journal of Curriculum Studies, 19*(4), 317–328.

Nguyen, T. T. M., Marlina, R., & Cao, T. H. P. (2021). How well do ELT textbooks prepare students to use English in global contexts? An evaluation of the Vietnamese English textbooks from an English as an international language (EIL) perspective. *Asian Englishes, 23*(2), 184–200.

Pajares, M. F. (1992). Teachers' beliefs and educational research: Cleaning up a messy construct. *Review of Educational Research, 62*(3), 307–332.

Pajares, M. F. (1993). Preservice teachers' beliefs: A focus for teacher education. *Action in Teacher Education, 15*(2), 45–54.

Richards, J. C. (1998). *Beyond Training*. Cambridge University Press.

Richards, J. C., & Pennington, M. (1998). The first year of teaching. In J. C. Richards (Ed.), *Beyond Training* (pp. 173–190). Cambridge: Cambridge University Press.

Roberts, J. (2016). *Language Teacher Education*. Routledge.

Rokeach, M. (1968). *Beliefs, attitudes, and values: A theory of organization and change*. Jossey-Bass.

Rowland, T. (2013). The Knowledge Quartet: The Genesis and Application of a Framework for Analysing Mathematics Teaching and Deepening Teachers' Mathematics Knowledge. *Sisyphus, 1*(3), 15–43.

Schön, D. A. (1983). *The Reflective Practitioner: How Professionals Think in Action*. Basic Books.

Schön, D. A. (1987). *Educating the Reflective Practitioner: Towards a New Design for Teaching and Learning in the Profession*. Jossey-Bass.

Segall, A. (2002). *Disturbing practice: Reading Teacher Education as Text*. Peter Lang.

Sercu, L., Bandura, E., Castro, P., Davcheva, L., Laskaridou, C., Lundgren, U., Garcia, M., & Ryan, P. (2005). *Foreign language teachers and intercultural competence: An international investigation*. Multilingual Matters.

Sharkey, J. (2004). ESOL Teachers' Knowledge of Context as Critical Mediator in Curriculum Development. *TESOL Quarterly, 38*(2), 279–299.

Shi, L., & Yang, L. (2014). A community of practice of teaching English writing in a Chinese university. *System*, *42*, 133–142.

Shulman, L. S. (1986). Those Who Understand: Knowledge Growth in Teaching. *Educational Researcher, 15*(2), 4–14.

Shulman, L. (1987). Knowledge and Teaching: Foundations of the New Reform. *Harvard Educational Review, 57*(1), 1–21.

Stuart, C., & Thurlow, D. (2000). Making it their own: Preservice teachers' experiences, beliefs, and classroom practices. *Journal of Teacher Education*, *51*(2), 113–121.

Van Velzen, C. P. (2013). *Guiding learning teaching* [Doctoral thesis]. Vrije Universiteit.

Van Velzen, C. P., & Timmermans, M. (2014). What can we learn from the shift towards a more school centred model in Netherlands? In K. Jones & E. White (Eds.), *Developing Outstanding Practice in School-based Teacher Education* (pp. 56–63). Critical Publishing.

Wang, J., & Odell, S. (2002). Mentored Learning to Teach According to Standards-Based Reform: A Critical Review. *Review of Educational Research, 72*, 481–546.

Yalcin Arslan, F. (2019). Reflection in pre-service teacher education: Exploring the nature of four EFL pre-service teachers' reflections. *Reflective Practice, 20*(1), 111–124.

Yost, D. S. (2006). Reflection and self-efficacy: Enhancing the retention of qualified teachers from a teacher education perspective. *Teacher Education Quarterly, 33*(4), 59–74.

Zuzovsky, R. (1995). Professional development of student teachers during preservice training. In R. Hoz & M. Silberstein (Eds.), *Partnerships of Schools and Institutions of Higher Education*. Ben Gurion.

# Reflective Practices in the InTASC Standards

*Sharifa S. Al-Rawahi and Sulaiman M. Al-Balushi*

**ABSTRACT**
This chapter examines the reflective practices emphasized in the Interstate Teacher Assessment and Support Consortium (InTASC) standards, specifically focusing on the Model Core Teaching Standards and Learning Progressions for Teachers. These standards, widely utilized by teacher preparation programs worldwide, including Sultan Qaboos University, are particularly interesting due to their emphasis on reflective practices. The chapter employs a qualitative approach to analyze the content of the standards document using thematic analysis. The main findings highlight that the standards document comprehensively addresses various aspects of reflective practices, emphasizing their importance in teacher evaluation. Topics explored include the concept of reflection, its significance, practical application, integration into teaching, and assessment methods. Each topic encompasses relevant subtopics. The chapter concludes with recommendations to enhance reflective practices among teacher candidates in teacher education programs, focusing on the InTASC standards.

## Introduction

Reflective practices have gained educational significance due to their impact on raising cognitive awareness, classroom practices, and educational beliefs (Abu Saleem, 2016; Sturkie, 2017). They also contribute to the development of teaching performance and the teacher's professional growth (Gungor, 2016). Research emphasizes that teachers should become reflective practitioners to improve their performance, a skill that can be acquired through training (Ngololo & Kanandjebo, 2021).

This chapter examines the application of the Interstate Teacher Assessment and Support Consortium (InTASC) standards in guiding the reflective practices of student teachers in the teacher preparation programmes at Sultan Qaboos University (SQU). It analyzes these standards to explore their treatment of the concept of reflection, the various types and characteristics of teacher reflection, and the different approaches to reflective practices. The analysis offers a framework for integrating reflective practices into teacher preparation programmes at SQU, as well as in other Omani and international teacher education programs seeking to align with InTASC standards or enhance the reflective practices of their pre-service teachers.

## Reflective Practices and Teacher Education Programs

John Dewey stresses the importance of reflective thinking and that reflection on practices contributes to improvement and development (Lupinski et al., 2012). Researchers and theorists have attempted to describe the different stages and mental processes associated with reflection as practitioners engage in their ability to better understand their beliefs and methods through this practice (Huma, 2017). Based on that, teacher preparation institutions have relied on the theory of reflection in designing programs to prepare student teachers and develop their skills during service (Huma, 2017).

The use of reflective practice in teacher preparation has grown dramatically, which benefits student teachers' professional efficacy (Arrastia et al., 2014; Davis et al., 2006; Huma, 2017; Mena-Marcos et al., 2013; Purcell & Schmitt, 2023). John Dewey and Donald Schön's concept of "reflection" has been evident in the literature, and it is now a crucial component of teacher education programs (Lupinski et al., 2012). Because reflection helps improve learning environments and their impact on student accomplishment, this favours how teachers develop their teaching competencies (Lupinski et al., 2012). This evolution in the use of reflection in teaching can be seen in how the student-teachers reflect while instructing, modifying their teaching according to what they learned from earlier reflections and impacting their present learning process (Purcell & Schmitt, 2023).

Reyes-Chua et al. (2020) stress the significance of student teachers' responsibilities in education and learning, emphasizing the need to teach them how to properly reflect during and after work (in-action reflection and on-action reflection). Teacher preparation programs are expected to encourage reflection and support ongoing development through writing and discussion of instructional strategies (Collin et al., 2013). Incorporating "reflection" into these programs encourages teachers to consider optimal practices, which has a favorable effect on teacher development and student progress (Lupinski et al., 2012).

In this chapter, reflection is defined as a process of self-monitoring aimed at enhancing a teacher's performance and fostering professional growth. This process involves identifying strengths and weaknesses, engaging in self-evaluation, problem-solving, and active participation, which includes making informed judgments. Reflection can be practiced individually or collaboratively, providing a flexible approach to continuous improvement and professional development.

## The Importance of Standards in Teacher Education Programs

The impetus for preparing teacher education programs and institutions for national accreditation by specialized professional associations and relevant accrediting agencies has provided an incentive to reassess and reformulate organizational structures, curriculum content, and practical experiences in teacher education programs (Kaufman, 2004). Regardless of the standards' quality, appropriate measurement indicators and systems must be established (Paliokas et al., 2017). Thus, at the global level, many countries and teacher preparation institutions have created specific standards lists for teacher preparation.

One of the responsibilities of teacher educators in universities is to use effective assessment tools to evaluate student teachers' knowledge and field performance. The InTASC standards are an important tool for this purpose, as they open a dialogue between students, teachers, and school administrators about using standards in teaching and encourage professional and ethical teaching (Kuo, 2018).

## International Accreditation of the Teacher Education Program at SQU

With the need for national standards for teacher preparation, international standards provide a basis for improving the quality of teacher preparation programs (Al-Balushi et al., 2022). The College of Education at Sultan Qaboos University (COE-SQU) began improving the quality of education early. It sought accreditation from the National Council for Accreditation of Teacher Education (NCATE), which later became the Council for the Accreditation of Educator Preparation (CAEP). Due to the lack of a national or regional accreditation body, the college turned to NCATE and obtained accreditation in 2016 for a period of seven years (2016–2022), and later in 2024, obtained academic accreditation from the Council for the Accreditation of Educators Preparation (CAEP). The college is among the few institutions in the Arab world that obtain this type of international accreditation for teacher preparation (Al-Balushi et al., 2020).

Given their differences from local admission policies, applying the CAEP standards to the Omani context was challenging for COE-SQU. However, the college successfully adapted the standards to the Omani context in collaboration with education experts. This involved developing new policies and making necessary reforms to meet accreditation requirements. The adaptation process and the specific changes made are detailed in the following section, providing valuable insights into the challenges and solutions in the context of international accreditation (Al-Balushi et al., 2020).

The CAEP standards indicated the importance of student teachers' acquiring the InTASC standards, especially in CAEP Standard One related to educational knowledge content. This standard requires that student teachers have a deep understanding and specialized knowledge that qualifies them to develop by demonstrating a complete understanding of the InTASC standards related to learners, learning, content, educational experiences, and professional responsibility (CAEP, 2019). The InTASC standards include ten main items, focusing on reflecting on the teaching practices to reach the required performance. Due to the importance of adopting standards that emphasize reflective practices in the teacher preparation program, COE-SQU has adopted the InTASC standards. The following section describes these standards in the teacher preparation program at Sultan Qaboos University.

## InTASC Standards in the Teacher Education Program at SQU

InTASC standards set expectations for the essential knowledge, critical dispositions, and performance required for high-quality teaching. "Performance" is considered primarily in these standards because it is observable and assessable in teaching practice. "Essential Knowledge" refers to the role of explicit and procedural knowledge necessary for effective practice. "Critical Dispositions" reflects the professional habits and ethical commitments that influence teachers' behaviour in real-world teaching practice (CCSSO, 2013). Therefore, COE-SQU sought to apply the InTASC standards in the teacher preparation program to reach higher educational levels and develop the teaching profession. The college has aligned the program outcomes with these standards, where student's work is evaluated according to them to improve teacher preparation and develop the educational process. The themes of these standards are linked to reflection, its concept, and its use, explicitly or implicitly.

## InTASC Standards Document

The InTASC document is organised as follows: First, an introduction and summary of the main teaching standards model, which describes the standards and objectives. Second, an overview of "Learning Progressions for Teachers" describes the development of teaching practice. Third, the ten primary standards are grouped into four general categories to organize the thinking process when using them. Each standard includes a few substandards in knowledge, behavior, and performance, corresponding to its learning progress. The standards are divided into domains as follows: the learner and learning, which includes standards 1 to 3; the content knowledge domain, which includes standards 4 and 5), the instructional practice domain, which includes standards 6 to 8; and finally, the professional responsibility domain, which includes standards 9 and10. The final section of the document includes a glossary and outline of the overarching topics in the standards, as well as the names of the committee members who formulated the standards and progress (CCSSO, 2013).

## Analysis of Reflective Practices in the InTASC Document

### Methodology

We used thematic analysis to analyse the InTASC document for the reflective practices. Thematic analysis is a qualitative technique that discovers the patterns and themes of qualitative data (Alhojailan & Ibrahim, 2012; Boyatzis, 1998). We began by "noticing" the emerging patterns of meanings and issues of importance in the raw data, which initially made it easy to classify the themes. Initial themes were used at the beginning of the document analysis to determine the theme categories and develop an initial set of codes. The inductive approach was also followed in the analysis of the InTASC document. The inductive approach is defined by Braun and Clarke (2006) as the process of coding data without attempting to fit it into a pre-existing coding system or the researcher's analytical concepts. This approach reflects how key concepts are drawn from the data rather than imposed in advance, which enhances the depth of understanding and analysis of important themes in the document.

## Analysis Procedures

The final themes were reached after passing through precise, detailed steps. It began with the "coding" process, which Strauss and Corbin (1998) define as the analytic processes through which data are fractured, conceptualized, and integrated to form theory (p.3). Coding is classifying and organizing data related to a specific point (Braun & Clarke, 2006; Elliott, 2018; Love, 2003). According to Bazeley (2013), coding is about creating categories and constructing a comprehensive picture of concepts the data emphasises.

The data were first read through in preparation for coding, known as "open coding." The analysis was further refined by repeatedly reading the data word by word to derive codes, with initial observations and impressions recorded, until themes were identified that formed the initial categories (Elo & Kyngäs, 2008; Hsieh & Shannon, 2005; Kibiswa, 2019; Potter & Levine-Donnerstein, 1999). After re-visiting the data, relationships between codes were identified to form categories. Subcategories were then organized and combined to reduce their number based on the purpose of the study, and patterns were identified at a higher level of abstraction (axial coding). Finally, the main categories were identified through "selective coding," and each category and code were defined (Elo & Kyngäs, 2008; Hsieh & Shannon, 2005; Kibiswa, 2019).

In the later stages of analysis, the focus was on clarifying, simplifying, and "reducing" the codes to limit the number of categories relevant to the emerging theory (Gibbs, 2012).

## Findings

The process of analysing the InTASC document using thematic analysis resulted in arriving at the following main themes:

1. The concept of reflection
2. The importance of reflection
3. Reflection as a practice
4. The use of reflection in teaching as a concept and practice
5. Evaluating reflective practices

Figure 2.1 shows a summary of the main and sub-themes.

**Figure 2.1:** Summary of Reflective Practices in the InTASC Standards Document.

## Theme One: The Concept of Reflection

The concept of reflection in the InTASC document explains that teachers self-evaluate and review their instructional practices and enhance their feedback to students with the aim of continuous improvement. Reflection in the InTASC document aims to critically examine teaching practices to improve student learning, including concepts such as analysis, improvement, deep understanding, and development. The following is an explanation of each of these emerging sub-themes.

### Analysis

The analysis process is an advanced and necessary stage of reflection. It is presented in the InTASC standards as a procedural practice for the teacher to understand the relationships between aspects of the educational process and learner development. This includes collecting and analyzing data to identify learning gaps and guide planning and teaching. It also includes identifying learner needs and engaging them in the analysis, with feedback for their development. This is illustrated, for example, by the following statement from the InTASC standards document: "The teacher engages learners in analyzing their own records and work samples about their progress toward learning objectives and to set new goals." (p. 32).

### Improvement and Development

The concept of improvement in the InTASC standards means improving performance or developing existing work as part of the reflection process. Improvement and development are natural outcomes of reflection, as they fall under its subcategories. These two concepts appear clearly in the InTASC document as the most closely related to reflection. In many ways, the concept of improvement appeared in the document with different meanings, some of which carry the same meaning as improvement: "to provide feedback in order to improve professional practice." (p. 12). As for development, it was also mentioned with the meaning of improvement: "The teacher provides options and resources to engage learners with the subject matter and to develop their skills in both collaborative and self-directed learning." (p. 23).

### Deep Understanding

"Deep understanding" is one of the meanings of reflection clearly stated in the InTASC standards. The document states that teachers should continually expand their understanding of learner diversity and its impact on learning while developing supports to deepen their understanding of academic content. Teachers should also use a variety of methods to connect learning to learners' interests and backgrounds, as illustrated by the paragraph: "By analyzing group discourse and learner work, the teacher discovers additional learner misconceptions and uses the processes, vocabulary, and strategic tools of the discipline to build accurate and deep understanding." (p. 25).

## Theme Two: The Importance of Reflection

Reflective practices are an important aspect of teaching, and reflective practices are an essential element of effective teaching and professional development. The InTASC standards emphasize teachers' need to reflect regularly to improve their practice, student learning, and professional development. The standards highlight their importance as integral to effective teaching and a guiding entry point for professional development. Teachers must reflect regularly on their teaching practices, students' learning, and professional development. The InTASC standards play a role in ensuring that high-quality education is provided – the one that meets the needs of all, as highlighted in Standard 9 of the document (Professional Learning and Ethical Practice), which states: "The teacher engages in ongoing professional learning and uses evidence to evaluate his/her practice continually." (p. 42).

This standard indicates that teachers should be reflective practitioners, continually evaluating and adjusting their teaching to meet the needs of students. Reflective practice involves reviewing experiences, identifying areas for improvement, and seeking feedback from colleagues and students to develop practices. This reflects teachers' creativity and professionalism in adapting instruction effectively and humanely. The InTASC standards emphasize the importance of reflective practice in teaching to promote ongoing teacher growth and development. By being reflective practitioners, teachers can improve their teaching practices and meet students' needs more effectively, contributing to their continued professional development. The frequency with which these practices appear in the standards document reflects their importance in developing performance.

## Theme Three: Reflection as a Practice

The results of the data analysis in this axis revealed two main sub-themes: the characteristics of reflection as a practice and the types of reflection. The following is an explanation of this.

### Characteristics of Reflection as a Practice

Reflection has several characteristics:

### Problem-Solving

The InTASC standards document emphasises the importance of problem-solving as a primary goal of reflective practices, as it appears clearly in multiple forms. The teachers may play this role or encourage their students to participate in solving problems, either individually or collectively, by applying knowledge to their daily lives. The document also highlights the importance of enhancing learners' abilities to identify problems and use critical thinking skills to explore appropriate solutions, including, for example: "The teacher engages learners in generating and evaluating new ideas and novel approaches, seeking inventive solutions to problems, and developing original work." (p. 27).

### Active Participation

Reflective practitioners are characterized by their active participation, which is a requirement of reflective practice (Eby & Kujawa, 1998). The InTASC highlights the role of the teacher in creating an appropriate learning environment, whether online or in person, to enhance learning outcomes. The teacher also manages the environment to encourage learners' participation and organizes time and space according to their interests, which makes it easier for them to choose appropriate methods and enhances their responsibility; for example: "The teacher communicates verbally and nonverbally in ways that demonstrate respect for and responsiveness to the cultural backgrounds and differing perspectives learners bring to the learning environment." (p. 21).

### Individual and Group Reflective Practice

The main goal of reflective practice, problem-solving, can be achieved through individual or group reflection. Individual reflection helps develop problem-solving skills, although this is difficult in university settings. Group reflection allows for collaboration and sharing of ideas, which enhances problem-solving effectiveness. This feature is evident in all InTASC standards related to knowledge, content, and level of progress, for example: "Use interactions with learners, families, and communities to understand better variations in development that can guide work with learners." (p. 18).

These group strategies demonstrate the importance of continuous teacher improvement. The InTASC document indicates that teachers should share the preparation plan with colleagues and obtain feedback before implementation, whether by joining a study group or using ready-made standards. The information gained should also be used to adapt instructional plans, sometimes known as lesson study, for example: "Share plan with key colleagues for feedback." (p. 42).

Reflective practice is "personal," as evidenced by the InTASC standards, emphasising the teacher's responsibility for each learner's learning. Learners have different skills and interests, and teaching strategies must be reviewed and designed according to this diversity and based on their prior knowledge and experience, enhancing their learning speed. Such attitudes are prominently expressed in the InTASC document: “The teacher creates developmentally appropriate instruction that considers individual learners’ strengths, interests, and needs and enables each learner to advance and accelerate his/her learning.” (p.16). At the individual level, a teacher should also practice reflective practice individually to improve his or her practice and the learning of his or her students, as evidenced by the following text: “Work with a coach/mentor to determine needs, set goals, and identify individually focused learning experiences to improve practice and student learning.” (p. 42).

## Self-assessment

Self-assessment appears in the InTASC standards as an essential reflective practice for both teacher and learner, used to identify strengths and areas for development. The teacher engages learners in assessing their strengths and identifies strategies to enhance their progress, which promotes individual and collective responsibility. It also supports learners’ autonomy. It guides them in identifying their learning needs while encouraging them to participate in decision-making and problem-solving. In addition, student records and work samples are used to build metacognitive strategies and make appropriate adjustments based on analysis of events, such as “The teacher engages learners in analyzing their own records and work samples about their progress toward learning objectives and to set new goals.” (p. 32). On the teacher’s side, the standards outline the use of various self-assessment methods, such as focus groups, to obtain feedback from colleagues, students, and families on the quality of the learning environment. It is also stressed that it is essential for the teacher to keep a self-assessment record of the variety of teaching strategies and the appropriateness and accuracy of the questions asked, which helps her improve her performance by obtaining feedback from colleagues. For example: “Use focus groups to get feedback from learners and families on the quality of the learning environment.” (p. 22).

## Decision Making

Reflective practice requires teachers to make critical decisions about teaching methods, which calls for the decision-making skill of “giving judgment.” The InTASC document shows that teachers collaborate with families and colleagues to promote learners' growth based on judgments about strengths and development priorities. Teachers should respect learners' needs and use this information to support their development and integrate their experiences and cultures into instruction. They also help learners reflect on their progress to promote their future growth: "The teacher engages learners in assessing their strengths and learning preferences and identifies various ways to promote each student's growth." (p. 19).

## Types of Reflection

The results of the data analysis showed various types and levels of reflection, each with its benefits and techniques. These types were reviewed in comparison with the educational literature, where they can be classified into three main types according to Van Manen's (1977) classification:

### Technical Reflection

This type of reflection is called "descriptive" and is considered the lowest level of reflection, as it focuses on strategies and methods for reaching specific goals. In this type, the teachers show their quest to convey information to learners through the use of various strategies, in line with the InTASC standards that emphasize providing a learning environment suitable for meeting the needs of learners, as the teachers help learners apply knowledge and skills in realistic contexts, work to develop more complex concepts, and provide opportunities to confirm learners' understanding through various methods that demonstrate the achievement of educational goals: "The teacher facilitates learners' use of current tools and resources to maximize content learning in varied contexts." (p. 27).

### Practical Reflection

Practical or procedural reflection includes applying practical methods in reflective practices. The document discusses using various tools to practice and evaluate reflection, as this practice is considered a means of improving teachers' performance in line with other professions (Glasswell & Ryan, 2017). When reflective practitioners begin to apply theories and procedures, they rise to a more advanced reflective level, moving from the technical level to the practical level. The data revealed some types of these practices, explicitly or implicitly, which can be classified into procedural and cognitive aspects. The following is an explanation of each aspect:

## First: The Procedural Aspect of Practical Reflection

The procedural aspect of the practical reflection includes different practices such as case studies, portfolios, reflective journals, discussion groups, peer observation, and video recordings. The following is an explanation of each type.

**Case Study.** One of the practical reflections related to the procedural aspect that appeared in the document is the "case study." The second standard of the InTASC document (Learning Differences) indicates that the teacher must use an understanding of individual differences, cultures and diverse societies to ensure inclusive educational environments that enable every learner to meet high standards, which means that there are case studies that fit the nature of the case that the teacher is dealing with. For example, this was explained in the "essential Knowledge" section of the InTASC standards in different ways, the most prominent of which is the following example: "The teacher understands students with exceptional needs, including those associated with disabilities and giftedness, and knows how to use strategies and resources to address these needs." (p. 17).

**Portfolios.** These are one of the methods of practical reflection and are a tool for final assessment, with the indication that they can be used technically to achieve the planned goals by preparing them electronically: "Examples of summative assessment include end-of-unit tests, final exams, semester exams, portfolios, capstone projects, performance demonstrations, state-mandated tests, the National Assessment of Educational Progress (NAEP)." (p. 48).

**Reflective Journals.** Reflective journals or daily diaries are tools for practical reflection, and this type appears in the InTASC document in its paper form as diaries or electronic forms as blogs and wikis. The importance of the teachers keeping a journal to document their metacognitive strategies is highlighted, which helps them to retrieve and analyze them alone or with a critical colleague: "Keep a journal on how teaching impacts student learning and identify potential areas of growth for self and learners." (p. 42). The teachers also encourage learners to create online accounts for expression and writing (e.g. blogs, wikis) to achieve learning goals and to benefit from others: "Develop a wiki for the sharing of research questions, processes, and findings related to the ethical practice of assessment." (p. 33).

**Discussion Groups.** The analysis of the InTASC standards document highlights the importance of group discussions for teachers and learners. Teachers should develop skills to improve learners' learning in collaboration with colleagues in the school. Learners should also be involved in discussions to enhance their ability to learn, exchange views, and communicate: "Participate in conversations and decision-making with colleagues and specialists who provide input, guidance, and assistance related to the needs of a particular set of learners to prepare for assessment." (p. 33).

**Peer Observation.** Peer observation is essential for practical reflection, and the InTASC document highlights its versatility. Teachers plan and adapt units of study and seek feedback from peers or critical teachers on implementation, facilitating performance improvement. At the learner level, teachers encourage students to share feedback based on standard criteria, helping them develop their skills and improve their performance, and this appears in a variety of ways in the document, for example: "Observe a colleague who uses varied roles in teaching and debrief ways to match roles with instructional purpose." (p. 39).

**Video Recordings.** The data analysis results showed that video recordings are an effective tool for practical reflection, and the InTASC document highlights their use in evaluating teaching practices. These recordings allow teachers to review and analyze their methods, which helps them improve planning for future lessons. Sometimes, the teacher may involve learners in this process: "Video record self in a group situation, analyze interaction, and set goals for improvement." (p. 47)

### Second: The Cognitive Aspect of Practical Reflection

The results of the data analysis showed a set of reflective practices related to the cognitive aspect of practical reflection, which relates to the role of teachers in professional development (Akbari et al., 2010). These practices call on teachers to follow up on developments in the educational process, which contributes to developing their skills and scientific knowledge. The cognitive aspect includes following the latest trends by reading professional literature, attending conferences and workshops, writing articles and blogs, and conducting procedural research. The following is an explanation of each of them:

**Reading Professional Literature.** Reading professional literature is an essential part of the cognitive aspect of practical reflection, which helps teachers to reflect on their teaching practices and stay informed about the latest educational trends. This practice highlights the role of virtual communities in promoting knowledge exchange among teachers and emphasizes the importance of reading current literature in organizational development and leadership. For learners, the teacher uses a variety of instructional strategies, such as reading and writing, to support learner communication, including engaging in writing on social media or blogs: "Access professional literature related to specific assessment needs of particular groups of learners." (p. 33). Attending conferences and training workshops. Attending professional conferences and training workshops is essential for teachers to keep up with educational developments while reflecting on their practices. The InTASC standards have shown the role of these practices in improving performance and assessing teachers' professional progress, whether in person or online: "Interact with colleagues at conferences sponsored by a professional association to learn and apply new developments in content and content pedagogy." (p. 25).

**Action Research.** Action Research is a tool for practical reflection that aims to develop the cognitive side of teachers, as it helps them follow educational developments and develop their research and problem-solving skills. The InTASC standards emphasize the importance of acquiring action research skills as a means of enhancing cooperation between teachers to conduct joint research and share results, which contributes to improving instructional practices and building research skills in the field of education: "Work with colleagues and specialists to apply action research practices to issues in improving assessment to better support learner growth." (p. 33).

## Critical Reflection

Since this type of reflection is the highest level in Van Manen's classification (Van Manen, 1977), it includes examining one's thoughts, feelings, and behaviors to identify underlying assumptions, biases, and values. Thus, it consists of the philosophy of teaching and a wide range of concepts, including the social, ethical, political, ideological, and moral dimensions of teaching practice (Cote Parra, 2012; Larrivee, 2008; Van Manen, 1977; Zeichner, 1981). The following is an explanation of what this type of reflection includes.

**Teaching Philosophy.** Although the term "teaching philosophy" is not explicitly mentioned, the document refers to the role of the teacher in building a unified vision and a supportive culture for learning, emphasising high expectations for learners' learning that seek to create learning environments that promote individual and collaborative learning and learner interaction. The importance of teachers' understanding of content and ability to apply knowledge to real-world issues is highlighted as the relationship between teacher and learner evolves from directive to collaborative, with the teacher acting as a facilitator to determine the course of action. For example, this is shown in the InTASC standards document: "The teacher plans instruction that supports every student in meeting rigorous learning goals by drawing upon knowledge of content areas, curriculum, cross-disciplinary skills, and pedagogy, as well as knowledge of learners and the community context." (pp. 34–35).

This is consistent with Soccorsi's (2013) study, which found that reflection after each teaching experience is essential for developing and refining a personal teaching philosophy, leading to teachers who are deeply committed to serving education.

**Ethical, Political and Social Dimensions.** In addition to the philosophy of teaching, the analysis of the document at the level of critical reflection shows the importance of linking teachers' practices to ethical, political and social aspects, with a focus on issues of equity, social justice and scientific ethics. The InTASC document devoted a "Critical Dispositions" section, representing professional habits and ethical commitments. It highlighted the concept of "equality of opportunity" implicitly in its context by using terms that indicate this, such as: "every learner" and "all learners," for example: "The teacher effectively uses multiple and appropriate types of assessment data to identify each student's learning needs and to develop differentiated learning experiences." (p. 30).

InTASC focused on the concept of equity by emphasizing educational practices that enabled learning for all and highlighted the role of the teacher in making informed decisions about how their identity affects perceptions and biases: "The teacher creates developmentally appropriate instruction that takes into account individual learners' strengths, interests, and needs and that enables each learner to advance and accelerate his/ her learning." (p. 16). As an important equity issue, teachers' efforts in the InTASC document were directed toward eliminating bias in educational practices: "The teacher works with others to minimize bias in assessment practices to ensure that all learners have a variety of opportunities to demonstrate their learning." (p. 33).

InTASC also presented the need to apply ethical issues in learners' learning and the principle of respect for others: "The teacher articulates explicit expectations for a safe, positive learning environment, including norms for behaviour that include respect for others, as well as responsibility for preparation and completion of work. S/he develops purposeful routines that support these norms." (p. 22).

In addition, the InTASC document explained the importance of teachers respecting linguistic and dialectal diversity and incorporating it into their teaching practices to enhance learners' engagement. It also referred to the concept of "Learners diversity," which includes the different cultures and needs of learners for whom English is a new language: "The teacher uses appropriate strategies and resources to adapt instruction to the needs of individuals and groups of learners." (p. 38).

On the social side, the InTASC standards document focused on the role of the teacher in employing resources inside and outside the school to support learners' learning and development, including engaging families and communities. It also helped connect learners with online development opportunities and face-to-face workshops. Additionally, it highlighted the role of the teacher in using technology to connect with colleagues to solve real-world issues, for example: "The teacher respects families' beliefs, norms, and expectations and seeks to work collaboratively with learners and families in setting and meeting challenging goals." (p. 45).

As Liu and Ball (2019) have shown, this expansion of the scope of critical reflection in the document can be attributed to the contradictory nature of the American public education system, which has always combined democratic impulses with social hierarchies. Despite efforts to improve teaching and teacher preparation over the past 50 years, the challenge of teaching for diversity and equity remains, calling for a rethinking of teacher preparation to teach diverse students.

## Theme Four: Employing Reflection in Teaching as a Concept and Practice

The importance of employing reflection in teaching lies in enabling student teachers to acquire reflection skills, which improves their teaching performance. Learning must be effective, based on self-activity and positive learner participation (Al-Adel et al., 2021). This fourth theme discusses the characteristics that a reflective teacher should have and the role of feedback in the teaching process to achieve improvement and development in the pillars of the educational process in general as factors that help employ reflection in teaching.

### Characteristics of the Reflective Teacher

The InTASC document emphasized the importance of the teacher's role in all of its ten standards, stressing the need for the reflective teacher to have specific characteristics that enable her to read events and situations deeply through analysis, synthesis, and investigation, which helps her understand what is happening and interpret it logically so that these characteristics are consistent with the skills of the twenty-first-century teacher. The following is an explanation of the most essential characteristics of the reflective teacher that appeared in the document:

### Continuous Analysis and Evaluation of Her Practices

The InTASC document indicated the importance of professional development in providing comprehensive and sustainable educational opportunities, aiming to expand teachers' professional knowledge base. Learning requires continuous evaluation and modification, as the teacher analyzes and evaluates her practices to identify strengths and priorities for development, and she can also request comments to obtain feedback. The formative evaluation process includes clarity of educational outcomes and success criteria, in addition to self-assessment and peer evaluation to enhance the learner's awareness of the importance of improvement: "Video record self in a group situation, analyze interaction, and set goals for improvement." (p. 47).

### Open-mindedness

This trait is evident in the InTASC standards document, by focusing on the importance of the teacher's understanding of individual differences and diverse cultures. The teacher practices reflection through peer assessment and observation, asking for feedback to improve her practice and using feedback from families and communities to review learning. This contributes to modification and development based on multiple perspectives. This reflects the concept of democratic education (Biesta, 2015). "The teacher communicates regularly with families to mutually understand learner development and engages the learner in understanding, analysing, and communicating their growth and needs" (p. 18).

### Self-directed and Independent

The InTASC document highlights the teacher's leadership role through her ability to make decisions related to learners' learning, which enables her to work independently and collaboratively. In addition, the teacher must guide learners toward independence and take responsibility for choosing appropriate methods for learning tasks, which contributes to producing good work as individuals: "The teacher leads in his/her classroom, assuming responsibility for and directing student learning toward high expectations" (p. 47).

### Responsibility

The teacher takes responsibility for the learning of all learners and shares it with peers, as highlighted in the InTASC standards through "professional responsibility" (standards 9 and 10). This attribute includes understanding learning styles and different development approaches, which motivates the teacher to implement appropriate learning experiences, such as linking concepts and encouraging critical and creative thinking. The document also encourages teachers to help learners take responsibility for their learning, which promotes the effective design and implementation of collaborative and self-directed learning and ensures partnership between teachers and learners for success: "The teacher seeks appropriate leadership roles and opportunities to take responsibility for learners' learning and advance the profession" (p. 47). This is consistent with Iqbal's (2017) study that reflective practices enable teachers to become successful decision-makers who take responsibility for their actions. She also agreed with Reyes-Chua et al. (2020) on the importance of teachers taking responsibility for the teaching and learning process in general.

## Feedback

The InTASC standards highlight the importance of providing feedback to teachers on their performance as part of continuous improvement and professional development, which contributes to promoting self-reflection and career advancement and improving the educational level of learners. The document also reverts the origin of the word "assessment" to a focus on providing guidance and feedback for growth and development. Feedback is stated in the InTASC standards as an explicit goal of the reflection process, to be provided critically and continuously for improvement and development. For example: "Mentors, coaches, and school leaders can use the progressions to provide feedback to teachers on their performance, including areas for growth and potential learning experiences as part of a continuous improvement process" (p. 12).

## Theme Five: Evaluative Reflective Practices

Reflective practice in education is a "learning-in-practice" process (Lisle, 2006, p. 117). Hence, the importance of linking reflective practices with teaching practices is that reflective practices are a thoughtful and systematic examination of teaching practices, as they include a critical analysis of the teacher and an evaluation of her teaching experiences, thus improving her teaching practices to facilitate student learning. This enhances the teacher's performance and facilitates student learning as we reflect on practice to generate ideas for improvement that may involve changing practice (Lisle, 2006). Therefore, evaluating teachers' learning outcomes is essential to determining their effectiveness (Belvis et al., 2013).

The InTASC standards document clarified that progress and progression are considered evaluation rules, including "descriptive" criteria that help the teacher or trainer compare performance and make formative judgments to support teacher growth. These gradations aim to improve teaching by providing descriptions of different levels of development of teaching practices and information for self-evaluation and reflection. The document links the assessment of reflective practices to the assessment of professional practice. For example, "Use protocols to guide reflective analysis and evaluation of practice." (p. 43).

The InTASC Standards document highlights the importance of reflective practice and evaluation of professional practice. Reflective practice is a means for teachers to analyze their teaching and identify areas for improvement critically. For example, Standard 8 (Instructional Strategies): "The teacher understands and uses a variety of instructional strategies to encourage learners to develop a deep understanding of content areas and their connections, and to build skills to apply knowledge in meaningful ways" (p. 39). This standard emphasizes the teachers' ability to evaluate their professional practice, which promotes analysis and reflection on instructional strategies and their impact on data-driven decision-making to support student learning. The InTASC Standards document also uses comprehensive evaluation mechanisms to ensure teachers' progress toward desired goals, focusing on various aspects of professional development. These can be summarized in the following points:

First, the teacher plays a vital role in nurturing learners' ability to critically evaluate the information and ideas they obtain from different resources: "The teacher guides learners in gathering, organizing and evaluating information and ideas from digital and other resources and different perspectives." (p. 29).

Second, the standards encourage teachers to create an interactive classroom environment with diversified teaching methods while engaging learners in evaluating this environment and proposing improvements: "The teacher uses a variety of methods to engage learners in evaluating the learning environment and collaborates with learners to make appropriate adjustments." (p. 21).

Third, InTASC standards guide the teacher to enhance learners' ability to reflect on their learning: "The teacher engages learners in assessing their strengths and learning preferences and identifies various ways to promote each student's growth" (p. 19).

Fourth, the standards emphasize the teacher's ability to collaborate with colleagues to improve the overall learning environment, including sharing best practices, pooling resources, and supporting professional development: "Collaborate with a colleague in a different discipline to design a problem-based instructional unit, analyze the contributions and limitations of different disciplines for that unit, and assess learning across the unit" (p. 28).

Fifth, InTASC's learning progression pathways assess teachers' commitment to continuous professional development through attending workshops, conferences, and participating in activities that keep them up to date with the latest teaching practices: "Based on reflection and other sources of feedback, the teacher takes responsibility for his/her self-assessment of practice and ongoing professional learning by seeking out and participating in professional learning experiences to address identified needs and areas of professional interest." (p. 42). This is to keep up with the latest educational developments and work to employ them in a manner that is appropriate to the educational environment. InTASC's assessment mechanisms provide a comprehensive approach to teachers' professional development, enabling them to continually assess their progress and adjust teaching techniques to ensure student success and progress.

## Conclusions, Recommendations and Limitations

In conclusion, this chapter emphasizes the critical role of the InTASC standards in shaping reflective practices among student teachers in Sultan Qaboos University's teacher preparation programmes. Using thematic analysis, the chapter explored how these widely recognized standards, which serve as a leading global framework for evaluating teachers, conceptualize, categorize, and apply reflection in teaching. The analysis highlights their adoption at SQU and other institutions to enhance the quality of teacher graduates. This exploration offers practical insights and a structured approach to embedding reflective practices, benefiting teacher preparation programmes not only at SQU but also across Oman and internationally, as they seek to adopt InTASC standards or strengthen the reflective competencies of their pre-service teachers.

The findings indicate that the standards comprehensively address various aspects of reflective practices, emphasizing their significance in teacher assessment, and they also provide a basis for improving the quality of teacher preparation programmes (Al-Balushi et al., 2022). Key themes identified include the concept of reflection, the value of reflection, reflection as a practice, integrating reflective practices into teaching, and evaluating these practices. Each theme encompasses several subtopics, providing a detailed framework for understanding and implementing reflective practices in teacher evaluation and professional development.

The InTASC standards emphasize the importance of reflective teaching practices in teacher preparation programs (CCSSO, 2013). The current chapter highlights some key recommendations based on these standards that underline the importance of reflective practices in enhancing teaching effectiveness and ensuring that teachers respond to the diverse needs of their students (CCSSO, 2013). We recommend developing curricula in teacher preparation programs to include critical thinking and reflective practices as indicated by the InTASC standards and providing opportunities to apply critical thinking and analysis skills. The study also recommends developing a culture of self-assessment and continuous improvement through collaborative reflection with colleagues, encouraging supervisor feedback, and emphasizing the importance of feedback from families and peers. The study also recommends linking theoretical knowledge to actual practices in the educational field. In addition, it is important to train academic supervisors on the reflective practices included in the InTASC standards so that they can apply them in supervising students. The study also recommends developing assessment tools based on the reflective practices included in the InTASC standards to be a unified and objective method of assessing reflective practices for pre-service teachers.

One area for improvement of the current study is the complexity of analyzing the reflective practices in the InTASC standards document as they appear outside the document. Therefore, it was necessary to search for the latent meanings of these reflective practices, code them into categories, and then topics representing the main folds of the data analysis results.

## References

Abu Saleem, I. M. (2016). The impact of the reflective practice of the university professor on improving his teaching performance. *Specialized International Educational Journal: Dar Simat for Studies and Research, 5*(2), 299–322.

Akbari, R., Behzadpoor, F., & Dadvand, B. (2010). Development of English language teaching reflection inventory. *System, 38*(2), 211–227. https://doi.org/10.1016/j.system.2010.03.003

Al-Adel, A., Al Dhafri, S., Kadhim, A., Alkharusi, H., Amer, T., & Al-Fori, S. (2021). Developing higher thinking skills for Omani student using effective learning strategies. *Journal of Arabic Studies in Education and Psychology, 130*, 23–65.

Al-Balushi, S. M., Al-Harthi, A. S. & Shahat, M. A. (2022). Teacher Education in Oman: Retrospectives and Prospects. In M. S. Khine (Ed.), *Handbook of Research on Teacher Education: Pedagogical Innovations and Practices in the Middle East* (pp. 87–102). Springer. https://doi.org/10.1007/978-981-19-2400-2_6

Al-Balushi, S. M., Emam, M. M. & Al-Abri, K. M. (2020). Leadership and teacher education in Oman. In R. Papa (Ed.), *Oxford Encyclopedia of Educational Administration.* Oxford University Press. https://doi.org/10.1093/acrefore/9780190264093.013.589

Alhojailan, M. I., & Ibrahim, M. (2012). Thematic analysis: A critical review of its process and evaluation. *West East Journal of Social Sciences, 1*(1), 39–47. https://2u.pw/jz13WA

Arrastia, M. C., Rawls, E. S., Brinkerhoff, E. H., & Roehrig, A. D. (2014). The nature of elementary preservice teachers' reflection during an early field experience. *Reflective Practice, 15*(4), 427–444. https://doi.org/10.1080/14623943.2014.900018

Bazeley, P. (2013). *Qualitative data analysis: Practical strategies*. Sage.

Belvis, E., Pineda, P., Armengol, C., & Moreno, V. (2013). Evaluation of reflective practice in teacher education. *European Journal of Teacher Education, 36*(3), 279–292. https://doi.org/10.1080/02619768.2012.718758

Biesta, G. J. (2015). *Beyond learning: Democratic education for a human future*. Routledge.

Boyatzis, R. E. (1998). *Transforming qualitative information: Thematic analysis and code development*. Sage.

Braun, V., & Clarke, V. (2006). Using thematic analysis in psychology [Abstract]. *Qualitative research in psychology*, *3*(2), 77–101. http://dx.doi.org/10.1191/1478088706qp063oa

CAEP (Council for Accreditation of Educator Preparation). (2019). *2013 CAEP Standards.* http://caepnet.org/standards/introduction

CCSSO (Council of Chief State School Officers). (2013). *InTASC Model Core Teaching Standards and Learning Progressions for Teachers 1.0*. https://ccsso.org/resource-library/intasc-model-core-teaching-standards-and-learning-progressions-teachers-10

Collin, S., Karsenti, T., & Komis, V. (2013). Reflective practice in initial teacher training: Critiques and perspectives. *Reflective Practice*, *14*(1), 104–117. https://doi.org/10.1080/14623943.2012.732935

Cote Parra, G. E. (2012). The role of reflection during the first teaching experience of foreign language pre-service teachers: An exploratory-case study. *Colombian Applied Linguistics Journal*, *14*(2), 24–34. https://doi.org/10.14483/udistrital.jour.calj.2012.2.a02

Davis, E. A., Petish, D., & Smithey, J. (2006). Challenges new science teachers face. *Review of Educational Research*, *76*(4), 607–651. https://doi.org/10.3102/00346543076004607

Elliott, V. (2018). Thinking about the coding process in qualitative data analysis. *Qualitative Report*, *23*(11). 2850–2861. https://nsuworks.nova.edu/tqr/%20vol23/iss11/14

Elo, S., & Kyngäs, H. (2008). The qualitative content analysis process. *Journal of Advanced Nursing*, *62*(1), 107–115. https://doi.org/10.1111/j.1365-2648.2007.04569.x

Gibbs, G. R. (2012). *Grounded theory, coding and computer-assisted analysis*. Policy Press.

Glasswell, K., & Ryan, J. (2017). Reflective practice in teacher professional standards: Reflection as mandatory practice. In *Reflective theory and practice in teacher education* (pp. 3–26). Springer.

Gungor, M. N. (2016). Turkish pre-service teachers' reflective practices in teaching English to young learners. *Australian Journal of Teacher Education*, *41*(2), 137–151.

Hsieh, H. F., & Shannon, S. E. (2005). Three approaches to qualitative content analysis. *Qualitative Health Research*, *15*(9), 1277–1288. https://doi.org/10.1177/1049732305276687

Huma, A. (2017). Improving Exercises of Reflective Thinking and Practice in Teacher Education at a State University in USA. *PJE, 34*(1), 113–126. https://doi.org/10.30971/pje.v34i1.194

Iqbal, M. Z. (2017). Reflection-in-Action: A Stimulus Reflective Practice for Professional Development of Student Teachers. *Bulletin of Education and Research, 39*(2), 65–82.

Kaufman, D. (2004). 14. Constructivist issues in language learning and teaching. *Annual Review of Applied Linguistics, 24*, 303–319. https://doi.org/10.1017/S0267190504000121

Kibiswa, N. K. (2019). Directed qualitative content analysis (DQlCA): A tool for conflict analysis. *The Qualitative Report, 24*(8), 2059–2079. https://doi.org/10.46743/2160-3715/2019.3778

Kuo, N.-C. (2018). Rethinking edTPA: The Use of InTASC Principles and Standards. *Journal of Educational Issues*, 4(1), 47–67. https://eric.ed.gov/?id=EJ1174471

Larrivee, B. (2008). Development of a tool to assess teachers' level of reflective practice. *Reflective Practice, 9*(3), 341–360. https://doi.org/10.1080/14623940802207451

Lisle, A. (2006). Maintaining interaction at the zone of proximal development through reflexive practice and action research. *Teacher Development, 10*(1), 117–143. https://doi.org/10.1080/13664530600587303

Liu, K., & Ball, A. F. (2019). Critical reflection and generativity: Toward a framework of transformative teacher education for diverse learners. *Review of Research in Education, 43*(1), 68–105. https://doi.org/10.3102/0091732X18822806

Love, P. (2003). Document analysis. In F. K. Stage & K. Manning (Eds.), *Research in the College Context: Approaches and Methods* (pp. 83–96). Routledge.

Lupinski, K., Jenkins, P., Beard, A., & Jones, L. (2012). Reflective Practice in Teacher Education Programs at a HBCU. *Educational Foundations, Summer*, 81–92. https://eric.ed.gov/?id=EJ1000232

Mena-Marcos, J., García-Rodríguez, M. L., & Tillema, H. (2013). Student teacher reflective writing: what does it reveal?. *European Journal of Teacher Education, 36*(2), 147–163. https://doi.org/10.1080/02619768.2012.713933

Ngololo, E. N., & Kanandjebo, L. N. (2021). Becoming Reflective Practitioners: Mathematics Student Teachers' Experiences. *Journal of Research and Advances in Mathematics Education*, 6(2), 128–141.

Paliokas, K., McWalters, P., & Diez, M. (2017). *The Interstate Teacher Assessment and Support Consortium (InTASC): An update on the model core teaching standards.*

Potter, W. J., & Levine-Donnerstein, D. (1999). Rethinking validity and reliability in content analysis. *Journal of Applied Communication Research, 27* (3), 258–284. https://doi.org/10.1080/00909889909365539

Purcell, M. L., & Schmitt, S. A. (2023). Strengthening preservice educator reflective practice through the use of personnel preparation standards. *Journal of Early Childhood Teacher Education*, 1–17. https://doi.org/10.1080/10901027.2023.2165984

Soccorsi, L. (2013). Instilling a personal teaching philosophy in pre-service teachers: Vitally important but not always easy to achieve. *Journal of Student Engagement: Education Matters*, *3*(1), 21–28.

Strauss, A., & Corbin, J. (1998). *Basics of Qualitative Research Techniques.* Sage.

Sturkie, L. M.(2017). *The Impact of a Reflective Practice Series on the Awareness Level of Six Teacher Candidates at a Public University in the Southeast.* [Doctoral dissertation, University of South Carolina]. https://scholarcommons.sc.edu/etd/4306

Van Manen, M. (1977). Linking of Being Ways. *Curriculum Inquiry, 6*(3), 205–228. https://doi.org/10.1080/03626784.1977.11075533

Zeichner, K. M. (1981). Reflective teaching and field-based experience in teacher education. *Interchange, 12*(4), 1–22. https://doi.org/10.1007/BF01807805

# Reflective Teaching Practices of Omani Pre-service Teachers: The Status Quo and Enhancement Mechanisms

*Mohamed Abdelraouf Attia Elsayed*

**ABSTRACT**

This paper aims to identify the level to which pre-service teachers at Sultan Qaboos University (SQU) use reflective teaching practices (RTPs), and if the level of these RTPs differ according to the variable of their academic major. This quantitative descriptive paper applied the questionnaire by Tok & Dolapçıoğlu (2013) on a sample composed of 119 of pre-service teachers at SQU. The results showed that respondents used RTPs at an acceptable level. These RTPs were ordered as follows: reflective teaching practices, self-evaluation, creating a reflective class climate, creating a learner-centered instructional environment, solving problems and making decisions about the future, valuing criticism, and finally openness to professional development. Data analysis revealed that there were statistically significant differences according to the variable of academic major in the direction of pre-service teachers whose major was social studies. The study proposed some mechanisms to enhance RTPs for pre-service teachers at SQU.

## Introduction

John Dewey was the first to introduce the reflection concept in his book "How We Think" (Dewey, 1933). Dewey's basic assumption was that good learning arises from the process of reflection, which meant later: deep thinking, critical thinking, problem solving, and higher-level thought. Dewey's reflective teaching practices (RTP) cannot be separated from observation and experience based on linking application to theory and active interaction with others by sharing what you have learned. RTP are mental processes concerned with solving problems, including insight based on the ability to analyze the situation, developing correct hypotheses, and evaluating all actions, decisions, and results (Abdul-Samie et al, 2022).

## Literature Review

To this day, there has been an increasing interest in Dewey's definition of reflective thinking as "active, persistent, and careful consideration of any belief or supposed form of knowledge in the light of the grounds that support it, and the further conclusions to which it tends" (1933, p. 6) and emphasis on teaching practices enhancing that reflective thinking as a key component of learning and that is explored in several studies. Both Maddux & Donnett (2015) and Dimova & Kamarska (2015) highlighted the importance of creating a situation of discomfort for learners and examining the warrants of settled belief. Gelfuso & Dennis (2014) further extrapolated the challenges and characteristics of reflective thought. Collier (1999) discussed the evolution of reflective dispositions and the different levels and stages of reflective judgment. These studies collectively emphasized the transformative potential of reflection in the learning process.

Moreover, RTP contributes to enhancing self-quality such as self-confidence, establishing supportive relationships between fellow teachers, improving the teacher's commitment to the profession, and stimulating teaching ability to develop strengths in performance and increasing the tendency toward reflection (Somerville & Keeling, 2004). Teachers can achieve that, for example, by implementing new instructional strategies based on feedback from observations and reflection, collaborating in a professional learning community to discuss their reflective practices, commitment to enhancing student learning experiences, and integrating technology that strengthens professional growth, reputation, and bonds.

Many studies asserted that the teacher's possession of RTP helps him/her to link new information to previous understanding, think about concepts, understand their thinking and learning strategies, analyze, evaluate, and apply new strategies in unfamiliar situations, and develop different kinds of communications and relationships. For example, Felten et al (2006) concluded that RTP is: the main link between community experience and academic learning, the intentional consideration of an experience in light of particular learning objectives, the process that helps students connect what they observe and experience in the community with their academic study, and the ability to speculate about one's own experience and generate from it some knowledge relevant to other experiences. Cruickshank & Applegate (1981) also emphasized that RTP encourages teachers to be students of teaching. Because RTP is a carefully organized form of peer teaching, it needs a group of interested teachers willing to teach in front of each other. To participate, teachers must spend time in preparation and reflection.

Regarding this significance, RTP is the ideal approach to teacher education. Through the use of semi-structured interviews, Mumthaz & Kgomotso

(2016) investigated the perceptions of teachers regarding critical RTP and found that teachers were reflecting-on-action and not reflecting-in-action. Such reflection was reactive, rather than guiding future actions.

In addition, Abdul-Samie et al.'s (2022) study found that RTP is an effective way to achieve the previously mentioned benefits on the one hand, and to deal with modern changes and trends in teaching and learning processes on the other hand. This is the suitable reaction to traditional teaching practices that have become unable to meet the needs of teachers concerning their practical problems on the third hand.

Hence, a large number of research studies have investigated engaging RTP in preservice teachers. As teacher education programs cannot simply address every student and every situation a prospective teacher will encounter, they must rather provide preservice teachers with a general knowledge base of pedagogical principles and practices and a strategy for adapting these principles and practices. Dewey's model of reflective practice serves as a method of adaptation, involving a systematic exploration of the motivations, techniques, resources, and outcomes associated with educational practices. This model allows practitioners to carefully analyze the circumstances and attitudes that either hinder or promote student success. Reflective teachers (1) respond to the specific educational and emotional needs of each student; (2) reflect on their personal goals and actions; and (3) continuously evaluate their teaching objectives, strategies, and resources (Ginsberg, 2023; Hasan & Abdulkarim, 2022; Norton, 1997).

RTP involves a process of self-examination and critical analysis of one's teaching methods and their impact on student learning (Gheith & Aljaberi, 2018). This approach is valuable in teaching, where it can enhance lesson delivery and student engagement (Huynh, 2022). However, it is important to critically evaluate different models of reflective teaching and make necessary modifications to address practical and ideological concerns (Gore, 1987). Furthermore, the integration of research and evidence-based knowledge is crucial in reflective practice, as it cannot only inform teaching and help raise standards of attainment (Newman, 1999), but it can also result in deeper learning about both the subject studied and the learner as well (Raber-Hedberg, 2009). In a broader context, RTP is considered a key lifelong learning skill that plays an essential role in teacher education. Consequently, the understanding of RTP has evolved across various disciplines and approaches, leading to distinctions among its concepts, types, and levels of reflection.

Finlay (2008) distinguished between two types of reflection: reflection-on-action, which involves thinking about events after they have occurred, and reflection-in-action, which refers to thinking that takes place during the activity itself. In reflection-on-action, practitioners engage in reviewing, describing, analyzing, and evaluating their previous practices to gain deeper insights and improve future applications. In contrast, reflection-in-action allows practitioners to assess their experiences and reactions as they happen. Due to the link between the practitioners' feelings and related theories, new quicker reactions to teaching scenarios can be promoted. Additionally, Cirocki and Widodo (2019) introduced a more widely recognized category called reflection-for-action, which focuses on planning future responses to enhance current practices.

Larrivee (2008) categorizes RTP into three levels: surface, pedagogical, and critical reflection. The first level primarily concentrates on the methods used to meet lesson objectives. The second level involves a deeper understanding of instructional theories and approaches. The highest and most significant level is critical reflection, which focuses on long-term objectives in teaching and learning.

Cirocki and Widodo (2019) proposed a four-component typology of RTP including reflection-before-lesson, reflection-during-lesson, reflection-after-lesson, and reflection-beyond-lesson. In the stage of "reflection-before-lesson", teachers need to focus on lesson objectives, learning outcomes, teaching methods, materials, activities, and classroom management. Then, addressing practical challenges and student needs becomes increasingly important in lesson planning. In the teaching process or reflection-during-lesson, "positive and negative surprises" take place that prompt teachers to respond with knowledge and adaptability. Reflection-after-lesson encourages teachers to evaluate their performance by observing and justifying how theories apply in their teaching contexts, aiming for improvement in future applications. Finally, reflection-beyond-lesson urges teachers to consider the "moral, political, and social issues" that affect their practice.

Based on the review, it is evident that there are different types of reflection that teachers and preservice teachers can utilize to reflect on their teaching or learning. This reflection helps them improve their practices and enhances their cognitive awareness of the reflective processes they engage in. Therefore, researchers worldwide have emphasized on the importance of providing practitioners with RTPs and professional competences which enable them to be involved in their expertise in hopes of enriching their experience and performance inside the classroom, and hence, enhancing the quality of teaching. This, certainly, requires attending workshops, seminars, short courses, or professional self-development largely dependent on the personal initiatives taken by the practitioners achieved by self-learning, research activities, and reflective practices. This means reinforcing RTPs is a long-term process which contributes to the development of new pedagogical theories and practices that undoubtedly support practitioners to highly improve performance (Aksu et al, 2023; Cadiz, 2021; Gheith & Aljaberi, 2018; Huynh, 2022; Keshek, 2019; Mathew et al, 2017; Tok & Dolapçıoğlu, 2013).

That is what UNESCO (2024) regarded for enabling the transformation of the teaching profession. Among these recommendations is:

> Policies should promote teaching as a collaborative profession, with adequate space, time and resources for collaborative planning, communities of practice, and reflective and reflexive practice by and among teachers, within and beyond their education institution. Such efforts can be supported by education authorities. Teachers should be encouraged to use interdisciplinary teams to teach core curricula content through thematic units. (p. 7)

Despite the world research interest in teaching and learning RTPs, such interest in the Omani context is still very little. However, theoretical interest in RTPs is determined on all educational stages.

In the Omani National Framework for the Teaching Profession issued by the Ministry of Education (2017), the second chapter specified nine professional standards for the competent Omani teacher according to his/her actual fields of work derived from his job duties and tasks. The fourth standard is: "The teacher reflects on practices to support sustainable professional development." This standard is achieved through the following indicators:

- Analyzing work outcomes and identifying strengths and development priorities in the professional aspect based on an evaluation of his/her classroom performance.
- Evaluating the effectiveness of teaching and learning practice.

- Benefiting from the feedback provided by colleagues and officials to improve his/her professional practices.
- Participation in professional development programs prepared by the competent authorities in the Ministry.
- Researching areas of professional development to develop personal skills.
- Keeping up with recent developments in educational theories, pedagogical practices, and his/her academic specialty.
- Contributing to professional learning communities and related school activities within the scope of the responsibilities assigned to him/her.

In response to both this Omani National Framework for the Teaching Profession as well as the Omani Authority for Academic Accreditation and Educational Quality Assurance, Sultan Qaboos University (2023) has prepared the "SQU Teaching and Learning Strategies Handbook" as a comprehensive guide designed to empower educators at SQU in their pursuit of excellence within the higher education landscape. This handbook presented a collection of proven strategies, innovative approaches, and practical tips to enhance teaching practices, engage students, and foster meaningful learning experiences. By exploring this document, a wide range of RTPs was included in many sections relating to learning objectives, teaching strategies, assessment tools, and all learning processes of reading, writing, and research projects whether learning is online, clinical, or fieldwork. The aim of that handbook was to allow opportunities for students to reflect on their individual participation, and the progress of the group. This should help them to identify ways to improve and develop their ability to collaborate effectively.

This paper aims to identify the level to which pre-service teachers at SQU use RTPs, and if the level of these RTPs differ according to the variable of their academic major. More precisely, this paper aims to answer the following questions:

- To what extent do Omani pre-service teachers at SQU use RTPs?
- Does the level of RTPs of Omani pre-service teachers differ according to their major?
- What are the proposed mechanisms to enhance RTPs for pre-service teachers at SQU?

## Methodology

This descriptive paper applied a RTPs questionnaire to all students of the Educational Qualification Diploma Program at SQU who were in the practical training period. The whole community represented 169 pre-service teachers, but only 119 (70.41%) responded to the questionnaire. Table 3.1 shows the characteristics of this sample and its distribution according to their major.

**Table 3.1:** Characteristics of the Questionnaire Respondents

| Major | Frequency | Percentage |
|---|---|---|
| English | 16 | 13.4 |
| Science & Math | 37 | 31.1 |
| Social studies | 21 | 17.6 |
| Islamic Education & Arabic | 25 | 21.0 |
| Music | 20 | 16.8 |
| Total | 119 | 100 |

The RTPs questionnaire adopted in this study was previously utilized by Tok & Dolapçıoğlu (2013). This questionnaire contained 28 items in 6 dimensions including: (1) creating a learner-centered instructional environment; (2) creating a reflective classroom Climate; (3) appreciating criticism; (4) self-evaluation; (5) solving problems and making decisions about the future; and (6) openness to professional development. The questionnaire responses ranged from a 5-dimensional scale (always=5; usually=4; hesitant=3; sometimes=2; and never=1). The questionnaire was translated into Arabic and presented to seven educational professors to judge its consistency with the Omani culture.

After some modifications, psychometric properties of that questionnaire were verified. Internal consistency was assured through conducting the questionnaire to a pilot sample of 25 pre-service teachers. Pearson correlation has been checked, and its values were significant at level of (0.01). Reliability was checked through Cronbach's Alpha. Table 3.2 shows Pearson Correlation for validity and Cronbach's Alpha for reliability.

**Table 3.2:** Pearson Correlation and Cronbach's Alpha

| Dimensions of the questionnaire | Items | Pearson Correlation | Cronbach's Alpha |
|---|---|---|---|
| Creating learner-centered instructional environment | 5 | .835** | .753 |
| Creating a reflective class climate | 5 | .726** | .772 |
| Valuing criticism | 4 | .706** | .776 |
| Self-evaluation | 4 | .829** | .773 |
| Solving problems and making decisions about the future | 5 | .847** | .759 |
| Openness to professional development | 5 | .814** | .757 |
| Total | 28 | --- | .878 |

After calculating the validity and reliability of the questionnaire, it was electronically sent to all students who were in the practical training via their formal e-mails. Data collected from the received completed questionnaires were scored, analyzed, and discussed. The questionnaire was analyzed according to the five-point Likert scale as Table 3.3 shows:

**Table 3.3:** The Extent of Means and Percentages of the Likert Scale

| Five-Response Likert Scale | Means | Percentages |
|---|---|---|
| Unacceptable practice level | 1.00 to less than 1.80 | Less than 36% |
| Low practice level | 1.80 to less than 2.60 | 20% to less than 52% |
| Medium practice level | 2.60 to less than 3.40 | 52% to less than 68% |
| Normal practice level | 3.40 to less than 4.20 | 68% to less than 84% |
| Acceptable practice level | 4.20 to less than 5.00 | 84% to 100% |

## Results

The statistical analysis of the sample responses indicated that pre-service teachers at SQU use RTPs at an acceptable level (M=4.25 & SD=0.423). Responses indicated the most practiced dimension was "Self-evaluation" (M=4.43 & SD=0.481), whereas the least practiced dimension was "Openness to professional development" (M=4.10 & SD=0.566). Table 3.4 shows the means and standard deviations of responses to the whole questionnaire.

**Table 3.4:** Means, Standard Deviations, and Percentages of the Sample Responses

| Reflective teaching practices | Mean | SD | % |
|---|---|---|---|
| 1) I plan for the teaching-learning process based on the skills and personal needs of students. | 4.18 | .965 | 83.6 |
| 2) I provide various activities (tests, homework, meeting with student or family, etc.) to determine students' learning levels. | 3.94 | 1.076 | 78.8 |
| 3) I evaluate the results of these activities. | 4.24 | .802 | 84.8 |
| 4) I give feedback about students' level of learning. | 4.53 | .649 | 90.6 |
| 5) I praise students who defend their views freely. | 4.62 | .689 | 92.4 |
| Creating learner-centered instructional environment | 4.30 | 0.570 | 86 |
| 6) I conduct lessons by relating the topics to students' own lives. | 4.51 | .636 | 90.2 |
| 7) I create a classroom environment where students can express themselves freely. | 4.39 | .654 | 87.8 |
| 8) I elicit students' views about the problems that emerge during class. | 4.28 | 1.057 | 85.6 |
| 9) I include students in in-class decision making. | 4.16 | .676 | 83.2 |
| 10) I facilitate students to share their feelings with me (interests, fears, anxieties, enthusiasm, etc.). | 4.45 | .733 | 89 |
| Creating a reflective class climate | 4.36 | 0.493 | 87.2 |
| 11) I enable my students to evaluate my teaching performance and attitudes in oral or written form. | 3.97 | .982 | 79.4 |
| 12) I change my teaching performance and attitudes based on my students' evaluation. | 4.14 | .816 | 82.8 |
| 13) I ask my colleagues to evaluate my teaching performance and attitudes. | 4.17 | .717 | 83.4 |
| 14) I consider my colleagues' criticism regarding my teaching performance and attitudes. | 4.16 | .823 | 83.2 |
| Valuing criticism | 4.11 | 0.588 | 82.2 |
| 15) I think over and over when deciding on teaching-learning processes (objectives, topics, methods, techniques, evaluation). | 4.17 | .729 | 83.4 |
| 16) I evaluate my strong and weak points in teaching. | 4.59 | .630 | 91.8 |
| 17) I conduct the practices that benefit my students/ yield results in their learning. | 4.56 | .633 | 91.2 |
| 18) I review my teaching practices. | 4.39 | .739 | 87.8 |

(*Continued*)

**Table 3.4:** *(Continued)*

| **Reflective teaching practices** | **Mean** | **SD** | **%** |
|---|---|---|---|
| Self-evaluation | 4.43 | 0.481 | 88.6 |
| 19) I think about improvements I can make when I am preparing this lesson in the future. | 4.50 | .623 | 90 |
| 20) I ask myself: what are the possible effects of the changes I can make? | 4.27 | .744 | 85.4 |
| 21) I think about using alternative methods. | 4.39 | .614 | 87.8 |
| 22) I determine the problems that occur in the lesson (students not understanding the topic, failure to attract interest, communication). | 4.10 | .764 | 82 |
| 23) I collect evidence that supports my decisions. | 3.83 | .905 | 76.6 |
| Solving problems and making decisions about the future | 4.22 | 0.498 | 84.4 |
| 24) I identify the areas where I need to develop. | 4.35 | .696 | 87 |
| 25) I follow professional publications and new developments. | 4.03 | .828 | 80.6 |
| 26) I discuss with my colleagues what we do in class, why we do this practice, whether these practices are effective. | 4.22 | .738 | 84.4 |
| 27) I make use of professional publications and new developments. | 4.17 | .680 | 83.4 |
| 28) I keep a diary to follow my professional development and see my shortcomings. | 3.72 | .956 | 74.4 |
| Openness to professional development | 4.10 | 0.566 | 82 |
| Total | 4.25 | 0.423 | 85 |

Analysis of the first dimension revealed that pre-service teachers at SQU used RTPs relating to "Creating learner-centered instructional environment" at an acceptable level (M=4.30 & SD=0.570). The sample practiced three items at an acceptable level and the highest one was Item No.5 "I praise students who defend their views freely" (92.4%), whereas there were two items which the sample practiced at a normal level and the least one was Item No.2 "I provide various activities to determine students' learning levels" (78.8%).

Data analysis of the second dimension revealed that the sample used RTPs relating to "Creating a reflective class climate" at an acceptable level

(M=4.36 & SD=0.493). The sample practiced four items at an acceptable level and the highest one was Item No.6 "I conduct lessons by relating the topics to students' own lives" (90.2%), whereas the Item No.9 "I include students in in-class decision making" came true at a normal level (83.2%).

The results of analyzing the third dimension showed that the sample used RTPs relating to "Valuing criticism" at a normal level as a whole (M=4.11 & SD=0.588) and in detail. The highest practice was Item No.13 "I ask my colleagues to evaluate my teaching performance and attitudes" (83.4%), whereas the lowest one was Item No.11 "I enable my students to evaluate my teaching performance and attitudes in oral or written form" (79.4%).

Analysis of the fourth dimension demonstrated that the sample used RTPs relating to "Self-evaluation" at an acceptable level (M=4.43 & SD=0.481). The sample practiced three items at an acceptable level and the highest one was Item No.16 "I evaluate my strong and weak points in teaching" (91.8%), whereas the Item No.15 "I think over and over when deciding on teaching-learning processes" came true at a normal level (83.4%).

The results of analyzing the fifth dimension revealed that the sample used RTPs relating to "solving problems and making decisions about the future" at an acceptable level (M=4.22 & SD=0.498). The sample practiced three items at an acceptable level and the highest one was Item No.19 "I think about improvements I can make when I am preparing this lesson in the future" (90%), whereas there were two items which sample practiced at a normal level and the least one was Item No.23 "I collect evidence that supports my decisions" (76.6%).

Data analysis of the sixth dimension indicated that the sample used RTPs relating to "Openness to professional development" at a normal level (M=4.10 & SD=0.566). The sample practiced two items at an acceptable level and the highest one was Item No.24 "I identify the areas where I need to develop" (87%), whereas there were three items which the sample practiced at a normal level and the least one was Item No.28 "I keep a diary to follow my professional development and see my shortcomings" (74.4%).

On the other hand, data analysis revealed that there were statistically significant differences, on the whole questionnaire, according to the variable of academic major as proved by Kruskal-Wallis Test (Chi-Square=13.702, Sig=0.008). The differences were in the direction of SQU pre-service teachers whose university major was social studies. Table 3.5 shows the statistical differences in the RTPs questionnaire according to the variable of major:

**Table 3.5:** The Statistical Differences on the RTPs Questionnaire

| Dimensions | Major | N | Mean | Chi-Square | Sig. |
|---|---|---|---|---|---|
| Creating learner-centered instructional environment | English | 16 | 67.44 | 10.146 | .038 |
| | Science & Math | 37 | 55.01 | | |
| | Social studies | 21 | 78.57 | | |
| | Islamic Education & Arabic | 25 | 49.92 | | |
| | Music | 20 | 56.38 | | |
| Creating a reflective class climate | English | 16 | 68.94 | 6.668 | .155 |
| | Science & Math | 37 | 54.74 | | |
| | Social studies | 21 | 73.38 | | |
| | Islamic Education & Arabic | 25 | 58.04 | | |
| | Music | 20 | 50.98 | | |
| Valuing criticism | English | 16 | 53.69 | 18.564 | .001 |
| | Science & Math | 37 | 52.57 | | |
| | Social studies | 21 | 88.60 | | |
| | Islamic Education & Arabic | 25 | 51.38 | | |
| | Music | 20 | 59.55 | | |
| Self-evaluation | English | 16 | 51.63 | 9.351 | .053 |
| | Science & Math | 37 | 60.97 | | |
| | Social studies | 21 | 77.02 | | |
| | Islamic Education & Arabic | 25 | 48.20 | | |
| | Music | 20 | 61.78 | | |
| | Total | 119 | | | |
| Solving problems and making decisions about the future | English | 16 | 56.13 | 6.519 | .164 |
| | Science & Math | 37 | 60.99 | | |
| | Social studies | 21 | 74.10 | | |
| | Islamic Education & Arabic | 25 | 48.80 | | |
| | Music | 20 | 60.48 | | |

| Dimensions | Major | N | Mean | Chi-Square | Sig. |
|---|---|---|---|---|---|
| Openness to professional development | English | 16 | 48.00 | 10.057 | .039 |
| | Science & Math | 37 | 54.73 | | |
| | Social studies | 21 | 77.64 | | |
| | Islamic Education & Arabic | 25 | 54.56 | | |
| | Music | 20 | 67.63 | | |
| Total of RTPs questionnaire | English | 16 | 55.81 | 13.702 | .008 |
| | Science & Math | 37 | 56.62 | | |
| | Social studies | 21 | 84.50 | | |
| | Islamic Education & Arabic | 25 | 49.40 | | |
| | Music | 20 | 57.13 | | |

## Discussion

The answers to the first question, "To what extent do pre-service teachers at SQU use RTPs?", revealed that the level of RTPs ranged from the normal level to the highest level. For the level of RTPs questionnaire dimensions, SQU pre-service teachers practiced four dimensions at an acceptable level, and two dimensions at a normal level as Figure 3.1 shows:

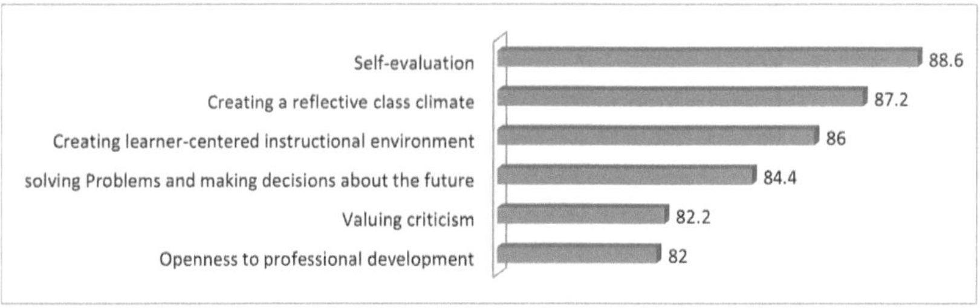


**Figure 3.1:** The Level of RTPs Questionnaire Dimensions.

As for the level of RTPs questionnaire items, SQU pre-service teachers used 15 RTPs at an acceptable level, ranging from M=4.22 to M=4.62, as well as using 13 RTPs at a normal level, ranging from M=3.72 to M=4.18.

This positive result demonstrates that SQU students implement RTPs and achieve their related and desired learning outcomes in a distinguished way (Planning and Statistics Department, 2022). In addition, SQU places the development of reflective teaching skills as a key priority in its teacher preparation programs. The university believes that these skills are necessary to develop effective teaching practices. The interest in these skills and practices is presented in an integrated manner within the pedagogical and specialized curricula of teacher preparation programs. This enhances students' understanding of RTPs importance and continuous application.

The university also provides numerous opportunities for students to implement RTPs during field training and class visits. This helps them develop their practical skills. Moreover, pre-service teachers receive continuous feedback from university professors and cooperating teachers as well as guidance and support provided to enhance their meditation skills.

In general, SQU encourages a culture of reflection and careful thinking and efficient teaching skills among pre-service teachers, as elaborated before via SQU Teaching and Learning Strategies Handbook (2023). SQU's interest in developing reflective teaching skills among pre-service teachers reflects its commitment to preparing distinguished teachers capable of continuous development of their pedagogical practices.

These results are consistent with many previous studies, such as Aksu et al (2023), Cadiz (2021), Gheith & Aljaberi (2018), and Tok & Dolapçıoğlu (2013), who collectively asserted that practitioners possess a high level of reflective practices.

On the other hand, the normal level of using RTPs relating to the two dimensions of valuing criticism and openness to professional development is due to the fact that the study sample is still in the field training period, which is one of the requirements for graduation. Thus, pre-service teachers often refrain from seeking evaluations of their teaching methods from peers or allowing students to share their opinions openly about their practices. This reluctance may stem from their fear of being judged by students or colleagues, particularly if their classroom deficiencies could adversely affect their graduation prospects. Additionally, the findings revealed that many preservice teachers do not maintain a diary to track their performance, follow their professional development, or follow and make use of professional publications, believing that practices mentioned in these last two dimensions are more suitable for in-service teachers.

Therefore, the respondents may lack the applicable knowledge regarding appreciating the criticism and sustainable professional development. As a whole, this result is rather consistent with both Gheith & Aljaberi (2018) and Tok & Dolapçıoğlu (2013) who indicated that practitioners lack sufficient field knowledge on reflective practices in the classroom.

The answer to the second question; "Does the level of RTPs of Omani pre-service teachers differ according to the variable of their academic major?", Table 5 showed that there were no statistically significant differences on three dimensions of RTPs questionnaire; "Creating a reflective class climate, Self-evaluation, and Solving problems and making decisions about the future", where the significance was more than 0.05. This indicates the consistency and lack of variation in the responses of the sample members and that there is no effect of the major variable on the RTPs of these three dimensions.

On the contrary, there were statistically significant differences on the other three dimensions of RTPs questionnaire; "Creating learner-centered instructional environment, Valuing criticism, and Openness to professional development", and all differences were in the direction of SQU pre-service teachers whose university major was social studies. As stated earlier, the level of RTPs relating to the other two dimensions is normal or below acceptable practice. This means that SQU pre-service teachers specialized in social studies use these RTPs less than their peers in other academic majors. This can be explained in the light of limited engagement with RTPs, or deficiency in their training or exposure to reflective practices. That is to say, the teacher education program for social studies may need more enhancements to better incorporate RTPs into its curriculum. This could involve integrating more practical experiences, workshops, or courses that focus on creating learner-centered environments, encouraging constructive criticism, and promoting professional development. Strategies could also include mentoring programs, peer evaluations, and opportunities for ongoing training. This result is rather consistent with Almusthi (2019) who concluded that there were difficulties facing social studies teachers when applying the active learning method, and then, limiting the time available for reflection and ongoing development of teaching practices.

## Conclusion

Enhancing RTPs for pre-service teachers takes time as it is a complex process that may require close attention to every aspect of a teacher education program. Most importantly, RTPs cannot be taught through a few simple techniques but requires education that transforms the ways of knowing and the views about knowledge. When RTPs becomes a habit of mind based on specific epistemic views that promote its development, then pre-service teachers can implement RTPs at the most acceptable level (Ostorga, 2006).

Accordingly, the most proposed mechanisms – extracted from an open-ended question at the end of the questionnaire – to enhance RTPs for pre-service teachers at SQU focused on diversification of instructional activities focusing on RTPs in the teacher education program such as: a) incorporating more explicit instruction, modeling, and practice of RTPs across the curriculum, b) expanding courses dedicated to RTPs, inquiry-based learning, and action research, c) ensuring pre-service teachers have ample opportunities to engage in reflective activities, such as writing reflective journals, conducting lesson studies, and facilitating peer-to-peer discussions, and d) spreading RTPs awareness among pre-service teachers via attending workshops, seminars, short courses, peers' classes, or professional teaching initiatives.

RTPs can also be enhanced by promoting mentorship and supervision during teaching practicum through providing extensive training for cooperating teachers and university supervisors on effective mentoring of RTPs, encouraging and supporting cooperating teachers to model and guide pre-service teachers in implementing RTPs, and establishing structured reflection sessions between pre-service teachers, cooperating teachers, and university supervisors to discuss and analyze teaching experiences. This is closely related to promoting communities of practice and peer learning through: facilitating the creation of peer support groups or professional learning communities among pre-service teachers to share experiences, discuss challenges, and collaboratively reflect on their practices, as well as encouraging pre-service teachers to observe each other's lessons and provide constructive feedback to foster a culture of collegial reflection.

In addition, enhancing RTPs cannot be separated from integrating technology-enhanced reflective tools. This can be achieved through leveraging digital platforms, such as online portfolios, blogs, and video analysis tools, to enable pre-service teachers to document, share, and critically examine their teaching practices. This requires the provision of training on the effective use of these technological tools to support reflective inquiry and evidence-based decision-making. The linkage between theory and practice can also be strengthened through: a) ensuring that the content covered in coursework is closely aligned with the realities of the Omani educational context and the challenges faced by teachers; b) encouraging pre-service teachers to make explicit connections between educational theories and their practical application in the classroom; and c) facilitating opportunities for pre-service teachers to engage in action research projects that address relevant issues in their local schools.

Finally, a culture of reflective practice at the institutional level should be fostered by: encouraging and supporting faculty members at SQU to model and integrate RTPs in their own teaching practices, establishing clear policies and structures that prioritize and recognize the development of reflective practitioners among pre-service and in-service teachers, and providing ongoing professional development opportunities for teacher educators to enhance their own competencies in facilitating RTPs.

Undoubtedly, the implementation of these proposed mechanisms would require a collaborative effort between the teacher education program, school partners, and the broader educational ecosystem in Oman. Sustained commitment and support from institutional leadership would be crucial for the effective enhancement of RTPs among pre-service teachers at SQU.

## References

Abdul-Samie, G., Salem, M., & Zidane, M. (2022). Reflective dialogue practices and their role in improving the teaching performance of faculty members in colleges of education: An analytical vision. *Education Journal (Al-Azhar)*, *41*(193), 231–262.

Aksu, D., Çalışır, M., & Sellüm, F. S. (2023). Reflective practices of pre-service teachers: Self-reflections on micro teaching. *Journal of Social Sciences and Education*, *6*(2), 254–274.

Almusthi, A. S. (2019). Challenges facing social studies teachers while applying the active learning strategies: Analytical descriptive study. *Journal of Educational and Psychological Sciences*, *3*(16), 101–129.

Cadiz, A. P. (2021). Pre-service teachers' reflective practice and their teaching practicum beliefs. *Jurnal Inovatif Ilmu Pendidikan*, *3*(2), 105–119.

Cirocki, A., & Widodo, H. P. (2019). Reflective practice in English language teaching in Indonesia: Shared practices from two teacher educators. *Iranian Journal of Language Teaching Research*, *7*(3 (Special Issue)), 15–35.

Collier, S. T. (1999). Characteristics of reflective thought during the student teaching experience. *Journal of Teacher Education, 50*(3), 173–181.

Cruickshank, D. R., & Applegate, J. H. (1981). Reflective teaching as a strategy for teacher growth. *Educational Leadership, 38*(7), 553–54.

Dewey, J. (1933). *How We Think: A Restatement of the Relation of Reflective Thinking to the Educative Process*. Prometheus.

Dimova, Y., & Kamarska, K. (2015). Rediscovering John Dewey's model of learning through reflective inquiry. *Problems of Education in the 21st Century, 63,* 29–29.

Felten, P., Gilchrist, L. Z., & Darby, A. (2006). Emotion and learning: feeling our way toward a new theory of reflection in service-learning. *Michigan Journal of Community Service Learning, 12*(2), 38–46.

Finlay, L. (2008). Reflecting on Reflective Practice. *Practice-Based Professional Learning Paper 52*, The Open University.

Gelfuso, A., & Dennis, D. V. (2014). Getting reflection off the page: The challenges of developing support structures for pre-service teacher reflection. *Teaching and teacher education, 38*, 1–11.

Ginsberg R. (2023). Preservice teacher action research: Making meaning and generating knowledge through inquiry. *Journal on efficiency and responsibility in education and science, 16*(1), 1–11.

Gheith, E., & Aljaberi, N. (2018). Reflective teaching practices in teachers and their attitudes toward professional self-development. *International Journal of Progressive Education, 14*(3), 160–179.

Gore, J. M. (1987). Reflecting on reflective teaching. *Journal of Teacher Education, 38*(2), 33–39.

Hasan, S., & Abdulkarim, S. (2022). John Dewey's intellectual form of educational philosophy in contemporary era. *Journal of Positive School Psychology, 6*(5), 4110–4118.

Huynh, H. T. (2022). Promoting Professional Development in Language Teaching through Reflective Practice. *Vietnam Journal of Education*, *6*(1), 62–68.

Keshek, M. (2019). The Reflective practices of teaching staff members at Damascus University and their relation to their job performance. *Association of Arab Universities Journal for Education and Psychology, 17*(3), 249–287.

Larrivee, B. (2008). Development of a tool to assess teachers' level of reflective practice. *Reflective practice, 9*(3), 341–360.

Maddux, H. C., & Donnett, D. (2015). John Dewey's Pragmatism: Implications for Reflection in Service-Learning. *Michigan Journal of Community Service Learning, 21*(2), 64–73.

Mathew, P., Mathew, P., & Pichette, P. J. (2017). Reflective practices: A means to teacher development. *Asia Pacific Journal of Contemporary Education and Communication Technology, 3*(1), 126–131.

Ministry of Education (2017). *The Omani national framework for the teaching profession.* Oman. www.edu.gov.om

Mumthaz, B., & Kgomotso, M. L. (2016). Teacher education and reflective practice programmes. *Journal of Educational Studies, 15*(1), 93–106.

Newman, S. (1999). Constructing and critiquing reflective practice. *Educational Action Research, 7*(1), 145–163.

Norton, J. L. (1997). Locus of control and reflective thinking in preservice teachers. *Education, 117*(3), 401–411.

Ostorga, A. N. (2006). Developing teachers who are reflective practitioners: A complex process. *Issues in Teacher Education, 15*(2), 5–20.

Planning and Statistics Department (2022). *Annual Statistics Book*. Sultan Qaboos University.

Raber-Hedberg, P. (2009). Learning through reflective classroom practice: Applications to educate the reflective manager. *Journal of Management Education, 33*(1), 10–36.

Somerville, D., & Keeling, J. (2004). A practical approach to promote reflective practice within nursing. *Nursing Times, 100*(12), 42–45.

Sultan Qaboos University (2023). *SQU Teaching and Learning Strategies Handbook*. Sultan Qaboos University.

Tok, Ş., & Dolapçıoğlu, S. D. (2013). Reflective teaching practices in Turkish primary school teachers. *Teacher Development, 17*(2), 265–287.

UNESCO (2024). *United Nations Secretary-General's High-Level Panel on the Teaching Profession. Recommendations and summary of deliberations: Transforming the teaching profession*. UNESCO.

PART II

# Reflective Practice for Continuing Professional Development and Quality Assurance

# Reshaping Teacher Beliefs

*Brian Poole*

**ABSTRACT**
Over the past three decades or more, an extensive scholarly literature on teacher beliefs has accumulated, and it is generally accepted that teacher beliefs play an important role in deciding what happens in classrooms and lecture theatres worldwide, because they tend to shape both what teachers do and what learning opportunities learners receive. In this chapter, data collected from lecturers at Majan University College during teaching-related staff development sessions over a 4-year period are used to illustrate and discuss sharply different beliefs about what constitutes effective teaching. The chapter concludes with possible ways in which opportunities can be created for lecturers to engage in reflective practice, thus potentially causing gradual shifts in both their pedagogical awareness and their behaviour in class.

## Introduction

It is generally accepted that teacher beliefs play an important role in deciding what happens in classrooms and lecture theatres worldwide (Farrell & Kun, 2008). Borg and Al Busaidi (2012, p. 6), for instance, put forward the view that "teachers' beliefs can powerfully shape both what teachers do and, consequently, the learning opportunities learners receive." Over the past three decades or more, an extensive scholarly literature on teacher beliefs has accumulated (see, for instance, Pajares, 1992; Calderhead, 1996; Ertmer, 2005; Borg 2011; Borg 2015; Wolf & Brown 2023), and it has been amply demonstrated that individual educators conceive of teaching in rather different ways. One important example of this is the distinction between teacher as learning facilitator and teacher as knowledge transmitter (Gow & Kember, 1993). In what follows, I use data collected from lecturers at Majan University College (MUC) during teaching-related staff development sessions in the 2016–2020 period to illustrate and discuss sharply different beliefs about what constitutes effective teaching. The data show that a significant minority of Majan staff instinctively advocate a transmission-based "jug and mug" approach to teaching (Postareff et al., 2023), and this is problematic as the College's teaching and learning philosophy, instantiated in key documents, is essentially constructivist in nature. Hence, the present paper also focuses on potential ways of fostering greater pedagogical awareness among lecturers who may hold unexamined and somewhat simplistic views on the nature of learning.

The data discussed in this paper arise from staff development sessions in which, as the person responsible for teaching quality at MUC, I asked my colleagues to submit anonymously brief written characterisations of 'good teaching' and 'an effective teacher'. It will be seen later that a proportion of the beliefs collected in this way are at variance with MUC's documented principles and strategies relating to learning and teaching—even though all academic staff are familiar with these through induction and through the day-to-day life of the College. We might wonder why this is so. Perhaps the beliefs are so deeply ingrained that the individuals concerned find it problematic to modify or discard them. Alternatively, certain key beliefs may be such an integral part of their teaching persona that they cannot be identified, detached, and held up for inspection and interrogation. In either case, any institution will find difficulty in bringing the beliefs and practices of certain teachers/lecturers more closely into line with its educational ethos.

This chapter proceeds in the following way. First, I provide information on the context in which I collected data on teacher beliefs. Next, I discuss various key concepts, drawing on relevant scholarly literature. I then describe data collection and discuss some of the problems in data interpretation. I conclude by indicating what, in my view, the data tell us about the beliefs of lecturers at MUC, and I then speculate about possible ways in which the transmission-related mindset of a minority of lecturers might be shifted so that they are more closely aligned with the institutional approach to teaching and learning. These ways include formal credit-rated courses in higher education pedagogy; in-house professional development sessions; reflective practice; and a systematic mentoring programme.

## Context

Majan University College (MUC) is the oldest private higher education institution in Oman, having been founded in 1995. It has the status of 'University College' under the Sultanate's tripartite classification system (College; University College; University) and delivers a range of undergraduate degrees in the areas of business, information technology and English language, in addition to hosting University of Bedfordshire (UoB) flying faculty delivering several master's degrees for which MUC staff provide local learning support. UoB is the College's main overseas partner and over more than 25 years the two institutions have collaborated closely on, for instance, programme franchising, programme validation, quality assurance, and programme delivery. As with all other similar institutions, the College's activities are also overseen and authorized by Oman's Ministry of Higher Education, Research and Innovation. Consequently, MUC can be regarded as a well-established higher education institution whose practices and standards comply with national and international expectations.

Naturally, given the fact that it has existed for almost thirty years and has reputable overseas partners, MUC has detailed documentation laying out the policies and procedures that direct all its activities, including learning and teaching. I shall now briefly describe some key points in relevant College documentation.

Notes appended to the College's teaching standards document (MUC Standards for Teaching and the Support of Learning, n.d.) suggest that "classroom interaction is a vital part of student learning" and go on to describe "teacher-centered classrooms" and long "teacher monologues" as undesirable and outdated. Instead, emphasis is placed on the co-construction of knowledge and on peer-assisted learning. Thus, MUC's approved documentation paints a picture of ideal learning and teaching processes and procedures within which teaching based on the transmission approach (as defined below) would have only very limited relevance.

It will additionally be understood from these extracts that MUC has committed itself to a learning environment in which teachers/lecturers are seen primarily as facilitators; in which old-fashioned 'stand and deliver' lecturing should be kept to a necessary minimum; and in which independent learning, peer-to-peer learning and classroom interaction are emphasized. A simple acronym, CREDO, is one of the means through which the College promotes its approach to teaching and learning among its academic staff.

C Combining innovative face to face teaching with smart use of technology
R Reducing the length of periods of lecturing
E Encouraging student participation
D Developing students as independent thinkers and learners
O Offering individual support to students

It is important to keep these features of the College's approach in mind as the teacher/lecturer beliefs collected from MUC academic staff are described.

## Selective Literature Review

To clarify what is meant by teacher or lecturer 'beliefs', it is helpful to consider the distinction between 'belief' and 'knowledge'. Many scholars have discussed the difficulty of defining these terms, in opposition to each other, in a way that is workable for the purposes of research. For example, Ertmer (2005, p. 28) argues that "part of the difficulty in defining teacher beliefs centers on determining if, and how, they differ from knowledge." Similarly, Feiman-Nemser and Floden (1986, p. 515) point out that "It does not follow that everything a teacher believes or is willing to act on merits the label 'knowledge'."

Of relevance here is the classical Greek distinction between *episteme* and *doxa*, which has endured for centuries in western philosophy. As Eisner (2002, pp. 375–76) notes, for the Greeks the term *episteme* denoted "true and certain knowledge," whereas *doxa* referred to a belief or opinion. But while the distinction seems fundamental it is not easy to operationalize. The philosopher Stephen Toulmin (1990), cited by Eisner (2002, p. 380), puts it this way:

> All our scientific explanations and critical readings start from, embody, or imply some interpretive standpoint, conceptual framework, or theoretical perspective… *episteme* was always too much to ask. Instead, the operative question is, which of our positions are rationally warranted, reasonable, or defensible – that is, well-founded rather than groundless opinions, sound *doxai* rather than shaky ones?

Notice that in the final question in this passage, Toulmin avoids both 'knowledge' and 'belief', substituting "positions" and "well-founded…opinions" though he does also refer to "sound *doxai*" which might be rendered in English as 'sound beliefs.' If we follow Toulmin there is no 'true and certain knowledge' and the distinction between 'knowledge' and 'belief' melts away. In addition, much work in the field of teacher beliefs sees them as just one element within a system of interacting forces underpinning either change or stasis in teacher behaviour and practices. See for instance the interconnected model of professional growth offered by Clarke and Hollingsworth (2002, p. 951). Overall, it seems plausible that if teachers could be persuaded to ask themselves which of their professional 'positions' are truly well-founded in research, and which are groundless, this might catalyse greater pedagogical awareness and growth.

It is also important to recognize that an individual teacher's beliefs (if they can be identified) are often at variance with his or her classroom practices. In other words, what teachers/lecturers say they believe may not be borne out in their classroom decision-making and behaviour. Tension between an individual teacher's espoused beliefs and what he or she does in class have been pointed out by numerous researchers—see, for instance, Fang (1996) and Phipps and Borg (2009). It should be borne in mind that simply because a pedagogue *says* he or she believes something about teaching or about being a good teacher, this does not automatically translate into that person's professional practices. Even if a teacher/lecturer states that good teaching entails the teacher's thoughts and ideas passing into the student's brain, this should not automatically mean that the person's classes generally progress according to a transmission model of teaching and learning (Cummins, 1989).

Richardson (1996, p. 103) sees teacher beliefs as "psychologically held understandings, premises, or propositions about the world that are felt to be true." Notice 'felt' rather than 'known.' In this paper teacher/lecturer beliefs will be dealt with specifically as propositions put forward by teachers/lecturers about the nature of good teaching or the characteristics of a good teacher. In Toulmin's terms these may be 'rationally warranted, reasonable, or defensible' or they may be 'groundless' in the sense that no sound research evidence supports them. These two groups of beliefs, and indeed other less determinate ones, may be seen as located on a cline or continuum.

When propositions put forward by teachers/lecturers are warranted (supported by research evidence) we might regard them as professional knowledge. On the other hand, some teacher beliefs may be essentially groundless. For instance, a teacher may believe that rote learning is universally effective. However, research has shown that, while aiding retention, it does not assist learners in transferring what they have learned to novel situations (see, for instance, Mayer 1995).

Having dealt briefly with teacher/lecturer beliefs, it is also important to consider what we mean by the transmission approach to teaching and learning. Freeman and McElhinny (1996, p. 264) describe this approach to teaching as follows: "In…teacher-centered classes, the teacher talks for most of the time as he or she transmits the curriculum content to the student population … and initiates the students' participation."

Freeman and McElhinny (1996) assert (citing Erickson 1996 and Savile-Troike 1996) that "research suggests that participation frameworks, or groupings of students and teachers for classroom activities…strongly influence the students' opportunities to talk and demonstrate achievement." More recent research reinforces the general finding that effective learning takes place, not through teacher-centered classroom practices, but through an environment in which both peer to peer and student-teacher interaction are encouraged. For instance, Walsh (2011, p. 22) argues, based on many years of research into classroom interaction and its effects, that it should have a greater similarity to everyday conversations, with more interruptions, requests for clarification and opportunities for the co-construction of meaning. Thus, the transmission approach to teaching, in which the lecturer declaims from the front of the room and generally asks questions to which he or she has a preferred or expected answer, may be seen as an outdated and partly discredited one, even though it may still hold sway in some universities around the world. Norton et al. (2005, p. 559) show that it is an orientation to teaching that is found more often in men than in women. Since the teacher/lecturer has considerable control when the transmission model of teaching is adopted, it may be seen as essentially based on behaviourist notions of learning. Four decades ago, Allwright (1984) showed that students' post hoc accounts of what was taught in one of their classes differ markedly. This alone provides evidence that a simplistic transmission-based understanding of teaching (from jug – the teacher – to mug – the student) is fundamentally flawed. Nevertheless, that understanding persists to some extent as a largely unwarranted teacher belief, as we shall see.

Having provided background and focus, I shall now proceed to consider the conduct of the present study.

## Methods

During the pre-Covid period, I gave the same interactive presentation to the academic staff of each of MUC's Faculties (Business Management, English Language Studies, and Information Technology). In total 56 of the then

73 full-time academic staff of the College (about 77 percent) attended one of the three sessions. Twenty-nine of the attendees were females and 44 were males. The largest group of staff (35 or 47.9 percent) was from India, with a further 9 (or 12.33 percent) from Pakistan, 6 Omani staff (8.22 percent), and 5 (6.85 percent) from the Philippines. Other nationalities represented included (in alphabetical order) British, Iranian, Kenyan, Lebanese, Nigerian, Palestinian, Sudanese, and Ukrainian. Since this group of lecturers is diverse in nationality (twelve nationalities in all) it seems likely that they will have been taught (as students) in a wide range of ways, thus emerging with rather different conceptions of 'good teaching' and 'good teachers.'

During each session I began by discussing the notion of teacher beliefs, bringing in the classical Greek notions of *episteme* and *doxa*. I then asked my colleagues to record on a slip of paper two of their own beliefs about either what constitutes good teaching or how we recognize a good teacher. Each belief was to be written as a single sentence. To preserve anonymity and to encourage openness, they were asked not to write their names, and I ensured that the papers were handed back (at the end of the session) in bulk, through an assistant. While most participants provided two beliefs, each in a single sentence, some wrote only one, while a few people wrote three or four. It is also possible that some individuals did not submit a response. Having read all the responses, I totaled them into 129 beliefs. However, this figure is contestable because of cases such as this:

Characteristics of a good teacher: patience; art of listening; empathy; demonstration of knowledge using practical examples; understanding the level of knowledge of the audience.

How many beliefs are provided here? Because this is difficult to decide, I have recorded this as a single item, and therefore (counter-intuitively) a single 'belief'—even though it consists of several component parts. However, most of the beliefs collected took the form of single propositions expressed in a sentence, such as the following examples:

A good teacher should be easy to understand.
A good teacher should be inspiring.
Effective teaching requires bridging theory and practice.
A good teacher values interaction with students.

After isolating 129 beliefs, I then moved to data categorisation. Both Bryan and Atwater (2002) and Richards et al. (2001) categorize teacher beliefs, but in each case the content or domain of the beliefs elicited is sharply different from those in the present study. It was therefore decided to allow categories to arise from the data through a content analysis, following a procedure like that adopted by Li (2012). I also used the freeware AntConc (Anthony, 2005), a concordancing tool which facilitates rapid identification of key words in written data and thus assists in the setting up of semantically based categories. I first transcribed all the data from the handwritten slips of paper. I then used AntConc (or sometimes, more simply, CTRL-F within MS Word) to search for key words. As a first step in analyzing the data (in total 1,489 running words), AntConc was used to pinpoint all cases of the words 'teacher' and 'teaching' and to show, in quickly readable form, the various linguistic contexts in which search words occur. In this way, 95 beliefs focusing on characteristics of good teachers and 34 beliefs about good teaching were identified. AntConc also facilitated the process of counting such words as 'empathy', 'communication' and 'patience', greatly aiding data categorization (through seeing key words in context) and the identification of category members. Through qualitative content analysis (via lexical semantic consideration of key words) I coded individual items, resulting in thirteen categories.

Although the assistance of AntConc concordancing freeware accelerated the process of finding specific words in the data, it did not significantly reduce the extent of subjectivity in coding the data. Individual respondents used different forms of words, even when expressing seemingly similar beliefs. I sometimes faced problems in deciding whether a given belief was sufficiently similar, semantically, to be assigned to the same category as another. Below are three indicative examples of the interpretative problems:

A good teacher is a facilitator and a motivator.
Good teaching should help students to unlearn and learn new developments/perspectives.
Good teaching means helping students to do the learning themselves.

I treat the first item as an exponent of both the belief category 'facilitation' and of the belief category 'motivation'. I added the second and third items (above) to 'facilitation' – even though no form of the words 'facilitate', or 'facilitation' appears in them. My justification is that 'helping' students to learn or to 'do the learning themselves' can be interpreted as facilitation. Such examples serve to illustrate the difficulty and degree of subjectivity involved in categorizing data of this kind.

We can now proceed to examine the beliefs elicited from the subjects. For reasons of space the full list of beliefs is not given here but may be obtained from the author.

## Findings

Having, in the previous section, discussed the complexity of the interpretative choices to be made in categorizing the data, I shall now reveal the categories which, in my view, do emerge. Tabulated data is available in the appendix.

Thirteen categories were identified in the data, but only a little more than half of the data is accounted for (70 out 129 items). 51 out of 95 beliefs about characteristics of a good teacher have been categorized as well as 19 out of 34 beliefs about what constitutes good teaching. The reason why almost half of the data has not been categorized is that it is so diverse – indicating, at least within this sample of lecturers, that beliefs about teaching and being a good teacher are idiosyncratic. Here are just a few examples which seem to be unique and therefore not to belong in any of the multi-item categories:

> Teaching and learning are two different things.
> A good teacher is one who creates healthy minds and wealthy careers.
> A good teacher must have a good temperament.
> A good teacher knows that s/he is not there to fill a bucket but to light a candle.
> Effective teaching is the process of building a nation.
> A good teacher must be able to go down to the level of understanding of the students.

While the 'transmission' category is the largest one (16 examples), it should be noted that this is not much more than 20 percent of the categorized examples, and that that many responses might be regarded as springing from more learner-centered sensibilities. Some examples are: 'facilitator/facilitation' (10 examples); 'relationship with students' (7 examples); interaction/interactive (4 examples); and empathizes/empathy (2 examples). There is clear evidence in the data indicating awareness among respondents about the importance of interaction, co-construction of knowledge and the role of the teacher as a facilitator. Nevertheless, the fact that the 'transmission' category forms the largest single group of responses is striking.

An OECD report (OECD, 2009) contrasts the transmission approach to teaching and learning with the view that the teacher is, or should be, primarily a facilitator – a view which is, of course, essentially constructivist in nature. The OECD report (OECD, 2009, p. 92) puts it this way:

> The direct transmission view of student learning implies that a teachers' role is to communicate knowledge in a clear and structured way, to explain correct solutions, to give students clear and resolvable problems, and to ensure calm and concentration in the classroom. In contrast, a constructivist view focuses on students not as passive recipients but as active participants in the process of acquiring knowledge. Teachers holding this view emphasize facilitating student inquiry, prefer to give students the chance to develop solutions to problems on their own, and allow students to play an active role in instructional activities.

It is precisely this second, constructivist, view of the learning and teaching process that is most strongly emphasized by MUC documentation, with its emphasis on such factors as classroom interaction, peer to peer learning, and independent learning. Yet, as the data in the appendix shows, more than 20 percent of the categorized beliefs (16/70) indicate a commitment to transmission-related notions.

Regardless of where these transmission-related beliefs emanate from (teacher education, personal experiences as a student, etc.), the question for MUC and for any other HEIs that encounter this phenomenon is whether they are amenable to change. As Li (2012, p. 34) puts it, "beliefs and perceptions are culturally bound," and when a body of teachers/lecturers springs from many national and cultural backgrounds it is inevitable that some of these will diverge from the norms upheld by particular institutions. At MUC, the documented approach to teaching emphasizes interactive classes and learner independence, so there is an apparent mismatch between the institutional ethos and the beliefs of about 20 percent of its teachers.

In the final section I shall suggest some ways forward, in terms of both practical solutions and further research.

## Possible Ways Forward

Categorization of the data collected in the present study shows that, while many lecturers hold beliefs about teaching and being a good teacher that sit comfortably with constructivist models of learning (such as beliefs about the importance of the teacher acting as a facilitator, and the need to promote teacher-student and student-student interaction), the largest single category of beliefs (constituting one eighth of the data) is that which contains beliefs associated with the transmission approach to teaching. Particularly in the Gulf context, where students typically learn through the medium of English and may have a limited command of the language, it is undesirable for lecturers to hold and act on such beliefs. Classes involving long lecturer monologues tend to result in students 'switching off', as it is difficult to maintain concentration for long periods when listening to a foreign language. As Klaassen (2008, p. 37) notes, based on her empirical research, attention span is considerably shorter when students listen to a foreign language and therefore innovative 'working methods' are needed to maintain students' attention.

MUC's teaching-related documentation states that 'lecturing and lecturer talking time' should be kept 'to a necessary minimum' and mentions 'short periods of lecturing…where appropriate.' Therefore, one reaction to these findings might be to tolerate the fact that some lecturers hold transmission-related views. Since only 22.86 percent of the collected beliefs (16/70) fall into this category, it seems reasonable to assume that relatively low levels of teacher-centered lecturing will take place in MUC classrooms and laboratories. However, this approach is defeatist. How can the beliefs and practices of transmission-focused lecturers be gradually shifted?

The tone of some of the transmission-related beliefs is striking and somewhat troubling:

A good teacher is one who makes the students understand what s/he taught them.

Good teaching happens when there is a transfer of knowledge from teacher to student.

Good teaching means imparting information to students.

A good teacher/lecturer is great in delivering information to his/her students.

A good teacher is one who transfers knowledge in an efficient way.

The writers of these five statements are so wedded to a 'jug and mug' view of teaching that they are unlikely to 'provide students with a variety of different learning experiences', as required by the College's approved documentation on learning and teaching. As has been shown by psychological research (see, for instance, Dweek, 2008), belief systems are fundamental not only to people's ambitions and goals but also to the way they interpret the external world and see patterns in their daily experiences. People also tend to adopt or absorb the beliefs of those they respect or identify with, and for educators this can mean internalizing beliefs about teaching from those they looked up to as 'good teachers' when they themselves were students (Lortie, 1975). It is a challenging task to reshape long held and deeply ingrained beliefs so that, in this case, they are more closely aligned with research findings and the College's teaching ethos. There are perhaps four principal ways in which this might be attempted: via formal credit-rated courses in higher education pedagogy; through professional development sessions; through reflective practice, and through some form of mentoring programme. These options overlap to some extent, but I shall deal with them in turn.

In the United Kingdom, many universities require new academic staff who have no, or relatively little, experience in teaching at higher education level to undergo formal study towards a postgraduate certificate or diploma. The programme structures and award titles differ, but they tend to be either postgraduate certificates (Sheffield Hallam University, Kingston University) or postgraduate diplomas (Oxford University). Similar programmes exist in other countries, for example at the National institute of Education in Singapore, and the Certificate in Learning and Teaching in Higher Education is increasingly offered internationally by the Higher Education Academy (UK). Greater adoption of such postgraduate certificates/diplomas in the Gulf region could raise awareness of innovative pedagogical approaches and techniques in higher education, and significantly shift the beliefs of lecturers who absorbed, teacher-centered education as children and young adults.

The second possible way forward is through professional development sessions. These could be developed and delivered in-house, with a range of colleagues leading individual sessions. In-house delivery could conceivably lead to a greater degree of trust and uninhibited interaction between participants, whilst the use of session leaders of different nationalities could defuse tensions around 'western' domination/neo-colonialism that might arise from the previous option. However, as has been noted (OECD, 2009, p. 90) although "professional development activities may change beliefs and attitudes" it is often the case that individuals with deeply ingrained see no reason to participate. Compulsory attendance, on the other hand, might stimulate resentment in some attendees and poison the atmosphere. The same can be said, of course, when an institution imposes compulsory study towards a postgraduate certificate or diploma.

The third potential option mentioned above is reflective practice (RP). Here I would like to make two points. Boud, Keogh and Walker (2013, p. 19) define RP as "an important human activity in which people recapture their experience, think about it, mull it over and evaluate it" and they go on to mention "intellectual and affective activities in which individuals engage to explore their experiences in order to lead to new understandings and appreciations." Many critiques of reflective practice have dwelt on the vagueness of some of the terms used to describe what goes on. For example, exactly how should a teacher/lecturer 'recapture' his or her in-class experiences and 'explore' them? Is it possible for ordinary people (as opposed, perhaps, to those trained in meditation) to isolate and dissect their own motivations, feelings and actions? In addition, as Smyth (1992, p. 285) puts it, "reflection can mean all things to all people" and at the same time is sometimes "trumpeted" as "something that is good or desirable...as virtuous as motherhood." A possible problem here is that those who cling to a transmission view of teaching may, in some cases, be rigid traditionalists. They may not be as open to reflective practice as those who are already willing to explore more innovative pedagogical approaches and techniques.

The fourth possible way forward is through some form of mentoring. The term 'mentor' owes its origins to Greek mythology, in which the fatherly Mentor took care of the absent Odysseus's son Telemakhos (Sands, Parson & Duane, 1992, p. 175). Mentoring relationships therefore typically involve an experienced academic (the mentor) seeking to guide, or catalyse the development of, a less experienced colleague (the mentee or protégé). However, more recently (Darwin & Palmer, 2009) it has been argued that this type of mentoring does little to promote wider team collaboration and provides mentees with restricted access to perspectives on higher education. Instead, 'mentoring circles' are advocated. In this model of mentoring, one mentor may work with a number of mentees, and the support and advice for individual mentees may come from any source within the group. A richer range of perspectives and ideas is generated in such mentoring circles and participants in the mentoring circles described by Darwin and Palmer at the University of Adelaide also noted "learning from others, hearing opinions from those more senior in the organization and meeting people you wouldn't normally meet…and (breaking down) feelings of isolation" (Darwin & Palmer, 2009, p. 132). Participants felt that meeting once per month was appropriate and also stressed the importance of focusing each session on a particular topic, such as time management, promotion, collaborative research or common frustrations. It would be possible to imagine such sessions focusing on topics such as teacher-centered versus student-centered learning, or on unpacking the notion of teacher/lecturer as facilitator. It is also important to note that the idea of mentoring circles fits well with norms of social interaction in Gulf societies (Alyousef, 2022, p. 16).

## Conclusion

To conclude, it has long been noted that teacher/lecturer beliefs are resistant to change. Having considered relevant literature, I suggest that mentoring circles might prove to be a fruitful way of seeking to modify the beliefs of educators in the Gulf region and elsewhere who currently think of teaching and learning in a transmission-based, 'jug and mug' way. It might also be valuable to explore ways in which mentorship can promote reflective practice (Pottinger et al., 2019).

## References

Allwright, R. (1984). Why don't learners learn what teachers teach?. In D. Singleton & D. Little (Eds.), *Language Learning in Formal and Informal Contexts* (pp. 3–18). IRAAL.

Alyousef, S. M. (2022). Patterns of social interaction and lifeways which affect health and healthcare of families in Saudi Arabia and the Gulf States. *Middle East Journal of Family Medicine*, 7(10), 14–23.

Anthony, L. (2005). AntConc: Design and development of a freeware corpus analysis toolkit for the technical writing classroom. In *2005*

*IEEE International Professional Communication Conference Proceedings, IPCC 2005* (pp. 729–737).

Borg, S. (2015). Researching teacher beliefs. In B. Paltridge & A. Phakiti (Eds.), *Research methods in applied linguistics: A practical resource* (pp. 487–504). Bloomsbury.

Borg, S. (2011). The impact of in-service teacher education on language teachers' beliefs. *System, 39*, 370–380.

Borg, S., & Al-Busaidi, S. (2012). *Learner autonomy: English language teachers' beliefs and practices*. British Council.

Boud, D., Keogh, R., & Walker, D. (Eds.). (2013). *Reflection: Turning Experience into Learning*. Routledge.

Bryan, L. & Atwater, M. (2002). Teacher beliefs and cultural models: A challenge for science teacher preparation programs. *Science Teacher Education*, *86*(6), 821–839.

Calderhead, J. (1996). Teachers: beliefs and knowledge. In D. Berliner & R. Calfee (Eds.), *Handbook of Educational Psychology* (pp. 709–725). Macmillan.

Clarke, D. and Hollingsworth, H. (2002). Elaborating a model of teacher professional growth. *Teaching and Teacher Education*, *18*, 947–967.

Cummins, J. (1989). The sanitized curriculum: educational disempowerment in a nation at risk. In D. Johnson & D. Ruen (Eds.), *Richness in Writing: Empowering ESL Students* (pp.19–38). Longman.

Darwin, A., & Palmer, E. (2009). Mentoring circles in higher education. *Higher Education Research & Development, 28*(2), 125–136.

Dweek, C. (2008). Can personality be changed? The role of beliefs in personality and change. *Current Directions in Psychological Science*, *17*, 391–394.

Eisner, E. (2002). From episteme to phronesis to artistry in the study and improvement of teaching. *Teaching and Teacher Education, 18*, 375–385.

Erickson, F. (1996). Ethnographic microanalysis. In S. L. McKay & N. Hornberger (Eds.), *Sociolinguistics and Language Teaching* (pp. 283–306). Cambridge University Press.

Ertmer, P. (2005). Teacher pedagogical beliefs: the final frontier in our quest for technology integration? *Educational Technology, Research and Development*, *53*(4), 25–39.

Fang, Z. (1996). A review of research on teacher beliefs and practices. *Educational Research*, *38*, 47–65.

Farrell, T. S. C., & Kun, S. T. K. (2008). Language policy, language teachers' beliefs, and classroom practices. *Applied Linguistics, 29*(3), 381–403.

Feiman-Nemser, S. & Floden, R. (1986). The cultures of teaching. In M. Wittrock (Ed.), *Handbook of research on teaching* (3rd edition, pp. 505–526). Macmillan.

Freeman, R. & McElhinny, B. (1996). Language and gender. In S. L. McKay & N. Hornberger (Eds.), *Sociolinguistics and Language Teaching* (pp. 218–282). Cambridge University Press.

Klaassen, R. (2008). Preparing lecturers for English-medium instruction. In R. Wilkinson & V. Zegers (Eds.), *Realizing content and language integration in higher education* (pp. 32–42). Maastricht University.

Li, L. (2012). Belief construction and development: two tales of non-native English-speaking student teachers in a TESOL programme. *Novitas-ROYAL (Research on Youth and Language)*, *6*(1), 33–58.

Lortie, D. (1975). *Schoolteacher: A sociological study.* University of Chicago Press.

Mayer, R.E. (1995). Cognitive theory for education: What teachers need to know. In N. M. Lambert & B. L. McCombs (Eds.). *How students learn—reforming school through learner-centered education* (pp. 353–378). American Psychological Association.

MUC. (n.d.). *Standards for Teaching and the Support of Learning.* Majan University College.

Norton, L., Richardson, T., Hartley, J., Newstead, S., & Mayes, J. (2005). Teachers' beliefs and intentions concerning teaching in higher education. *Higher Education*, *50*(4), 537–571.

OECD. (2009). *Creating Effective Teaching and Learning Environments.* https://www.oecd.org/edu/school/43023606.pdf

Pajares, M. F. (1992). Teachers' beliefs and educational research: Cleaning up a messy construct. *Review of Educational Research*, *62*(3), 307–332.

Postareff, L., Lahdenperä, J., Hailikari, T., & Parpala, A. (2024). The dimensions of approaches to teaching in higher education: a new analysis of teaching profiles. *Higher Education*, *88*, 37–59. https://doi.org/10.1007/s10734-023-01104-x

Pottinger, E., Dyer, R., & Akard, J. (2019). Reflective practice through mentorship: A program reflection. *Journal of Instructional Research*, *8*(2), 62–69.

Richards, J., Gallo, P., & Renandya, W. (2001). Exploring teachers' beliefs and the processes of change. *PAC Journal*, *1*(1), 41–62.

Richardson, V. (1996). The role of attitudes and beliefs in learning to teach. In J. Sikula (Ed.), *Handbook of Research on Teacher Education* (pp.102–119). Macmillan.

Savile-Troike, M. (1996). The ethnography of communication. In S. L. McKay & N. Hornberger (Eds.), *Sociolinguistics and Language Teaching* (pp. 351–382). Cambridge University Press.

Sands, R. G., Parson, L. A., & Duane, J. (1991). Faculty mentoring faculty in a public university. *The Journal of Higher Education, 62*(2), 174–193.

Smyth, J. (1992). Teachers' work and the politics of reflection. *American Educational Research Journal*, *29*, 267–300.

Toulmin, S. (1990). *Cosmopolis: The hidden agenda of modernity*. The Free Press.

Walsh, S. (2011). *Exploring Classroom Discourse: Language in Action*. Routledge.

Wolf, S., & Brown, A. (2023). Teacher beliefs and student learning. *Human Development*, *67*(1): 37–54. https://doi.org/10.1159/000529450

## Appendix: Categorization of the Data

| # | Category | Total examples | Teacher/ Teaching | Typical exponent | Comments |
|---|---|---|---|---|---|
| 1 | Transmission | 16 | 10/6 | A good teacher delivers knowledge to students. | |
| 2 | Facilitator/ Facilitation | 10 | 7/3 | A good teacher acts as a facilitator. | |

*(Continued)*

(*Continued*)

| # | Category | Total examples | Teacher/ Teaching | Typical exponent | Comments |
|---|---|---|---|---|---|
| 3 | Inspires/ Inspiring | 7 | 5/2 | A good teacher inspires students to excel. | |
| 3 | Relationship with Students | 7 | 7/0 | A good teacher maintains a good rapport with students. | The examples in this category are linguistically diverse. They involve words such as 'rapport', 'friendly' and 'approachable'. |
| 3 | Communicates/ Communicator | 7 | 4/3 | A good teacher is an effective communicator. | |
| 6 | Motivates/ Motivation | 6 | 4/2 | A good teacher is one who motivates students. | It might be argued that the 'inspires' and 'motivates' categories could be combined. |
| 7 | Interaction/ Interactive | 4 | 2/2 | Effective teaching is interactive. | |
| 8 | Patient/ Patience | 3 | 3/0 | A good teacher shows patience in making students understand. | This example ('*making* students understand') might also be allocated to the transmission category. |
| 9 | Listening | 2 | 2/0 | Listening is more important than speaking for a good teacher. | |
| 9 | Empathizes/ Empathy | 2 | 2/0 | A good teacher empathizes with the students. | These two examples could perhaps be placed in the 'relationship' category. |
| 9 | Relating Theory to Practice | 2 | 1/1 | Effective teaching requires bridging theory and practice. | |

| # | Category | Total examples | Teacher/ Teaching | Typical exponent | Comments |
|---|---|---|---|---|---|
| 9 | Shaping Students | 2 | 2/0 | A good teacher is one who moulds/ creates good human beings. | |
| 9 | Prior Knowledge | 2 | 2/0 | Good teachers take into account prior knowledge. | |
| | Totals | 70 | 51/19 | | |

# Observation of Teaching and Reflective Practices for Sustainable Enhancement of Teaching Quality in Higher Education

*Sulaiman Al Hasani*

**ABSTRACT**
Educational institutions are striving to elevate their teaching and learning practices, ensuring they are quality-driven and student-centric. Teaching observations play an instrumental role in enhancing teaching quality in higher education and support the growth and professional development of educators. This book chapter explores teaching observation practices, emphasizing their developmental and reflective nature, and examines their methodologies, objectives, and impact on professional growth and the quality of education. The chapter looks at best practices and the impact of teaching observations, specifically peer observation of teaching, and emphasizes how leveraging technological advancements transforms observation practices for sustainable enhancement of teaching quality. The book chapter outlines the pillars constituting an ideal observation structure: pre-observation preparation, evidence collection, observer analysis, self-analysis and reflection, discussion of observation outcomes, and action plan formulation. It shares best practices from the higher education sector. The chapter will also discuss the necessary policy frameworks and forms of infrastructure essential to support teaching observations. Additionally, it will address the strategic aspects of engaging relevant stakeholders to create a culture of continuous improvement and excellence in teaching and learning through structured observation practices.

## Introduction

Teaching quality in higher education is fundamental to student success and institutional reputation. High-quality teaching practices are essential for developing critical thinking, enhancing student engagement, and improving learning outcomes. Institutions that prioritize teaching excellence produce competent graduates and contribute to the broader educational landscape by setting standards and sharing best practices (Netshifhefhe et al., 2016).

Teaching observations serve as a pivotal tool and are considered one of the most effective tools for both educators' professional development and the enhancement of teaching quality. Teaching observations are structured evaluations of classroom instruction, typically conducted by peers, administrators, or educational researchers. Their primary purpose is to assess and improve teaching practices through systematic, evidence-based feedback.

Observations aim to identify both strengths and areas for development in teaching, provide platform for professional growth and enhancing student learning outcomes. These observations can be formative, aimed at professional development, or summative, contributing to performance evaluations and institutional accountability (Fletcher, 2018). For the purpose of this chapter, the focus will be on summative/developmental teaching observation and the reflective practices aimed for sustainable enhancement of teaching quality in Higher Education.

Systematically observing and reflecting on teaching practices can provide valuable insights to educators into their instructional methods and student engagement, interactions, and their ways of learning. The teaching observation process coupled with constructive feedback and reflective practices can encourage a culture of continuous improvement, where feedback is used constructively to refine teaching strategies and educators reflect on their practices and plan their growth and improvements (Hendry & Oliver, 2012). Teaching observations also provide opportunities for learning and the dissemination of effective and best teaching practices across the institution (Hendry & Oliver, 2012).

This chapter aims to explore the role of teaching observations in enhancing teaching quality through reflective practices and provide a comprehensive understanding of how teaching observations and reflective practices contribute to the continuous and sustainable improvement of teaching quality in higher education. This chapter examines the different methodologies of teaching observations and their objectives. Additionally, it explores the methodologies, objectives, and impacts of reflective practices within teaching observations. Furthermore, the chapter discusses how technological advancements are transforming these practices, ensuring sustainable enhancement of teaching quality. The chapter also enumerates the key components that ensure the success of teaching observations and what ideal observation of teaching structure looks like. Additionally, the chapter provides educators practical recommendations for implementing effective teaching observations and showcases best practices in teaching observation with a focus on peer observation of teaching. Moreover, the chapter discusses the necessary policies and infrastructure to support teaching observations and what policy frameworks and infrastructure ought to be in place to ensure successful observation of teaching. Last but not least, the importance of engaging stakeholders and involving educators, administrators, and policymakers in the process is underscored.

## Definition and Significance of Teaching Observation

Teaching observation usually refers to the systematic and intentional process of attending and observing teaching practices directly or through recorded sessions for the purpose of analyzing and assessing these practices. It plays a critical role in educational settings, serving as a tool for both formative and summative assessments (Richards & Farrell, 2011; Yiend et al., 2014). Formatively, it aids educators in identifying areas of improvement and providing guided support for their professional growth and development, while summatively, it provides data for performance evaluations and accountability measures (Richards & Farrell, 2011). The significance of teaching observation is due to its ability to enhance teaching and learning quality in the institution by providing objective feedback and promote collaborative continuous improvement. Studies have shown that regular and effective teaching observations lead to enhanced instructional strategies and improved student learning outcomes (Danielson, 2013). There are a number of types and methodologies of teaching observations, which can vary greatly in their purpose and approach, each contributing uniquely to the professional development of educators and the overall quality of education. Understanding the different types of teaching observations can help educators, administrators, and institutions effectively utilize these tools and capitalize on their potentials. Some examples of different types of teaching observations include: 1) Student-led teaching observation, where students take an active role in observing and providing feedback on teaching practices; 2) Mentor observation for new or less experienced educators, where a mentor educator, often with considerable experience and expertise, observes the mentee's classroom to offer guidance and feedback; 3) Administrative observation, which serves a more evaluative purpose, where administrators or academic leaders conduct these observations to assess instructors' performance against standardized rubrics or criteria; 4) Self-observation, which is intended to empower educators to take control of their professional development, usually done by recording their own lessons and reviewing the footage to reflect on their practices, identify areas for improvement, and develop strategies to enhance their effectiveness; 5)

Peer observation, also referred to as Peer Observation of Teaching (POT) (Sullivan et al., 2012; Rauch & Whittaker, 1999; Flores, 2019; Whittaker et al., 2023; Skoog, 1980). Peer Observation of Teaching (POT) is the focus of this chapter.

Widely recognized and practiced, POT is a structured process in which educators observe each other's teaching practices to provide feedback. POT is referred to as one of the significant tools for enhancing the effectiveness of teaching and learning practices. Studies have shown that POT is considered as an effective method for enhancing teaching performance and contributes greatly to educators' professional development and growth. Educators receive specific, actionable feedback from their peers that helps them improve their instructional methods. This process benefits both the observee and the observer, therefore, contributing to mutual professional development (Siddiqui et al., 2007). It provides opportunities for educators to learn from each other and integrate best practices into their own teaching (Paul, 2021). The developmental feedback received through POT helps educators refine their instructional techniques, which is critical for continuous improvement (Sullivan et al., 2012). Furthermore, POT encourages the sharing of best practices and supports the development of a cohesive academic community (Bell & Mladenovic, 2008). Through this collaborative process, educators can transform their educational perspectives and build stronger professional relationships (Hendry et al., 2014). Furthermore, POT helps educators develop reflective practice skills, allowing them to critically evaluate their teaching and make informed changes to improve student learning outcomes (Yiend et al., 2014). The feedback and reflections generated during POT sessions encourage educators to consider their roles as professional educators and to seek relevant developmental processes (Eri, 2014). When implemented effectively, peer observation can significantly enhance the quality of teaching and learning. Programs that include structured pre-observation meetings, observation sessions, and post-observation reflections are particularly successful in promoting educator development and improving instructional practices (Norbury, 2001). Educators report that POT helps them gain new insights and feel more confident in their teaching abilities (Rauch & Whittaker, 1999). POT has been shown to significantly enhance the content and delivery of instruction, leading to better student outcomes (Skoog, 1980).

As seen in the literature, there are significant benefits to POT and it is considered to be an effective educator development tool. Despite its potential benefits, POT carries several negative connotations that can impact its effectiveness and acceptance among educators. It is worth exploring the challenges associated with POT to understand how these can be mitigated to ensure effective utilization of this tool. The following section discusses challenges such as stress and anxiety associated with POT, the perception of superficiality and compliance, the influence of political and power dynamics, the lack of adequate training and preparation, and the decoupling from formal staff development processes.

One of the primary negative connotations of POT is the stress and anxiety it can induce in both observers and observees. Observers may feel more stress than observees due to the responsibility of providing constructive feedback. This added pressure can affect the observer's performance and the quality of feedback provided (Kohut et al., 2007). For observees, having a peer in the classroom can create a sense of being judged, leading to discomfort and vulnerability. This environment may hinder the natural flow of teaching and learning activities, impacting the overall effectiveness of the observation process (Sullivan et al., 2012). Another significant issue with peer observation is its potential to be perceived as a superficial exercise rather than a meaningful developmental process. When POT is implemented primarily to meet external requirements or compliance standards, it can be seen as a "tick box" activity rather than a tool for genuine professional growth (Chamberlain et al., 2011). This perception can diminish the motivation of educators to engage fully with the process, reducing its potential impact. Additionally, a managerial and compliance-driven approach can lead to resistance among faculty members, who may view the process as an imposition rather than a beneficial practice (Shortland, 2004). Peer observation can also exacerbate existing political and power dynamics within academic departments. The process may be influenced by personal biases and relationships, affecting the objectivity and fairness of the feedback provided (Hammersley-Fletcher & Orsmond, 2004). Negative assessments during peer feedback can lead to defensive reactions, straining professional relationships and hindering collaboration and openness. This dynamic can create a hostile environment, making it difficult for educators to accept and act on feedback constructively (Batlle & Seedhouse, 2020). Adequate training for peer observers is often lacking, leading to inconsistencies in the quality and usefulness of feedback (Kohut et al., 2007). Observers may not feel sufficiently prepared to conduct effective observations and provide constructive feedback, which can undermine the developmental goals of POT (Kohut et al., 2007). Without proper training, the process may fail to meet its intended outcomes, resulting in a wasted opportunity for professional growth (Blackwell, 1996). Finally, peer observation is sometimes decoupled from formal staff development processes, making it unclear how the outcomes of observations are integrated into professional growth initiatives. This separation can diminish the perceived value of PoT and its impact on teaching quality (Chamberlain et al., 2011). When peer observation is not linked to broader staff development programs, its potential benefits are not fully realized, and educators may not see the process as a valuable component of their professional development. The following sections of the chapter identify the areas to overcome the challenges associated with PoT and how to make the process more effective.

## Peer Observation of Teaching and Reflective Practices in Education

In order to have an effective teaching observation, there must be a strong emphasis on teaching observation as a reflective practice. So, how are reflective practices linked to teaching observation, and why is this link important? In general, reflective practices are essential for continuous personal and professional development. They are defined as the process of engaging in deep thought about an individual's actions, learnings and experiences to gain understandings and improve future practices. There are a number of core principles that support reflective practice, including self-awareness, critical analysis, and continuous learning. Various models guide reflective practices, each offering unique frameworks for introspection and growth. Schön's Reflective Practitioner emphasizes the importance of reflection-in-action and reflection-on-action, promoting adaptability and informed decision-making in complex situations (Schön, 1983). Gibbs' Reflective Cycle provides a structured approach to reflection, encouraging individuals to systematically evaluate their experiences through stages of description, feelings, evaluation, analysis, conclusion, and action plan (Gibbs, 1988). Kolb's Experiential Learning Cycle highlights the iterative nature of learning from experience through a cycle of concrete experience, reflective observation, abstract conceptualization, and active experimentation (Kolb, 1984). Rolfe et al.'s Reflective Model simplifies the process into three fundamental questions: What? So what? Now what? (Rolfe et al., 2001). These models are complemented by techniques that enhance reflective practice, such as journaling, which involves regularly recording thoughts and experiences to track progress and insights; critical incident analysis, which focuses on examining significant events to understand their impact and underlying factors; and reflective dialogue and discussions, which encourage sharing and analyzing experiences with peers to gain diverse perspectives and deepen understanding. By understanding these frameworks and models, one can see the importance of incorporating reflective practices in teaching observation. Through these practices and frameworks, individuals can systematically reflect on their experiences from observing or being observed, leading to enhanced self-awareness and professional growth. By integrating observation and reflection into their routine, educators can create a dynamic and responsive teaching environment. An educator reflecting on their teaching experiences can develop a deeper understanding of their professional practice, leading to more effective and responsive teaching strategies. Integrating teaching observations with reflective practices creates a comprehensive approach to professional development. Observations provide external feedback, while reflective practices encourage internal evaluation, resulting in a balanced and holistic view of teaching performance (Farrell, 2015).. Research additionally indicates that integrating teaching observation and reflective practices can significantly enhance teaching effectiveness due to the fact that observations provide concrete data that can inform reflective practice, which should result in making self-evaluation more focused and actionable (Farrell, 2015). Reflective practices support educators internalize the feedback received from observations and apply it to their teaching in meaningful ways (Larrivee, 2000). Ultimately, the synergy between observation and reflection provides a robust and a sustainable model of teaching enhancement, ensuring that educational practices evolve to meet the changing needs of students, institutions and the community at large.

So how this can be done effectively and how can we integrate reflective practices in the teaching observation process? Effective integration requires a structured framework where observations are followed by reflective sessions. This could involve pre-observation meetings to set goals, post-observation debriefings to discuss findings, and reflective journaling to process and apply feedback. Such a framework ensures that both observation and reflection are purposeful and aligned with the overall goals of professional development (Cosh, 1999). This approach enhances individual teaching practices as well as contributing to a collaborative professional culture where continuous improvement is valued and pursued (Jay & Johnson, 2002). As the main focus of this chapter is Peer observation of Teaching (POT), the following section highlights the methodologies and process of POT and how reflective practices are integrated in the process.

## Methodologies of Peer Observation of Teaching

The first step is pre-observation preparation; this phase involves setting clear objectives and goals for the observation, which may include assessing specific teaching strategies, student engagement techniques, or classroom management skills. This is initiated and led by the observee. This phase also involves the observer reviewing the course content to understand the lesson's context and expectations. A pre-observation meeting between the observer and the observee is essential for aligning expectations and discussing areas where the observee seeks feedback. Danielson (2007) emphasizes the importance of such meetings in establishing mutually agreed-upon goals and understanding the instructional context (Siddiqui et al., 2007). As this is led by the observee, it reaffirms the importance of the developmental aspect of the observation and focuses the discussion around the delivery and teaching strategies.

The second step is the actual observation, during which evidence is collected through various means to provide a comprehensive evaluation of teaching practices. Detailed observation notes capture specific instructional methods and student reactions, and technology such as the use of video recordings to offer a complete view of classroom dynamics (leveraging technology to enhance the process of teaching observation is explored later in this chapter). Additionally, gathering indirect feedback from students provides insights into their engagement and understanding of the material. Marshall (2009) highlights the significance of using multiple forms of evidence to ensure a well-rounded observation of teaching practices (Sullivan et al., 2012). This step is then followed by a post-observation discussion between the observer and the observee, immediately after the observation session, to ensure that thoughts and observation notes are current, relevant, and accurate.

The post-observation meeting provides an opportunity for the observer and instructor to discuss the findings collaboratively. This discussion should lead to actionable insights that the instructor can implement in future lessons. Hattie and Timperley (2007) indicate that collaborative discussions help instructors understand and apply feedback more effectively. The collaborative nature of this discussion ensures that the instructor feels supported and empowered to make necessary adjustments to their teaching practices (Yiend et al., 2014). The observer analyzes the collected evidence to identify patterns and areas for improvements. This analysis should focus on providing constructive feedback that supports the observee's professional development. Effective feedback is specific, actionable, and aimed at promoting growth. Identifying patterns in the instructor's teaching methods and student interactions is crucial for offering meaningful insights that can lead to improved instructional practices (Bell & Mladenovic, 2008).

The analysis and feedback are then shared with the observee who is expected to engage in self-analysis and reflection, which is a critical component of the observation process. Reviewing the collected evidence allows the observee to gain a deeper understanding of their teaching practices. Guided reflection involves answering specific questions about what strategies worked well and what areas need improvement. This step encourages educators to critically analyze their actions and decisions (Hammersley-Fletcher & Orsmond, 2005). Models of reflection such as Schön's Reflective Practitioner (Schön, 1983), Gibbs' Reflective Cycle (Gibbs, 1988) or Kolb's Experiential Learning Cycle can be used.

The final part of the cycle of the observation process is the formulation of an action plan based on the discussion outcomes. This plan includes specific goals to address identified areas for improvement, strategies to achieve these goals, and timelines for implementation. Guskey (2002) asserts that effective professional development involves setting clear goals, developing strategies, and monitoring progress over time. The action plan serves as a roadmap for the instructor, guiding them in making targeted improvements to their teaching practices (Sullivan et al., 2012).

The POT process is depicted in Figure 5.1:

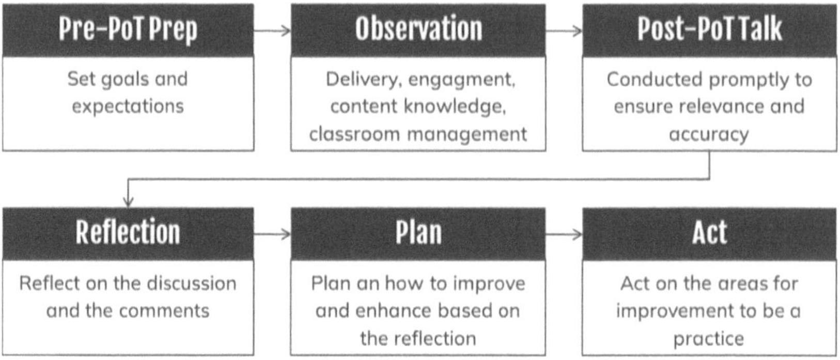


**Figure 5.1:** The Process of Peer Observation of Teaching (POT).

## Best Practices for Implementing Effective Teaching Observations

The first step in implementing effective teaching observations is to establish clear objectives and set clear expectations. Defining the purpose of the teaching observation and providing the framework for what the observation aims to achieve, whether it is improving instructional methods, assessing teacher performance, or as a professional development tool, makes the outcomes of the observations more meaningful and actionable. Equally, the training of the observers is crucial to ensure consistency and reliability in observations. The training needs to be focused on accurately identifying and evaluating teaching practices. Training can include understanding the observation tools, learning to identify key teaching behaviors, and practicing with sample observations. Furthermore, a supportive environment is essential for implementing effective teaching observation, educators should feel that observations are conducted to help them develop and grow rather than to criticize or judge. A supportive environment encourages openness and honesty, which can lead to more productive feedback sessions. Such a supportive environment encourages collaborative reflection that involves teachers and observers discussing the observations together to reflect on what went well and what could be improved. This promotes a culture of continuous learning and professional development.

Recently, there has been a drive to utilize technology to reduce the effort and administrative tasks associated with the academic workload. Institutions can also leverage technology to enhance the efficiency and effectiveness of teaching observations. The use of technology in teaching observations helps to overcome traditional limitations, such as observer bias and the logistical challenges of coordinating in-person observations, thereby allowing a more reflective and improvement-oriented observation culture (Bielefeldt, 2012). Technology facilitates the collection of objective data, enables more detailed analysis, and supports the professional development of educators through enhanced feedback mechanisms. Tools such as video recordings and automated behavior measurement systems can provide objective data and allow for detailed analysis and, therefore, effective implementation of the teaching observation.

Video recording of the real-time classroom activities and interactions can be a very powerful tool for teaching observations, the recordings can be reviewed and analyzed in detail by the educator instructing the class or by an observer. Video recording of classroom activities enables multiple reviews and the identification of specific teaching behaviors and student responses (Beck et al., 2002). Another useful technology for the teaching observation is online feedback platforms where observers can input their observation comments and other details related to the observation digitally. Such platforms streamline the process of providing and receiving feedback (Irvin et al., 2016). With such comments and data received from different sources within the institution, data analytics tools are essential to analyze large volumes of observation data to identify patterns and trends that help the institution identify areas of strength and areas for improvements in their practices. Data analytics tools can provide quantitative metrics on various aspects of teaching, such as student engagement, instructional strategies, and classroom management techniques. Ultimately, educators and institutions can make informed decisions based on empirical evidence, leading to targeted interventions and more effective teaching practices (Parker et al., 2019). An example of such platforms and software is the Generalized Observation and Reflection Platform (GORP) which is a digital tool for developing customizable observation protocols, as well as for collecting, analyzing, and reporting quantitative observation data. It enhances collaboration between educators by facilitating the articulation and setting of goals for classroom practices. GORP provides both visual and quantitative data that complement traditional qualitative observations, making it a comprehensive tool for pedagogical partnerships (Donahoe et al., 2023).

Overall, technology can be utilized in enabling educators to track progress and identify areas for professional development, ensuring that interventions are based on solid evidence. Moreover, technology can be used to reduce the administrative burden associated with traditional observation methods, making the process more efficient and less time-consuming. This efficiency allows educators to focus more on improving their teaching practices rather than on the logistics of observations.

## GCET: An Example of Teaching Observation and Reflective Practice

The Global College of Engineering and Technology (GCET), Muscat, Oman in partnership with the University of the West of England (UWE), Bristol, UK (GCET-UWE) partnership provides a valuable example of how teaching observation and reflective practice can significantly impact both students and staff (Global College of Engineering and Technology, 2021; University of the West of England, 2021). This partnership has brought opportunities through staff development initiatives like the Postgraduate Certificate in Academic Practice (PCAP). The PCAP program is a comprehensive professional development initiative aimed at enhancing the teaching and assessment skills of academics. Through structured modules and reflective practices, this program enables faculty members to critically evaluate their teaching methods and strategies, building an environment of continuous improvement especially for a growing college where the majority of the staff are early-mid career.

Teaching Observation in Practice: One of the core elements of the PCAP program is the emphasis on teaching observations. As part of the program, academics are observed by external experts from the partner institution as well as participating in structured developmental peer observations where they observe each other's teaching sessions and provide constructive feedback. This process is guided by specific criteria that focus on various aspects of teaching, such as student engagement, clarity of instruction, and the use of learning technologies. The observed sessions are followed by reflective discussions, where the observer and the observee collaboratively analyze the teaching practice, identify strengths, and discuss areas for improvement. The observation sessions happen during the first module of the PCAP as well as at the end of the programme, where the progress is assessed and evaluated.

The teaching observation component of the PCAP program provides immediate and actionable feedback to academics, encouraging them to critically reflect on their teaching practices. At GCET, many academics are either early in their careers or have not previously engaged in a systematic, structured approach to enhancing their teaching methods. Through these observations, educators have come to recognize the importance of diversifying their teaching strategies to accommodate various learning styles and student needs. This awareness has led to the adoption of more inclusive and student-centered teaching methods, directly enhancing the quality of the learning experience.

The impact of these improvements is significant. Over 80% of the academics who enrolled in and completed the program have reported enhanced teaching styles, greater engagement with students, and an improved ability to reflect on and refine their teaching methods. This continuous process of reflection and adaptation not only benefits the educators but also creates a more dynamic and responsive learning environment for students, fostering better educational outcomes.

Reflective practice is a core component of the teaching observation process within the PCAP program. Academics are encouraged to engage in deep reflection on their teaching practices, not only after receiving feedback from peer or external observations but also through their own independent reflections. This reflective process often involves the use of reflective journals, where educators document their experiences, challenges, and insights gained from both their teaching and the feedback received.

The program also incorporates technology to support reflective practices effectively. A user-friendly journaling platform, PebblePad, is utilized, enabling academics to easily record and organize their reflections. Additionally, classrooms are equipped to allow staff to record their teaching sessions, providing them the opportunity to review their performance critically. These recordings can also be shared with external observers from UWE for further feedback when needed. This integration of technology facilitates a continuous cycle of reflection and improvement, enhancing both teaching practices and learning outcomes (Global College of Engineering and Technology, 2021).

Through reflective practice, academics develop a heightened awareness of their teaching methodologies and the impact these methods have on student learning. By reflecting on feedback from peer observations, educators have refined their approach to formative assessment, incorporating a variety of feedback mechanisms designed to promote learning. This includes using immediate feedback tools—some of which are innovative—such as recording their feedback while annotating student work. Additionally, they have developed formative assessments that align more closely with learning outcomes and effectively utilize technology to enhance the learning process such as Mentimeter, Kahoot and other platforms.

The impact of teaching observation and reflective practice facilitated by the GCET-UWE partnership extends beyond individual educators to significantly benefit students. As academics enhance their teaching strategies through these reflective practices, students experience more engaging and effective learning environments. The use of innovative teaching methods and technologies, which many educators have adopted post-observation, helps cater to diverse learning needs and create a more inclusive classroom environment. Furthermore, the emphasis on formative assessment encourages students to actively participate in their learning process, receiving ongoing feedback that helps them improve their performance. This was evident through the module report reflection as well as the performance of the students and their engagement when compared to pre-PCAP modules' reports.

For the staff, PCAP program report a deeper understanding of research-based teaching and an ability to apply this knowledge to their own practice. They feel more confident in their roles, more adept at utilizing learning technologies, and more capable of designing assessments that truly measure student learning outcomes.

## Essential Policy Frameworks for Teaching Observations

For the effective implementation of teaching observations and reflective practices within an institution, establishing a robust policy framework is critical. Such frameworks should clearly outline the objectives, processes, and intended outcomes of teaching observations to ensure consistency and transparency as well as help setting the expectations. Therefore, there should be policies in place that define the purpose of observations, whether for formative feedback, summative evaluation, or professional development, and ensure that these purposes are communicated to all stakeholders. Clear guidelines on the roles and responsibilities of observers and observees, the frequency of observations, and the use of observation data are essential components of an effective policy framework (Compton, 2016).

It is potent to leverage technology to enhance the efficiency and effectiveness of teaching observations. Therefore, essential technological tools including video recording equipment, online feedback platforms, and data analytics software should be available to facilitate teaching observations. Additionally, comprehensive training and development programs for both observers and observees are essential. Training should cover the use of observation tools and the provided IT infrastructure, techniques for providing constructive feedback, and strategies for reflective practice. Observers need to be skilled in identifying and evaluating key teaching behaviors and in using observation protocols reliably. Continuous professional development opportunities should be available to ensure that all participants are up-to-date with the latest best practices in teaching and learning Eddy et al., 2015). Teaching observation also requires administrative support for its effective implementation. Institutions need to allocate resources for training, provide technical support for the use of technology, and ensure that observation schedules are managed effectively. Administrative staff can help coordinate the logistics of observations, such as scheduling, data collection, and reporting. Support from administrators also involves ensuring that the observation process is aligned with broader institutional goals and policies, and that it contributes to the overall mission of enhancing teaching quality (O'Leary & Savage, 2020).

## Engaging Stakeholders in Teaching Observations

Teaching observations, like any other process and system in an institution, require engagement and buy-in from all stakeholders to be successful and sustainable. Stakeholder involvement and engagement ensure that the perspectives and needs of all parties involved, including faculty members, students, administrators, and external evaluators, are considered and addressed. Such an inclusive approach promotes a sense of ownership and commitment to the process, which ultimately leads to more meaningful and actionable outcomes. When stakeholders are actively involved, they are more likely to support and participate in teaching observations, thereby enhancing the quality of education (Hatzipanagos & Lygo-Baker, 2006).

There are a number of strategies institutions can adopt for engaging faculty members, students, administrators, and external evaluators. Starting with the faculty members who are the core of this process, engaging them can be achieved through training sessions and raising their awareness of the importance of teaching observations. Additionally, involving them in collaborative observation models such as peer observations as a developmental tool. This approach provides faculty with the right mindset on how to approach teaching observations and provides them with constructive feedback for the purpose of promoting professional development and the sharing of best practices (Pressick-Kilborn & te Riele, 2008). As some have the negative connotation due to the feeling of being judged, encouraging voluntary participation among faculty members and ensuring that observations are non-evaluative and aimed at professional growth can reduce anxiety and increase acceptance.

Students can provide valuable insights into teaching effectiveness, therefore, involving them in the observation process, either through feedback mechanisms or as part of collaborative observation teams, can enhance the relevance and impact of the observations. Structured frameworks for student feedback can ensure that their input is constructive and focused on specific aspects of teaching (Kandiko Howson & Weller, 2016). Engaging them involves demonstrating the value of observations in enhancing teaching quality and students' learning outcomes. Similarly, administrators play a crucial role in providing the necessary support and resources for teaching observations. Engaging them involves raising their awareness of the alignment of the teaching observation process with the institution's teaching standards and goals.

On a larger scale, institutions need to adopt and encourage a culture of collaboration among faculty members, students, and administrators which builds a supportive environment where continuous improvement is valued. Such an environment and culture also benefit from recognizing and rewarding excellence in teaching, which can motivate educators to engage in continuous improvement and support. Institutions can establish awards, grants, or public acknowledgments for exemplary teaching practices identified through observations. Such methods are proven to be effective in incentivizing high-quality teaching and highlight effective practices that others can emulate.

## Conclusion

This chapter presents the critical role of teaching observations and reflective practices in achieving sustainable enhancement of teaching quality in higher education. Teaching observations offer educators valuable insights into their instructional strategies, student engagement, and overall teaching effectiveness. When coupling these observations with reflective practices, educators can identify areas for improvement and also engage in continuous professional growth.

Peer Observation of Teaching (POT) in higher education is considered as a tool for collaboration and mutual professional development. POT enhances both the teaching practices and the academic community when executed with clear objectives, appropriate training, and robust policy frameworks. Reflective practices, integrated with POT, empower educators to critically evaluate their methodologies, apply feedback constructively, and innovate in their instructional approaches.

The integration of technology further strengthens the impact of teaching observations. Tools such as video recordings and data analytics enable more detailed, objective, and actionable feedback, while platforms like PebblePad facilitate structured reflective practices. The chapter also highlighted the case study from the GCET-UWE partnership to exemplify the potential of structured teaching observation programs. Educators at GCET have demonstrated noteworthy improvements in their teaching styles, student engagement, and reflective practices following their participation in the PCAP programme.

The chapter also acknowledges the challenges associated with teaching observations, such as stress, perceptions of compliance, and power dynamics. Addressing these challenges requires a supportive institutional culture, comprehensive training for participants, policy infrastructure and clear communication of the developmental purpose of observations. To ensure the success and sustainability of teaching observations, engaging all stakeholders; faculty, students, administrators, and external evaluators is imperative.

## References


Batlle, J., & Seedhouse, P. (2020). The hidden impact of peer observation: Analyzing the invisible and visible. *Educational Review, 72*(1), 1–15.

Bielefeldt, T. (2012). Guidance for technology decisions from classroom observation. *Journal of Research on Technology in Education, 44*(3), 205–223.

Blackwell, R. (1996). Peer observation and feedback: A staff development tool for adult educators. *Australian Journal of Adult and Community Education, 36*(3), 195–210.

Chamberlain, J., D'Artrey, M., & Rowe, D. (2011). Peer observation of teaching: A decoupled process. *Journal of Further and Higher Education, 35*(3), 337–347.

Cosh, J. (1999). Peer observation: A reflective model. *ELT Journal, 53*(1), 22–27.

Danielson, C. (2013). *The Framework for Teaching: Evaluation Instrument*. The Danielson Group.

Donahoe, K., Staggs, S., & Vargas, S. (2023). GORP: Generalized Observation and Reflection Platform. *Technology and Teacher Education, 31*(4), 445–465.

Farrell, T. S. C. (2015). *Reflective language teaching: From research to practice*. Bloomsbury Publishing.

Fletcher, A. (2018). Observing educators: Professional development through observation. *Educational Research and Reviews, 13*(6), 232–239.

Flores, M. (2019). Learning to be a teacher: mentoring, collaboration and professional practice. *European Journal of Teacher Education, 42*(5), 535–538.

Gibbs, G. (1988). *Learning by doing: A guide to teaching and learning methods*. Further Education Unit. Global College of Engineering and Technology (2021). *GCET newsletter: 2nd issue*. https://gcet.edu.om/wp-content/uploads/2021/Newsletter/GCET%20NEWSLETTER%202ND%20ISSUE.pdf

Guskey, T. R. (2002). Professional development and teacher change. *Teachers and Teaching, 8*(3), 381–391.

Hammersley-Fletcher, L., & Orsmond, P. (2005). Reflecting on reflective practices within peer observation. *Studies in Higher Education, 30*(2), 213–224.

Hendry, G. D., & Oliver, G. R. (2012). Seeing is believing: The benefits of peer observation. *Higher Education Research & Development, 31*(4), 572–582.

Jay, J. K., & Johnson, K. L. (2002). Capturing complexity: A typology of reflective practice for teacher education. *Teaching and Teacher Education, 18*(1), 73–85.

Kohut, G. F., Burnap, C., & Yon, M. G. (2007). Peer observation of teaching: Perceptions of the observer and the observed. *College Teaching, 55*(1), 19–25.

Kolb, D. A. (1984). *Experiential learning: Experience as the source of learning and development*. Prentice-Hall.

Larrivee, B. (2000). Transforming teaching practice: Becoming the critically reflective educator. *Reflective Practice, 1*(3), 293–307.

Netshifhefhe, L., Nobongoza, V., & Maphosa, C. (2016). Quality Assuring Teaching and Learning Processes in Higher Education: A Critical Appraisal. *Journal of Communication, 7*, 65–78. https://doi.org/10.1080/0976691X.2016.11884884.

O'Leary, M., & Savage, S. (2020). *Classroom observation: A guide to the effective observation of teaching and learning*. Routledge.

Rauch, K., & Whittaker, C. (1999). Observation and Feedback during Student Teaching: Learning from Peers. *Action in teacher education, 21*, 67–78.

Richards, J. C., & Farrell, T. S. C. (2011). *Practice Teaching: A Reflective Approach*. Cambridge University Press.

Rolfe, G., Freshwater, D., & Jasper, M. (2001). *Critical reflection in nursing and the helping professions: A user's guide*. Palgrave Macmillan.

Schön, D. A. (1983). *The reflective practitioner: How professionals think in action*. Basic Books.

Shortland, S. (2004). Peer observation: A tool for staff development or compliance?. *Journal of Further and Higher Education, 28*(2), 219–228.

Skoog, G. (1980). Peer evaluation in higher education: An analysis and a framework for development. *Journal of Educational Administration, 18*(2), 203–215.

Sullivan, P. B., Buckle, A., Nicky, G., & Atkinson, S. H. (2012). Peer observation of teaching as a faculty development tool. *BMC Medical Education, 12*, 1–6.

University of the West of England (2021). PGCert Academic Practice. University of the West of England. https://info.uwe.ac.uk/programmes/specification.asp?file=X90K-7452.pdf

Whittaker, E., Pathak, A., Piya, S., Cary, L., & Harden, J. (2023). Peer observation of student-led teaching. *Medical Teacher, 45*, 1300–1303.

Yiend, J., Weller, S., & Kinchin, I. (2014). Peer observation of teaching: The interaction between peer review and developmental models of practice. *Teaching in Higher Education, 19*(6), 703–713.

# A Reflective Journey to Professional Development: Advance HE Fellowship Experience

*Mohammed Siddique*

**ABSTRACT**

Reflective practices are considered fundamental to enhancing professional development and ensuring adequate focus on evaluating one's experience. Learning from experience by taking time to reflect enables individuals to attain better insights and understand critical issues. In Higher Education (HE), rational decision making, critical thinking, quality teaching and collaborative practices are critical to achieving teaching excellence and effective leadership. This chapter explores my experience of self-reflection as part of the process of applying for Senior Fellowship of the UK's Advance HE while undertaking a key leadership role in an Omani Higher Education Institution (HEI). This includes reflecting on professional work completed in quality assurance and program development. Additionally, reflection on my interaction with students and staff has brought about impactful changes in program delivery. This is evident from successful initiatives in planning, reviewing the curriculum, enriching teaching with advancement in Information Communication and Technology (ICT) based on teaching standards, mentoring colleagues, sharing good practices in teaching, learning and assessments. Furthermore, by using guiding principles as a reflective practitioner, effective changes can be achieved by following a systematic approach to investigating issues from different perspectives, understanding strengths and limitations, and ensuring smooth operations in HEIs.

## Introduction

Reflective practice is a discipline where learning transpires based on experience through self-reflection and standard practices. It ensures learning by giving adequate time and attention to reflect on and interpret experience. It is necessary for bringing effective changes through planning, acting and reflecting in the learning cycle. Reflective practices are evaluated based on experience and structured reflection. These include creating an action plan, exploring alternatives and devising strong questions based on choosing a critical incident. Although HEIs aim at developing critical thinkers, analysts, subject experts and policymakers, transforming their students' knowledge into practice can present a challenge (Dall'Alba & Barnacle, 2007). Reflective practice requires reflective collaboration with students. This can be based on addressing students' interests and needs while designing and planning in-class activities, discussions, and effective communication to develop trust leading to tangible actions in the learning process (Fragouli, 2023). Furthermore, reflective thinking and teaching leads to more effective teaching by exploring teaching pedagogies, academic preparation, understanding learner needs, and navigating cultural aspects.

Reflective practices are guided by certain principles that are key factors in working towards teaching excellence. To follow them, collaborative working, a range of communication platforms, innovative pedagogies and assessment models are required. These factors include thorough subject knowledge, cognizance of prior learning and scaffolding, inclusivity in teaching, passion, effective curriculum and effective assessments of learning outcomes (McHanwell & Robson, 2018). In this chapter, effective leadership and quality teaching are discussed based on reflective practices. These are discussed based on my experience of applying for Senior Fellowship of the UK's Advance HE (SFHEA). The discussion includes outcomes attained from professional practices, leadership roles involved and evaluation of various academic practices.

## Reflective and Professional Practices

The process of reflective practice helps improve performance by enhancing understanding and contributing towards knowledge and actively reflecting on experiences. Reviewing reflective teaching, student engagement and professional integrity supports understanding of a need for pedagogical change that can be implemented through collective consensus of teachers' well-being, approach towards students on professional ethics and engagement (Tao, 2013). The well-being of teachers refers to their abilities, concentration, motivation and satisfaction in the professional environment.

## UK Professional Standards Framework (UKPSF)

The UK Professional Standards Framework (UKPSF) is a recognised framework used in the higher education as a tool to benchmark success concerning teaching and learning support (AdvanceHE, 2023a). The UKPSF consists of professional standards and the guidelines for teaching professionals in higher education. This framework recognises the significance of determining roles of teaching and learning in HE. It describes the key characteristics of a qualifying profile and the dimensions of these roles through evaluation based on evidence provided. As depicted in Figure 6.1, the dimensions include areas of activity, core knowledge and professional values which contribute to the enhancement of students' learning experience.

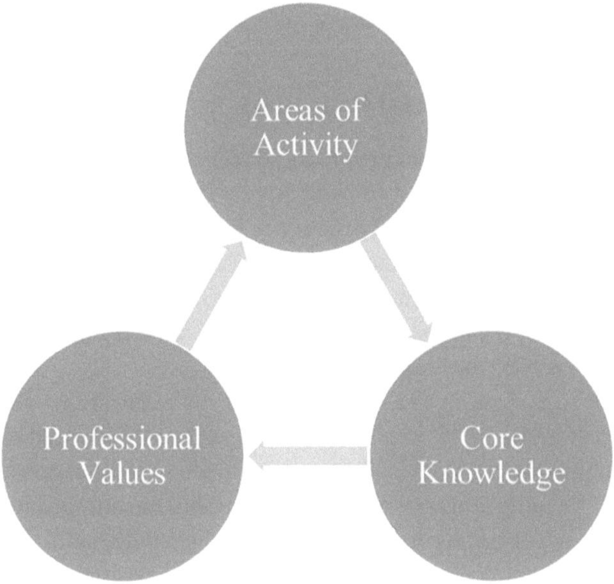


**Figure 6.1:** UK Professional Standards Framework (AdvanceHE, 2023a).

Recognition as a Senior Fellow requires evidence-based fulfilment of the requirements of Descriptor-3 of Advance HE's UKPSF framework. Descriptor-3 ensures that there is valid evidence for a comprehensive understanding of reflective practices and approaches to teaching and learning that contributes towards higher quality of learning by students. It involves reflection on the key contributions towards teaching and learning by demonstrating thorough understanding of effective teaching practices (AdvanceHE, 2023b). Descriptor 3 necessitates evidence of successful engagement and commitment towards all areas of activity, core knowledge, professional values, pedagogic research, professional development and successful leadership roles. Moreover, reflective elucidation is required from experience in a leadership role in an HE institutional context that supports learning at Level 4 or above of the Framework for Higher Education Qualifications (FHEQ). Evidence of an applicant's career milestones and contribution towards teaching and learning needs to be collated. Areas of achievement such as research, teaching and learning initiatives and professional practices are very valuable as part of the application for Senior Fellowship, as is experience gained from advisory roles, mentoring, leadership or management roles and other collaborative activities.

## Account of Professional Practices

The application of professional practices and reflection on thoughtful decision making is essentially required to be aligned with the UKPSF. In the reflective commentary, my individual experience based on my job profile and the institutional context was discussed, showing evidence of real-life examples of practice in teaching and learning. The application focused on providing a strong rationale for the decisions taken for the success and impact of scholarly activities on teaching and learning.

The Reflective Area of Practices (RAP) in my application reflected my contribution towards staff recruitment and mentoring of new staff to aid their integration into the work environment. It included sharing of good practices in teaching, learning and assessment. For example, I encouraged new staff to follow a student-centric approach by providing them with hands-on practical activities. As part of staff development, I delivered a session on the effective use of video clips to all academic colleagues that helped them in updating their module pages with relevant teaching material. As an outcome of such practices, the staff retention rate increased to more than 95% in my Faculty.

## Leadership, Management and Organizational Roles

To enhance learning by developing the curriculum, strategic planning is required at the faculty level. For example, the maintenance of appropriate class sized ensures an effective learning environment where peer to peer and student to teacher interaction is highest (Johnson & Johnson, 2008). As a Director of Studies (DoS), my participation in teaching and learning and the quality enhancement process included the designing of new programs and organizing of staff teams to support the required curriculum upgrades. I ensured that the curriculum was reviewed and updated to reflect student needs and align it with the latest trends in the industry. The coordination and support for the team in designing curricula helped foster innovation in teaching, learning and assessment methods and aided the acquisition of key skills by students. This process aligns well with the achievement of professional values and use of core knowledge promoted by Advance HE.

Academic advisers should perceive their role as critical in terms of monitoring students' attendance, performance, supporting and motivating them to be independent learners (Keengwe et al., 2012). I, in consultation with the Chair of the institution's Quality Assurance and Enhancement Committee (QAEC), initiated the process of counselling students who were not progressing in their studies, listening to their issues and proposing a proper study plan. This was achieved by recording the issues in a student management system and following up with the academic advisers who provided these students with the required support. For example, a student was struggling with a particular module's assessment. A different assessment strategy was proposed consisting of a report instead of a written exam. The new assignment description addressing the same learning outcomes of the module was designed by the module team and the student was able to complete this assessment. I also arranged workshops on exam writing skills, academic integrity and referencing. As an outcome, the report on progression in the 2023–2024 academic year showed that 82% of the students at risk progressed in their studies. The entire process has helped many students to overcome their challenges and influenced staff members to support their academic advisees rigorously.

## Evaluation of Academic Practices

Reflection through evaluating experience is based on reflecting on actions that enable individuals to get an in-depth insight into the learning process. It is central to safeguarding against making impulsive decisions. During my application for SFHEA, I had the opportunity to reflect on my contribution and the influence I had on my colleagues in the smooth execution of HEI operations. With a succession of academic promotions, I contributed to the Faculty of Information Technology as a Senior Lecturer, Program Manager, Director of Studies (DoS) and later at the institutional level as Head of Registry Systems and Examinations (HoRSE). This contribution was both academic and administrative in nature. My work in quality assurance and program development required my extensive involvement in evaluating the existing curriculum and enriching it with technological advances in line with established HE teaching standards. This required academic judgement to successfully implement effective initiatives in planning and reviewing the curriculum by interacting with colleagues and students. Moreover, the variety of assessments helped in evaluating the effectiveness of teaching based on module assessment strategies. The engagement and mentoring with the new academic staff proved to be a useful opportunity to share good practices in teaching, learning and assessments. Additionally, coordinating module delivery, assessing students, reviewing and updating the teaching material and peer review of colleagues positively impacted the overall program delivery which was acknowledged by the students and the external examiners.

The administrative roles are critical in terms of supporting and managing staff and student-related operations. Being a DoS and later as HoRSE, my active contribution helped in taking important decisions in day-to-day operations such as planning, execution and reviewing the registration process, academic advising and the examination schedule. The section below elaborates two case studies describing my leadership role in monitoring and reviewing existing programs, and developing new academic programs in the Faculty of IT.

## Case Study 1: Monitoring and Structured Deployment of Periodic Review of Existing and New Academic Programs/Pathways

### Context

This case study focuses on the periodic review and new program development processes conducted over an academic year, elaborating my role as a Program Review Team Lead (PRTL) leading the entire approval processes. My initiatives helped reflect on the existing teaching, learning and education practices to improve and enhance them contributing to the HEI's teaching standards. Normally, the review of these programs is conducted every four to five years ensuring that standards are maintained as per the HEI's quality assurance policies (El-Khawas et al., 1998). I delegated certain responsibilities to colleagues and supported them in identifying resources and preparing self-reflection and evaluation documents through a series of meetings. One of the key achievements from this practice was the designing of a new bachelor's program in Computing, with Oil and Gas, Banking Information Systems and Software Engineering pathways. These were approved by the QAEC, an independent international review panel from our affiliated university and the Ministry of Higher Education, Research and Innovation (MoHERI) in Oman. Coordination with the team was needed to collect feedback from various stakeholders such as existing students, staff, College's QAEC, external examiners, Industry Advisory Panel (IAP) members, and subject experts. Additionally, in a subsequent academic year, in a new role as Head of Registry Systems and Examinations (HoRSE), my participation in the periodic review of existing and new programs at the HEI level as well as providing system support in naming conventions of modules and programs helped in achieving Advance HE's requirements for Senior Fellowship. This includes leading the HEI team in reviewing and updating the graduate attributes contributing towards updating curriculum designing of all programmes.

## Initiatives and Approach

As a PRTL, one of my main goals was to lead the program review process and update the curriculum. This involved reflective practices carried out in the HEI for over a period of five years. I had an opportunity to attend a workshop on program accreditation by the Center for Learning Innovations & Customized Knowledge Solutions. This workshop gave me an insight into some of the important processes, information and approvals required by coordinating with the team. I identified specific actions to be taken to maximize the success of the entire review process that were addressed through eight important stages. The first stage consisted of self-evaluation of programs on offer by holistically reviewing them based on validity, currency, and industry trends. In stage 2, changes to the programs were proposed based on data collection and surveys from stakeholders. This was supported by self-reflection on existing practices, rationale for changes, motivation, and relevant evidence. During stage 3, team meetings were conducted with the IAP and external examiners to discuss the new proposals. A series of formal and informal visits were made at industrial sites to gather the skills demand across business domain. Stage 4 required benchmarking of programs with local, regional, and international HEIs pertaining to similar provider, competitor, and aspirational targets. This process included my extensive role in reviewing the modules and constructively aligning them to the UK's Quality Assurance Agency (QAA), subject benchmark statements, Body of Knowledge and the FHEQ as documented in the Course Information Forms. The subsequent stages included the documentation and defense of the proposed programs at the Faculty, QAEC, University and MoHERI levels, which were successfully carried in coordination with the HEI's QAEC.

### Achievements and Implications

The reflective practices I followed during my lead role in conducting review of existing programmes, designing new programmes and executing other faculty operations that were in line with the Strategic Plan of the HEI are evident from the description provided in the below section. The curriculum development and review are an important criterion that HEIs need to achieve as set by the Oman Authority for Academic Accreditation and Quality Assurance of Education (OAAAQA, 2018). As an outcome from the review processes, one of the approved Computing programs (Oil and Gas) was unique in the entire Gulf region and attracted a large number of students. The HEI was recognized for maintaining good curriculum standards across its programs. The students on the programs have an opportunity to study modules that correspond to the latest market trends and are of international standard. This was confirmed by the external examiners from various UK HEIs, as quoted in their report that "the curriculum is current and varied teaching and assessment strategies are highly appropriate. Academic standards at the HEI are excellent and comparable to standards at similar educational institutions in the UK". My involvement in reflecting on the complete processes and my contribution gave me an enriching experience towards my professional development.

## Case Study 2: Integration of IoT Functionalities and Simulations with Cisco® Packet Tracer into a Networking Program

### Context

In this case study, my initiative with regard to reflecting on module delivery and its contents are discussed. As a module coordinator of the Computer Network Programming (CNP) module from a networking program, I led the module team in reviewing the module contents and its assessments. Advances in network infrastructure, its solutions and rapid development in Internet of Things (IoT) applications address innovation to technology-enhanced learning (Coccoli et al., 2016). This helps to expose students to the newest technologies and support in achieving hands-on industry standards practical experience by integrating IoT functionalities and simulations using Cisco® Packet Tracer. My aim was to re-design the module in order to build a pragmatic model and develop cognitive network programming. The process involves self-reflection on existing practices of instilling different skill sets within student groups. I integrated the Cisco® Networking Academy training course material by balancing networking and programming knowledge as part of the module syllabus. The revised module allows creating specifications, setting up basic computer networks, adding smart IoT devices, and creating back-end intelligence through microcontroller examples. Additionally, the main categories added in the IoT simulations are smart devices, actuators, micro-controllers, and the sensors. The contents are delivered using advanced IoT, Python or Java language, Blockly programming, security and analytics.

## Initiatives and Approach

As a DoS, my passion and my role prompted me to review and suggest updates in the curriculum as per industry trends. The content of the CNP module was reviewed and updated based on its learning outcomes, aims and objectives addressing the concerns arising from student forums such as Academic Program Committee (APC), APMR and the student feedback action plans. The periodic review of the networking program was an opportunity to reflect on this module contents. Advanced network programming requires packages, input/output streaming, and extensive file handling to build client-server architecture and address security concerns in the network systems (Gordieiev et al., 2016). The client-server based web services domain such as REST architecture and JSON technologies requires the Integrated Development Environment (IDE) settings to configure APIs and execute applications using web server (John & Siddique, 2021). Hence, I coordinated with the module team to start the use of an Eclipse IDE tool, configured on Java and host websites using an Apache Tomcat web server. IoT devices usually are configured using Java, Python or Visual programming and can be implemented through practical simulations as part of the in-class activities

(Finardi, 2018). Hence, the configuration of IoT functionalities in the network designs was introduced using Eclipse IDE. This initiative is influenced by my previous industry experience, attending a FOSS (Free and Open-Source Software) conference and other workshops. The Faculty staff specialized in networking and the module team gave a very positive response upon the completion of documentation. Additionally, I encouraged students to enroll on similar professional courses that I offered as a registered tutor in CISCO® NetAcademy.

### Achievements and Implications

By reflecting on the past three years of module delivery, I led the team to explore possibilities in addressing this concern and add more hands-on practical activities to ensure that students gain industry standard practical experience. Comparative analysis of students' results before after the proposed changes in the curriculum showed a significant improvement. It also directly influenced the students to work on topics such as smart home and smart parking which are related to IoT using Arduino, Raspberry Pi, etc. Our external examiners praised these projects for using the latest technologies leading towards industries standard projects. Most of the networking students in their final technology project are designing and developing network designs that focus on upgrading the network infrastructure of companies. Many of these projects are now being built with IoT features. The staff and student feedback on this initiative has been positive. With this successful initiative, the professional requirements for Senior Fellowship of Advance HE were achieved.

## Characteristics of a Reflective Practitioner

Through deeper reflection and allotment of time to make sense of their previous work and honestly challenge assumptions, teachers can enhance their professional practice. Relevant reflective practices include reflecting, planning actions, implementing and evaluating the achievements considering the criticality and taking actions as a meaningful reflection (Mohamed et al., 2022). Tacit and explicit knowledge with the addition of relevant information and wisdom enables reflection to be practiced as a methodology, which leads to becoming a more successful reflective practitioner (Sasaki, 2024).

These reflective practices have contributed to my professional development and personal growth. The characteristics required for being a reflective practitioner are illustrated in Figure 6.2 below.

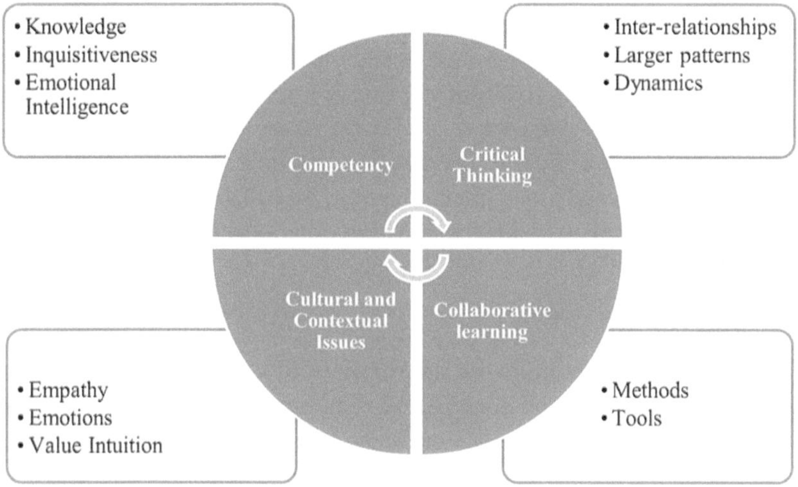


**Figure 6.2:** Characteristics of a Reflective Practitioner.

The acquisition of knowledge, inquisitiveness and possession of emotional intelligence contribute towards self-reflection on the experiences. This emphasises important characteristics of possessing competency in professional and personal growth. The competency of the practitioner enables them to adapt and improve in their practice. Some of the key components include the acquisition of knowledge required for performing tasks effectively and inquisitiveness that encourages continuous learning and gaining deeper understanding of concepts. Critical analysis of inter-relationships and their dynamics helps in understanding larger patterns and examining issues with a different perspective. This approach supports the investigation of problems and identification of root causes. It can be achieved with an in-depth awareness of the context and evaluation of its implications by examining the inter-dependence of various entities or ideas.

The cultural aspect is important, and the context of learning requires giving value to intuitions, emphasizing empathy and emotions. These are deeply subjective recognising cultural norms shaped by values and collaboration.

An empathetic approach to the social and environmental challenges individuals to deal with relationships and diverse perspectives, precluding misinterpretations of context. This approach enables the free and fair expression of emotions, and values the ability to sense common understanding among different individuals.

Further, collaborative learning is an add-on toward self-reflection by using different tools and techniques for learning. It fosters teamwork, engaging in exchanges of diverse perspectives and constructive dialogue towards problem solving. This is achievable using various methods such as peer teaching, group discussions and use of interactive tools for collaboration contributing towards an inclusive and effective learning experience.

## Conclusion

Reflective practice requires an approach to follow adaptive, generative and radical learning and understand their importance in contributing toward quality teaching. Collaborative sessions, addressing problems using problem-solving skills as a response through self-reflection, enhance learning and teaching (Sandars et al., 2023). This approach necessitates understanding the context and taking various initiatives towards knowledge development. From reflecting on the areas of professional practices and the case studies, it was possible to have a clear understanding of the strengths as well as limitations. My contribution detailed in Case Study 1 led to the proposed programs being approved by necessary entities and a subsequent significant number of new student recruits. Good practices such as reaching out to stakeholders, conducting a market study, and prioritizing student and alumni interaction and industrial trends were shared between different Faculties of the HEI. As noted in Case Study 2, the students from the revised networking program will be exposed to Cisco® Packet Tracer's latest version that utilizes advanced features such as IoT using Blockly and other programming languages. This will contribute to the students' high-quality learning experience. Further, this module will also help students to work on advanced industry-standard projects that can include IoT rather than traditional network designs. Overall, all of these practices presented in my SFHEA application have been shared with my colleagues for their suggestions and I have continued to learn from their expertise.

## References

Advance HE (2023a). *Professional Standards Framework for teaching and supporting learning in Higher Education*. Advance HE. https://advance-he.ac.uk/knowledge-hub/professional-standards-framework-teaching-and-supporting-learning-higher-education-0

Advance HE (2023b). *Senior Fellowship of the Higher Education Academy.* Advance HE.

Maresca, P., Stanganelli, L., & Coccoli, M. (2016). Teaching Computer Programming Through Hands-on Labs on Cognitive Computing. *Distributed Multimedia Systems.*

Dall'Alba, G., & Barnacle, R. (2007). An ontological turn for higher education. *Studies in Higher Education, 32*(6), 679–691. https://doi.org/10.1080/03075070701685130

Sands, R. H., Parson, L. A., & Duane, J. (1991). Faculty mentoring faculty in a public university. *Journal of Higher Education, 62*(2), 174–193.

Finardi, A. (2018). *IoT Simulations with Cisco Packet Tracer.* https://ieeexplore.ieee.org/document/9476125/

Fragouli, E. (2023). Reviewing & Reflecting Upon Practices of Collaboration in Higher Education. *European Journal of Contemporary Education and E-Learning, 1*(2), 23–32. https://doi.org/10.59324/ejceel.2023.1(2).03

Gordieiev, O., Lobur, T., & Kozak, R. (2016). Integrating Cisco Systems' Educational Programs in ICT Security Academic Curricula. *Information & Security: An International Journal, 35*, 151–163. https://doi.org/10.11610/isij.3508

John, E., & Siddique, M. (2021). *2021 International Conference on Decision Aid Sciences and Application (DASA)*, pp. 231–235. DOI: 10.1109/DASA53625.2021.9682324

Johnson, R. T., & Johnson, D. W. (2008). Active Learning: Cooperation in the Classroom. *The Annual Report of Educational Psychology in Japan, 47*, 29–30. https://doi.org/10.5926/arepj1962.47.0_29

Keengwe, J., Schnellert, G., & Mills, C. (2012). Laptop initiative: Impact on instructional technology integration and student learning. *Education and Information Technologies, 17*(2), 137–146. https://doi.org/10.1007/s10639-010-9150-8

McHanwell, P. S., & Robson, P. S. (2018). *Guiding Principles for Teaching Promotions*. Advance HE.

Mohamed, M., Rashid, R. A., & Alqaryouti, M. H. (2022). Conceptualizing the complexity of reflective practice in education. *Frontiers in Psychology, 13*, 1008234. https://doi.org/10.3389/fpsyg.2022.1008234

OAAAQA (2018). *Institutional Standards Assessment Manual*. The Oman Authority for Academic Accreditation and Quality Assurance of Education. https://oaaaqa.gov.om/About-the-OAAA/OAAA-Manuals

Sandars, J., Allan, D., & Price, J. (2024). Reflective practice by health professions educators to enhance learning and teaching: AMEE Guide No. 166. *Medical Teacher, 46*(7), 864–873. https://doi.org/10.1080/0142159X.2023.2259071

Sasaki, H. (2024). Workshops to Enhance Teachers' Reflection as Reflective Practitioners and to Help Them Gain Professional Capacities for Education for Sustainable Development: A Case Study of Japanese Prospective Teachers. In H. Fujii & S.-K. Lee (Eds.), *Science Education for Sustainable Development in Asia* (pp. 301–324). Springer Nature. https://doi.org/10.1007/978-981-99-8711-5_18

Tao, S. (2013). Why are teachers absent? Utilising the Capability Approach and Critical Realism to explain teacher performance in Tanzania. *International Journal of Educational Development, 33*(1), 2–14. https://doi.org/10.1016/j.ijedudev.2012.01.003

PART III

# Reflective Practice in the Context of New Challenges and Opportunities Connected with Artificial Intelligence

# Human Minds, AI Hands: Reflections on Using AI in Academic Research

*Mohamed Salah El Din*

**ABSTRACT**
The year 2023 witnessed a dramatic shift to AI adoption across multiple fields, and academic research is no exception. The use of generative AI models has become an essential skill for researchers, especially with their expansive capabilities in the research landscape. This chapter provides a reflection on the ethical and responsible use of Generative Artificial Intelligence in enhancing the quality and productivity of academic research. AI supports scholars in a variety of forms, such as identifying and refining research topics, summarizing papers, improving review of literature, identifying research gaps, analyzing and visualizing data, formatting references, proofreading manuscripts and offering constructive feedback. However, despite its numerous abilities, AI lacks human creativity and critical thinking, thus it should not replace researchers. Moreover, there are major concerns associated with its use, including data privacy, academic integrity, and AI dependency. Alternatively, AI could be utilized as a research assistant, supporting researchers to write high quality papers. This chapter sheds light on the focal areas where AI could be harnessed as a valuable tool in academic research, providing practical examples from international as well as personal experiences, and thereby transferring this knowledge to fellow academics. It promotes a greater comprehension of AI's capabilities and constraints as a research assistant by encouraging academics to reflect on their use of this transformative technology. The chapter aims to achieve these objectives while considering AI challenges, balancing the adoption of technology and academic norms and ethics.

## Introduction

Research is a central foundation of academic life. Besides being part of the job description, it is crucial for academic institutions to produce knowledge, enhance the learning process, reputation, ranking, and society's welfare (Jalal, 2020; Pal & Sarkar, 2020; Sysoieva & Sokolova, 2020).

However, the academic environment is becoming more demanding and competitive, especially when it comes to research. In addition to the increased teaching and administrative workloads after the Covid-19 pandemic, faculty members face constant pressure to publish in leading journals, obtain research grants and participate in research competitions (Nicholls et al., 2022). Universities became obsessed with quantitative measures of performance. Research targets are translated into number of publications, citations, ranking and other metrics, emphasizing quantity over quality of published work

(Watermeyer et al., 2023). This intensive requirement in a "Publish or Perish" culture is incentivizing researchers to publish more work to preserve their reputation in the academic community (Lund et al., 2023), secure earnings and obtain academic positions (Fischer, 2023; Jalal, 2020).

As a result of this strain, academic staff suffer from overwork, stress, burnout, anxiety, depression, and mental health issues (Janib et al., 2021; Mondal et al., 2023; Nicholls et al., 2022). Seeking a better work-life balance, academics either resign and find other jobs or stay in the field and quiet quit the industry, focusing solely on their main educational tasks. This usually comes on the expense of their main role as knowledge producers (Watermeyer et al., 2023). In other words, overburdening academic staff with increased research output targets leads to job dissatisfaction and poor performance (Janib et al., 2021).

In this context, Artificial Intelligence (AI) has emerged as a pivotal tool that can assist researchers in overcoming research challenges (Al Harrasi & Salah El Din, 2024; Hashem et al., 2024). Generative AI (GAI), a subset of the wider concept of AI, is considered a significant advancement that is disrupting the academic landscape. GAI models use sophisticated algorithms and vast amounts of data to replicate human ability in generating new content including text, audio, music, pictures, videos, and other material (Bail, 2024; Huang & Le, 2021).

Notable examples of GAI models include Large Language Models (LLMs), which replicate human abilities in comprehending language and providing responses to user queries. A prominent LLM model is Open AI's ChatGPT, which can generate new content and assist in various tasks effectively (Hai, 2023; Lund et al., 2023). The responsible and ethical use of Generative AI (GAI) applications provides an invaluable solution to researchers, allowing them to be more productive and efficient. This includes automating some routine activities, enhancing, and facilitating faster academic writing, drafting research questions and hypotheses, summarizing literature, translating, and generating citations and analyzing data. Nonetheless, the use of GAI in research comes with an array of risks, challenges, and limitations that researchers should consider before using it in research (Al Harrasi & Salah El Din, 2024; Watermeyer et al., 2023).

This chapter synthesizes the existing literature on the use of Generative AI in academic research to provide a comprehensive reflection of the potential responsible use of generative artificial intelligence as a research assistant, enhancing the productivity and quality of academic research. The chapter aims to identify the limitations and challenges of generative AI in academic research; explore the possible uses of Gen AI in academic research process; and speculate on the future prospects of AI and its impact on academic research.

## Barriers, Challenges and Limitations of Using AI in Academic Research

Despite the enormous potential of adopting GAI in academic research, there are substantial challenges and limitations. These difficulties fall into five key categories: ethical and legal concerns, technological constraints, cognitive and sociocultural impact, socio-economic impact and access and representation. Figure 7.1 provides a visual representation of these categories.

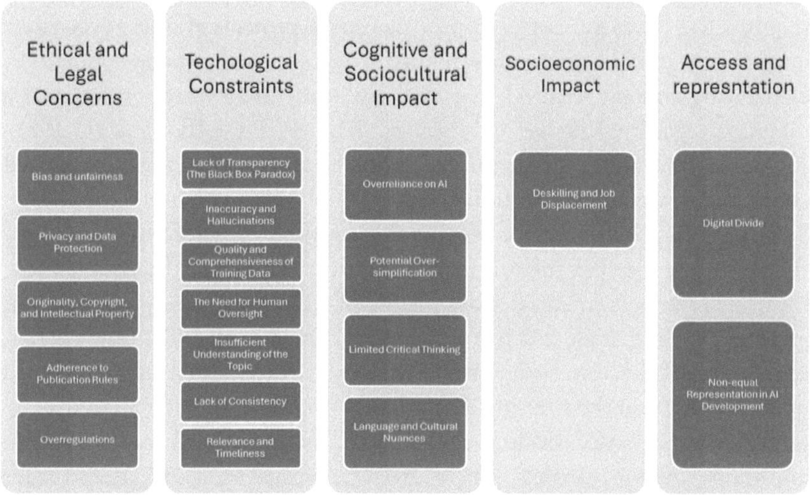


**Figure 7.1:** Barriers, Challenges and Limitations of AI in Academic Research.

### Ethical and Legal Concerns

Generative AI models are trained on vast amounts of datasets and use their sophisticated algorithms to generate new content. However, these models are usually biased, due to the inherent bias in the training data itself.

As a result, a GAI system may reinforce and amplify these biases and stereotypes, leading to unfair results, including bias against race, gender, and other societal groups (Baldassarre et al., 2024; Calamur & Ghosh, 2024; Fui-Hoon Nah et al., 2023; Manduchi et al., 2024; Satyam & Geetha, 2023). To overcome bias challenge, it is integral that organizations developing GAI models ensure that both training data and models' algorithms are bias-free (Zlateva et al., 2024). This entails a rigorous critical evaluation of the training data sources, to assure their comprehensiveness and diversity. Moreover, it is essential to develop models that can minimize bias and unfairness in their responses (Ferrara, 2023). Finally, researchers should be mindful of this challenge when they utilize GAI in academic research and take necessary precautions to avoid the blind use of GAI without careful verification (Ma & Zhao, 2024).

According to Golda et al. (2024), personal information fed into GAI models could be used for training purposes, content generation or revealing personal characteristics of users, thereby compromising their anonymity. This requires the development of appropriate data protection and governance mechanisms in addition to conformance to data security laws and regulations. Generating content with AI, especially in academic research, represents a dilemma regarding Intellectual Property Rights (IPR) (Zhong et al., 2023). There are continuing deliberations on the legal situations of AI generated content (Anechitaoe, 2023; Indri Hapsari et al., 2024; Zlateva et al., 2024). Since Gen AI models are not accountable for their produced material, they should not be listed as co-authors for scientific papers. For the same reason, scientific reviewers should declare the use of AI in the review process (Lund et al., 2023; Tang et al., 2024). Furthermore, Wang et al. (2024) suggest that authors should receive compensation for their copyrighted material based on its inclusion in the training data of the AI model, ensuring fair and integrable distribution of royalties. In addition, there is a need for explainable and transparent AI models, where users can verify their output and trace the sources of the generated content (Blau et al., 2024; Jaiswal et al., 2023).

The rapid integration of GAI in academic research has forced journals to reassess their publication guidelines (Inam et al., 2024). Most journals do not allow GAI to be listed as a co-author or advocate the declaration of AI use for accepting manuscripts (Tang et al., 2024), while others like Science have adopted a stricter policy, by rejecting papers partially written by AI (Lund et al., 2023). To verify the originality of submitted manuscripts, some journals use AI detectors. Applications such as Papermill Alarm for detecting fake and fraudulent papers, and Proofig for identifying manipulated images, are frequently used to prevent the improper utilization of AI in research (Hosseini & Resnik, 2024). On the other hand, using GAI in the peer review process indicates a lack of proper governance, possibly undermining its credibility and objectivity (Mollaki, 2024).

It is imperative that the use of AI in academic research is organized and regulated to address ethical, societal and legal concerns. However, overregulation may limit innovation, slow down investments, and deprive researchers from its potential benefits (Baldassarre et al., 2024). Moreover, it could stifle scientific advancements (Feuerriegel et al., 2024), undermine interdisciplinary collaboration and raise compliance costs (Dwivedi et al., 2023). A balanced approach in regulating the use of AI in academic research, focusing on key risks including bias, data protection and privacy, to find a middle ground between the required academic freedom for creative research and ethical governance of AI applications. As a result, a responsible integration of generative AI in research will be fostered, allowing researchers to increase productivity and enhance research quality (Baldassarre et al., 2024; Ekundayo et al., 2024; Manduchi et al., 2024).

## Technological Constraints

GAI developers hide the basic foundations of their models to protect intellectual property. As a result, users provide inputs to the model (prompts) and get outputs (responses) without understanding how the system functions (Barbalau et al., 2020)(B˘ Arb˘ Al˘ Au et al., 2020. This is often referred to as the "Black Box Paradox", which poses a major challenge in trusting AI decision making Fui-Hoon Nah et al., 2023). GAI developers should introduce explainable AI, which provides a rationale for its decision-making process, allowing researchers to rely on its output with high levels of confidence and detect AI biases and mistakes (Bail, 2024; Satyam & Geetha, 2023; Zlateva et al., 2024. Additionally, creators of AI models should disclose limitations and confidence assessments for their models (Blau et al., 2024). GAI hallucinations happen when it generates inaccurate or misleading information. They result from vague user prompts or errors in training algorithms (Gu, 2024; Lemos, 2024). As AI responses are usually given with high levels of confidence, AI hallucination can lead to misinformation, faulty decision making

(Aditya, 2024; Baldassarre et al., 2024; Gu, 2024), and legal actions (Fischer, 2023). Elali & Rachid (2023) used ChatGPT to write a complete research paper and found that the responses included fabricated data that is not easily detected, thereby undermining the integrity of research. Accordingly, there is a need to devise an algorithmic solution in the core of GAI systems, to identify fabricated information (Manduchi et al., 2024).

GAI models generate output by resembling the patterns and structures they learnt from the training data, which may sometimes be incomplete, biased, or include errors. Consequently, the ability of Generative AI models to provide reliable and factual responses depends heavily on the quality, inclusivity and diversity of training data (Bandi et al., 2023; Zerka et al., 2020). In other words, the quality of GAI' output is as good as the data that it trained on (Gu, 2024). This poses a serious issue for scholars who use GAI in research, who may unknowingly depend on mistaken or biased information, thereby jeopardizing the credibility of their findings. Therefore, it is essentials that researchers understand the limitations and problems of using GAI in research, so that they can exercise caution and verify results while depending on GAI tools (Dwivedi et al., 2023; Grimes et al., 2023).

Generative AI models should not be governed only by technology; they require human supervision to confront their associated hazards. This includes ensuring ethical and responsible use, identifying and eliminating bias, managing copyright issues, verifying information accuracy, adhering to legal requirements, integrating with human knowledge, and finally, guaranteeing continuous improvement (Blau et al., 2024; Woodruff et al., 2024). Similarly, Bowman et al. (2022) argue that this oversight is getting more critical as the performance of GAI models becomes closer to human capabilities. Insufficient understanding of the topic. Some users use generative AI models and search engines interchangeably to search for information and get answers for their questions, even though they are completely different in their functionality and purpose. Search engines like Google locate and rank web pages according to keywords, thereby providing users with a list of links to explore. On the other hand, GAI models generate original content, answer queries and summarize documents based on large language models' capabilities, by comprehending and responding to user inputs. This is achieved by aggregating and synthesizing information from multiple sources and depending on probabilities to predict the next word in the sequence. So, they may not understand the topic and possibly provide inaccurate responses (Dwivedi et al., 2023; Manduchi et al., 2024; Sun et al., 2024).

Researchers should be able to follow the same methodology and reach similar results. One of the main challenges of GAI is generating inconsistent output. It varies due to different reasons, mainly inconsistency in training data (Bail, 2024; Di Sarno et al., 2024; Spennemann, 2023) and architectural limitations of the model itself. Hence, the model responses could be unreliable and variable (Xie et al., 2023). Bail (2024) identifies three main reasons for inconsistency in GAI's output. To begin with, these models are probabilistic in nature. They tend to give different outcomes even if the same prompt was repeated. This is due to their choice of the most likely outcome, rather than selecting the most reasonable or correct one. Next, their response is extremely sensitive to the user's input. Slight differences in users' repeated prompts may lead to noticeable variations in the models' outputs. Finally, GAI models evolve over time over time, which leads to changes in their responses, adding to their limitation of inconsistent results. Additionally, large language models use static trained data to generate new content, making them unable to keep track of new information and updates (Spennemann, 2023). However, even this static training data is not guaranteed to be totally retained in the models' memory. GAI models tend to forget, and their performance usually deteriorates over time. This phenomenon is known as "Catastrophic Forgetting." GAI developers are required to continuously train these models to ensure the quality and accuracy of their responses (Feuerriegel et al., 2024; Shi et al., 2024).

## Cognitive and Socio-cultural Impacts

The convenience and efficiency of generative AI models encourage researchers to get quick and easy answers to their questions, sometimes without verification or checking of the information. This may undermine the research process and negatively impact users' cognitive abilities (Iskender, 2023). Overreliance on AI can lead to a decline in human skills and serious negative impacts on mental health. This includes memory loss, shorter attention spans, difficulties in information sharing, social isolation, decreased human interactions, and undermined self-confidence (Dergaa et al., 2024; Zlateva et al., 2024).

As GAI models lack reasoning and proper analysis capabilities, they tend to over-simplify complex knowledge. This may produce misleading results, sometimes presenting facts inaccurately or offering insufficient answers (Rodriguez Schon & Colombi, 2024). Research shows that GAI models generally have limited critical thinking ability, which is fundamental to academic research (Dwivedi et al., 2023; Lund et al., 2023) Their output is usually descriptive and superficial. Besides, they struggle to incorporate feedback to correct text deficiencies and hence provide the same level of output quality (Spennemann, 2023).

Despite the global use of GAI models, they usually neglect cultural diversities (Manduchi et al., 2024). Most GenAI models have received sufficient training only on a handful of languages, particularly English, Chinese, and Japanese, which makes their capabilities in generating content in other language limited and undependable (Ahuja et al., 2023; Ye et al., 2024). In their study, Tao et al. (2023) found that these models favor English-speaking and European values, leading to varying effects on users around the world. This culture bias may cause and accelerate western culture dominance, especially with the growing use of GAI over time.

## Socio-economic Effects

The use of AI in academic publishing and peer review process may lead to deskilling. With its ability to streamline processes, a human factor will not be needed for most of the tasks, which could lead to job displacement (Gendron et al., 2022). On the other hand, the effect extends to necessitating essential skills for researchers in the era of AI. Researchers should learn to use new GAI platforms to compete in the new research landscape (Bian, 2024).

### Access and Representation

The growing incorporation of AI in different domains widens the digital divide, the increasing gap between individuals around the world, where usually people from wealthy nations are more likely to access and utilize GAI, while others in poor areas of the world could be deprived from this ability. This impact extends to the job market, where new jobs that require specific AI skills are created (Bozkurt, 2023; Capraro et al., 2024). Furthermore, there is a need for simpler GAI models with more convenient user interfaces to facilitate their deployment in research. Also, introducing training initiatives for researchers and knowledge sharing programs can overcome such difficulty and enhance their technical knowledge (Ekundayo et al., 2024). Finally, it is imperative to ensure equality and fairness while providing access to these models, including people with different disabilities (Satyam & Geetha, 2023).

Moreover, GAI models are predominantly developed by men from specific racial and academic backgrounds. Underrepresentation of women and minorities can lead to bias and unfairness in AI models (UN, 2022). Including a diverse variety of stakeholders in the GAI development process is essential to fostering equality and inclusion. It has been proposed that applying human-focused design principles, which incorporate a variety of viewpoints and ensure that the system serves the needs of all users, can help to overcome biases in AI (Chen et al., 2023).

## Ethical use in Academic Research

GAI has the potential to boost the quality and the productivity of scholarly work in different areas such as data analysis, automation of time-consuming tasks and creative problem solving. Nevertheless, the inclusion of GAI in research requires collaborative efforts from stakeholders to promote ethical use, facilitate multidisciplinary research, overcome its challenges, and ensure data governance and security (Al Harrasi & Salah El Din, 2024; Malik et al., 2023).

### Brainstorming

GAI is instrumental in facilitating brainstorming, idea generation and critical thinking (Pu et al., 2024; Schmidt et al., 2023). With the notable capacity to skim through large datasets, it can identify trends and themes that researchers are not able to recognize easily. GAI can refine research topics and formulate research questions (Hutson, 2024). Joosten et al. (2024) recommend that GAI should be used as a partner to the human user in the brainstorming process, thereby increasing productivity and efficiency. Tools like ChatGPT and Perplexity are valuable in supporting interdisciplinary research by synthesizing information from different sources, enabling a more holistic perspective (Ekundayo et al., 2024).

### Conducting a Literature Review

Finding relevant sources and writing literature reviews is one of the most time-consuming elements of academic research. GAI systems can smoothen the literature review writing process by examining and synthesizing vast amounts of research papers based on the research topic. Web-based applications such as Elicit, Consensus, Scopus AI and Scite.ai can read and arrange papers, find relevant information based on specific search criteria, identify research gaps, create quick literature reviews, and manage and export citations for verification processes (Aguilera-Cora et al., 2024; Hutson, 2024). Moreover, chatbots such as ChatGPT and Gemini have proved to be beneficial in simplifying complex scientific concepts and summarizing texts. However, these platforms are not suited to writing coherent literature reviews due to potential hallucinations and inability to cite actual sources (Acheampong & Nyaaba, 2024).

## Writing a Research Methodology Section

Researchers can use GAI applications to aid in selecting the appropriate research methodology, design, and data collection methods, especially in qualitative research approaches (Acheampong & Nyaaba, 2024; Aguilera-Cora et al., 2024). Rahman et al. (2023) note that ChatGPT can provide invaluable insights on methodological choices to take while writing a research paper, provided that scholars write an accurate and proper prompt. However, Dönmez et al. (2023) highlight the importance of human oversight, as GAI can give inaccurate information about research methods. Researchers should not depend merely on these tools. Instead, they should be used as guides rather than single resources for methodological elements. Additionally, GAI has the capability to introduce new methodologies that can change academic norms (Ekundayo et al., 2024).

## Conducting Data Analysis

The considerable and spontaneous impact of GAI on academic research is its ability to transform data analysis. GAI solutions can automate processes that usually require a great amount of human input. In the context of qualitative studies, these tools can identify patterns, comprehend emotional tones, and forecast upcoming trends, exposing significant insights that could have been overlooked in case of traditional thematic analysis (Christou, 2023; Ekundayo et al., 2024; Platt & Platt, 2023). In addition, Generative AI models have demonstrated their value in enhancing survey procedures, online experiments, content analysis and agent-based modeling, which are frequently used methods to understand and analyze human behavior (Bail, 2024). Besides, automation of data analysis increases the speed, efficiency, and quality of the entire process, thereby enabling the discovery of novel insights that could not be easily found by traditional research methods (Liu et al., 2023).

### Conducting a Peer Review

Peer review suffers from key challenges, including ambiguity, subjectivity, bias, shortage and inferior quality, and deficiency in reviewing interdisciplinary research (Carruthers, 2020; He et al., 2022; Hutson, 2024; Silva & Nazarovets, 2022; Wicherts, 2016; Woods et al., 2022). According to research, AI is already altering the peer review process and alleviating its challenges by offering objective, fair and consistent reviews (Carabantes et al., 2023; Checco et al., 2021; Drori & Te'eni, 2024; Hutson, 2024). In this regard, academic reviewers can train GAI models such as ChatGPT or Google Gemini to perform the review process efficiently based on predetermined criteria. However, some AI limitations exist including limited critical ability and models' bias, which need to be addressed and mitigated for better reviews (Lund et al., 2023; Salah et al., 2023).

### Support in Academic Writing

GAI is very efficient in automating tedious and time-consuming tasks such as proofreading, grammar checking, paraphrasing, and structuring research papers. GAI-powered applications like Quillbot, Grammarly and ChatPDF offer language editing services with simple and convenient tools (Adams & Chuah, 2022; Bulatovic et al., 2024). Research has indicated a positive relationship between the use of Grammarly and Quilbot and writer's self-confidence and output quality (Astuti & Sumarni, 2023; Latifah et al., 2024; Yilong Su, 2024). Nevertheless, contrary to what some academics believe, using AI to proofread and correct minor grammar and language mistakes in manuscripts can lead to rejections, as most journals use AI-detection software to identify its use (Dönmz et al., 2023). Adams & Chuah (2022) highlight that researchers should limit their use of GAI in the writing process to providing recommendations for better academic writing quality, focusing on macro issues such as text coherence and cohesion. Moreover, overreliance on GAI platforms undermines researchers' understanding of cognitive abilities and academic writing skills (Latifah et al., 2024).

## Future Prospects of using GAI in Academic Research

Generative AI is increasingly being integrated into various stages of the research process. Its pace of adoption is expected to become faster as scholars target higher productivity and efficiency of the research process. As AI technologies evolve, their integration will become more evident and transformative (Al Harrasi & Salah El Din, 2024; Grimes et al., 2023). One of the prominent possibilities of AI is reshaping existing research methodologies. This is supported by the promised speed and analytical capabilities of AI, enabling researchers to discover patterns and identify relationships that was difficult to uncover via conventional methods (Ekundayo et al., 2024). Furthermore, there is a wide scope for using GAI as a research assistant. In this scenario, researchers can utilize the technical capabilities of GAI in automating different stages of research, facilitating the process and gaining efficiency. GAI can assist in repetitive and time-consuming tasks such as semantic search, data cleaning, literature review synthesis, pattern recognition and formatting manuscripts. On the other hand, Researchers can concentrate on creative and cognitive tasks of the scientific research. This human-AI collaboration opens the door for more impactful and innovative research findings (Lund et al., 2023).

Nonetheless, researchers should carefully establish ethical approaches to use GAI in research, while considering its associated risks, such as data privacy, over-reliance, and other ethical and technological challenges (Al Harrasi & Salah El Din, 2024). The shift towards ethical GAI utilization in research requires an active governance from higher education institutions, by building integration frameworks, setting clear policies, continuous monitoring and evaluation and collaboration with other stakeholders like policymakers, and GAI technology providers (Dwivedi et al., 2023; Grimes et al., 2023).

## Conclusion

Generative Artificial Intelligence (GAI) has emerged as a revolutionary tool that can assist researchers to keep pace with increased publication targets and intensive academic pressure. This is accomplished by automating time-consuming processes, enhancing research efficiency and quality, and paving new ways for scholarly explorations. However, harnessing this massive power in research requires active supervision and careful consideration of the numerous challenges and limitations of GAI models to avoid compromising on the academic quality of research. Scholars need to be aware of the ethical and legal concerns, technological constraints, cognitive and socio-cultural challenges, socio-economic impact, and access and representation issues. This emphasizes the need for a mindful and careful approach, ensuring that GAI can enhance the research quality while preserving academic integrity.

Tools such as OpenAI's ChatGPT, Google Gemini, Consensus, Scopus AI, Perplexity, among others, are pivotal in different stages of research, including idea generation and brainstorming, literature review writing and synthesizing, selection of proper research methodologies, conducting data analysis and supporting academic writing. Nonetheless, beyond the current uses and the immediate challenges of deploying GAI in academic research, it will have a striking influence on the academic landscape. As noticed, GAI tools are developing, and their capabilities are becoming greater with time. Consequently, their use in research is expected to increase in the upcoming years. Their impact may surpass simple automation of tasks, to devising new research methodologies and changing academic norms.

Finally, harnessing the full potential of GAI in academic research entails a collaborative, multidisciplinary and balanced approach that includes the viewpoints of various stakeholders such as academic staff, academic journals, GAI developers and legislators. There should be a consensus on drafting proper guidelines for the use of GAI applications that mitigate its risks and challenges. Meanwhile, researchers should ensure active use of these tools by understanding their limitations and ensuring human oversight while seeking automation.

## References

Acheampong, K. O., & Nyaaba, M. (2024). Review of Qualitative Research in the Era of Generative Artificial Intelligence. *SSRN Electronic Journal*. https://doi.org/https://doi.org/10.2139/ssrn.4686920

Adams, D., & Chuah, K.-M. (2022). Artificial Intelligence-Based Tools in Research Writing. In P. P. Churi, S. Joshi, M. Elhoseny & A. Omrane (Eds.), *Artificial Intelligence in Higher Education: A Practical Approach* (pp. 169–184). CRC Press. 169–184. https://doi.org/10.1201/9781003184157-9

Aditya, G. (2024). Understanding and Addressing AI Hallucinations in Healthcare and Life Sciences. *International Journal of Health Sciences, 7*(3), 1–11. https://doi.org/10.47941/ijhs.1862

Aguilera-Cora, E., Lopezosa, C., Fernández-Cavia, J., & Codina, L. (2024a). Accelerating research processes with Scopus AI: A place branding case study. *Revista Panamericana de Comunicación, 6*(1). https://doi.org/10.21555/rpc.v6i1.3088

Ahuja, K., Diddee, H., Hada, R., Ochieng, M., Ramesh, K., Jain, P., Nambi, A., Ganu, T., Segal, S., Axmed, M., Bali, K., & Sitaram, S. (2023). *MEGA: Multilingual Evaluation of Generative AI.* http://arxiv.org/abs/2303.12528

Al Harrasi, N. & Salah El Din, M. (2024). Future Horizons: Exploring Artificial Intelligence's Role in Shaping Research Landscapes. In N. Al Harrasi & M. Salah El Din (Eds.), *Utilizing AI for Assessment, Grading, and Feedback in Higher Education* (pp. 114–134). IGI Global Scientific Publishing. https://doi.org/10.4018/979-8-3693-2145-4.ch005

Anechitaoe, C. (2023). Intellectual Property versus Artificial Intelligence. *Ovidius University Annals, Economic Sciences Series* (pp. 2–6), Ovidius University of Constantza, Faculty of Economic Sciences.

Astuti, D., & Sumarni, S. (2023). Grammarly in students' self-directed learning for writing skills: Advantages and disadvantages. *INSANIA: Jurnal Pemikiran Alternatif Kependidikan*. https://doi.org/10.24090/insania.v28i1a.8899

Barbalau, A., Cosma, A., Ionescu, R.T., & Popescu, M.C. (2020). Black-Box Ripper: Copying black-box models using generative evolutionary algorithms. *ArXiv, abs/2010.11158*.

Bail, C. A. (2024). PERSPECTIVE Can Generative AI improve social science? https://doi.org/10.1073/pnas.2314021121/-/DCSupplemental

Baldassarre, M.T., Caivano, D., Fernandez Nieto, B., Gigante, D., & Ragone, A. (2023). The Social Impact of Generative AI: An Analysis on ChatGPT. *Proceedings of the 2023 ACM Conference on Information Technology for Social Good*. https://doi.org/10.1145/3582515.3609555

Bandi, A., Adapa, P. V. S. R., & Kuchi, Y. E. V. P. K. (2023). The Power of Generative AI: A Review of Requirements, Models, Input–Output Formats, Evaluation Metrics, and Challenges. *Future Internet, 15*(8), 260. https://doi.org/10.3390/fi15080260

Acheampong, K. O., & Nyaaba, M. (2024). Review of Qualitative Research in the Era of Generative Artificial Intelligence. *SSRN Electronic Journal*. https://doi.org/https://doi.org/10.2139/ssrn.4686920

Adams, D., & Chuah, K.-M. (2022). Artificial Intelligence-Based Tools in Research Writing. In *Artificial Intelligence in Higher Education* (1st ed., pp. 169–184). CRC Press. https://doi.org/10.1201/9781003184157-9

Aditya, G. (2024). Understanding and Addressing AI Hallucinations in Healthcare and Life Sciences. *International Journal of Health Sciences*, 7(3), 1–11. https://doi.org/10.47941/ijhs.1862

Aguilera-Cora, E., Lopezosa, C., Fernández-Cavia, J., & Codina, L. (2024a). Accelerating research processes with Scopus AI: A place branding case study. *Revista Panamericana de Comunicación*, *6*(1). https://doi.org/10.21555/rpc.v6i1.3088

Ahuja, K., Diddee, H., Hada, R., Ochieng, M., Ramesh, K., Jain, P., Nambi, A., Ganu, T., Segal, S., Axmed, M., Bali, K., & Sitaram, S. (2023). *MEGA: Multilingual Evaluation of Generative AI*. http://arxiv.org/abs/2303.12528

Al Harrasi, N., & Salah El Din, M. (2024). Future Horizons: Exploring Artificial Intelligence's Role in Shaping Research Landscapes. In N. Al Harrasi & M. Salah El Din (Eds.), *Utilizing AI for Assessment, Grading, and Feedback in Higher Education* (pp. 114–134). IGI Global Scientific Publishing. https://doi.org/10.4018/979-8-3693-2145-4.ch005

Anechitaoe, C. (2023). Intellectual Property versus Artificial Intelligence. *Ovidius University of Constantza, Faculty of Economic Sciences*, *1*, 2–6.

Astuti, D., & Sumarni, S. (2023). Grammarly in Students' Self-Directed Learning for Writing Skills: Advantages and Disadvantages. *Insania Jurnal Pemikiran Alternatif Kependidikan*, *28*(1a), 36–50. https://doi.org/10.24090/insania.v28i1a.8899

Bail, C. A. (2024). PERSPECTIVE Can Generative AI improve social science? *PNAS*, *121*(21). https://doi.org/10.1073/pnas.2314021121/-/DCSupplemental

Baldassarre, M. T., Caivano, D., Nieto, B. F., Gigante, D., & Ragone, A. (2024). *The Social Impact of Generative AI: An Analysis on ChatGPT*. 363–373. https://doi.org/10.1145/3582515.3609555

Bandi, A., Adapa, P. V. S. R., & Kuchi, Y. E. V. P. K. (2023). The Power of Generative AI: A Review of Requirements, Models, Input–Output Formats, Evaluation Metrics, and Challenges. In *Future Internet* (Vol. 15, Issue 8). Multidisciplinary Digital Publishing Institute (MDPI). https://doi.org/10.3390/fi15080260

Barbalau, A., Cosma, A., Ionescu, R. T., & Popescu, M. (2020). *Black-Box Ripper: Copying black-box models using generative evolutionary algorithms.* https://github.com/antoniobarbalau/black-box-ripper.

Bian, Z. (2024). Research on the Impact of Artificial Intelligence on the Labor Market. *Business, Economics and Management EMFRM, 2023*, 1036–1041.

Blau, W., Cerf, V. G., Enriquez, J., Francisco, J. S., Gasser, U., Gray, M. L., Greaves, M., Grosz, B. J., Jamieson, K. H., Haug, G. H., Hennessy, J. L., Horvitz, E., Kaiser, D. I., London, A. J., Lovell-Badge, R., McNutt, M. K., Minow, M., Mitchell, T. M., Ness, S., … Witherell, M. (2024). Protecting scientific integrity in an age of generative AI. *Proceedings of the National Academy of Sciences of the United States of America*, *121*(22), e2407886121. https://doi.org/10.1073/pnas.2407886121

Bowman, S. R., Jeeyoon, H., Perez, E., Chen, E., Craig, P., Heiner, S., Lukosuite, K., Askell, A., Jones, A., Chen, A., Goldie, A., Mirhoseini, A., Cameron, M., Olah, C., Daniela, A., Amodei, D., Drain, D., Dustin, L., Eli, T.-J., … Kaplan, J. (2022). *Measuring Progress on Scalable Oversight for Large Language Models*. https://doi.org/10.48550/arxiv.2211.03540

Bozkurt, A. (2023). *Challenging the Status Quo and Exploring the New Boundaries in the Age of Algorithms: Reimagining the Role of Generative AI in Distance Education and Online Learning. 18*(1). https://doi.org/10.5281/zenodo.7755273

Bulatovic, V., Mirovic, I., & Kaurin, T. (2024). Analyzing Grammarly software for corrective feedback: Teacher's perspective on affordances, limitations and implementation. *Focus on ELT Journal*, *6*(1), 74–86. https://doi.org/10.14744/felt.6.1.6

Calamur, H., & Ghosh, R. (2024). Adapting Peer Review for the Future: Digital Disruptions and Trust in Peer Review. *Learned Publishing*, *37*(1), 49–54. https://doi.org/10.1002/leap.1594

Capraro, V., Lentsch, A., Acemoglu, D., Akgun, S., Akhmedova, A., Bilancini, E., Bonnefon, J.-F., Brañas-Garza, P., Butera, L., Douglas, K. M.,

Everett, J., Gigerenzer, G., Greenhow, C., Hashimoto, D., Holt-Lunstad, J., Jetten, J., Johnson, S., Longoni, C., Lunn, P., … Viale, R. (2024). The Impact of Generative Artificial Intelligence on Socioeconomic Inequalities and Policy Making. *PNAS Nexus*, *3*(6), 191. https://doi.org/10.2139/ssrn.4666103

Carabantes, D., González-Geraldo, J. L., & Jover, G. (2023). ChatGPT could be the reviewer of your next scientific paper. Evidence on the limits of AI-assisted academic reviews. *Profesional de La Informacion*, *32*(5). https://doi.org/10.3145/epi.2023.sep.16

Carruthers, J. (2020). Peer Review: Not in Crisis … but Vibrant in Its Growing Diversity. *South African Journal of Science*, *116*(9/10). https://doi.org/10.17159/sajs.2020/8853

Checco, A., Bracciale, L., Loreti, P., Pinfield, S., & Bianchi, G. (2021). AI-assisted Peer Review. *Humanities and Social Sciences Communications*, *8*(1). https://doi.org/10.1057/s41599-020-00703-8

Chen, Y., Clayton, E. W., Novak, L. L., Anders, S., & Malin, B. (2023). Human-Centered Design to Address Biases in Artificial Intelligence. *Journal of Medical Internet Research*, *25*, e43251. https://doi.org/10.2196/43251

Christou, P. (2023). How to Use Artificial Intelligence (AI) as a Resource, ow Methodological and Analysis Tool in Qualitative Research? *Qualitative Report*, *28*(7), 1968–1980. https://doi.org/10.46743/2160-3715/2023.6406

Dergaa, I., Ben Saad, H., Glenn, J. M., Amamou, B., Ben Aissa, M., Guelmami, N., Fekih-Romdhane, F., & Chamari, K. (2024). From tools to threats: a reflection on the impact of artificial intelligence chatbots on cognitive health. *Frontiers in Psychology*, *15*. https://doi.org/10.3389/fpsyg.2024.1259845

Di Sarno, L., Caroselli, A., Tonin, G., Graglia, B., Pansini, V., Causio, F. A., Gatto, A., & Chiaretti, A. (2024). Artificial Intelligence in Pediatric Emergency Medicine: Applications, Challenges, and Future Perspectives. *Biomedicines*, *12*(6), 1220. https://doi.org/10.3390/biomedicines12061220

Dönmez, I., Idil, S., & Gulen, S. (2023). Conducting Academic Research with the AI Interface ChatGPT: Challenges and Opportunities.

*Technology, Engineering, Mathematics and Art Education*, *6*(2), 101–118. https://doi.org/10.55290/steam.1263404

Drori, I., & Te'eni, D. (2024). Human-in-the-Loop AI Reviewing: Feasibility, Opportunities, and Risks. *Journal of the Association for Information Systems*, *25*(1), 98–109. https://doi.org/10.17705/1jais.00867

Dwivedi, Y. K., Kshetri, N., Hughes, L., Slade, E. L., Jeyaraj, A., Kar, A. K., Baabdullah, A. M., Koohang, A., Raghavan, V., Ahuja, M., Albanna, H., Albashrawi, M. A., Al-Busaidi, A. S., Balakrishnan, J., Barlette, Y., Basu, S., Bose, I., Brooks, L., Buhalis, D., … Wright, R. (2023). "So what if ChatGPT wrote it?" Multidisciplinary perspectives on opportunities, challenges and implications of generative conversational AI for research, practice and policy. *International Journal of Information Management*, *71*. https://doi.org/10.1016/j.ijinfomgt.2023.102642

Ekundayo, T., Khan, Z., & Nuzhat, S. (2024). Evaluating the Influence of Artificial Intelligence on Scholarly Research: A Study Focused on Academics. *Human Behavior and Emerging Technologies*. https://doi.org/10.1155/2024/8713718

Elali, F. R., & Rachid, L. N. (2023). AI-generated research paper fabrication and plagiarism in the scientific community. In *Patterns* (Vol. 4, Issue 3). Cell Press. https://doi.org/10.1016/j.patter.2023.100706

Ferrara, E. (2023). Fairness and Bias in Artificial Intelligence: A Brief Survey of Sources, Impacts, and Mitigation Strategies. *Sci*, *6*(1), 3. https://doi.org/10.3390/sci6010003

Feuerriegel, S., Hartmann, J., Janiesch, C., & Zschech, P. (2024). Generative AI. *Business and Information Systems Engineering*, *66*(1), 111–126. https://doi.org/10.1007/s12599-023-00834-7

Fischer, J. E. (2023). Generative AI Considered Harmful. *Proceedings of the 5th International Conference on Conversational User Interfaces, CUI 2023*, 1–5. https://doi.org/10.1145/3571884.3603756

Fui-Hoon Nah, F., Zheng, R., Cai, J., Siau, K., & Chen, L. (2023). Generative AI and ChatGPT: Applications, challenges, and AI-human collaboration. *Journal of Information Technology Case and Application Research*, *25*(3), 277–304. https://doi.org/10.1080/15228053.2023.2233814

Gendron, Y., Andrew, J., & Cooper, C. (2022). The perils of artificial intelligence in academic publishing. *Critical Perspectives on Accounting*, *87*, 102411. https://doi.org/https://doi.org/10.1016/j.cpa.2021.102411

Golda, A., Mekonen, K., Pandey, A., Singh, A., Hassija, V., Chamola, V., & Sikdar, B. (2024). Privacy and Security Concerns in Generative AI: A Comprehensive Survey. *IEEE Access*, *12*, 48126–48144. https://doi.org/10.1109/ACCESS.2024.3381611

Grimes, M., von Krogh, G., Feuerriegel, S., Rink, F., & Gruber, M. (2023). From Scarcity to Abundance: Scholars and Scholarship in an Age of Generative Artificial Intelligence. *Academy of Management Journal*, *66*(6), 1617–1624. https://doi.org/10.5465/amj.2023.4006

Gu, J. (2024). *Responsible Generative AI: What to Generate and What Not*. http://arxiv.org/abs/2404.05783

Hai, H. N. (2023). *ChatGPT: The Evolution of Natural Language Processing*. https://doi.org/10.22541/au.167935454.46075854/v1

Hashem, R., Ali, N., El Zein, F., Fidalgo, P., & Abu Khurma, O. (2024). AI to the rescue: Exploring the potential of ChatGPT as a teacher ally for workload relief and burnout prevention. *Research and Practice in Technology Enhanced Learning*, *19*, 023. https://doi.org/10.58459/rptel.2024.19023

He, Y., Tian, K., & Xu, X. (2022). A Validation Study on the Factors Affecting the Practice Modes of Open Peer Review. *Scientometrics*, *128*(1), 587–607. https://doi.org/10.1007/s11192-022-04552-x

Hosseini, M., & Resnik, D. B. (2024). Guidance needed for using artificial intelligence to screen journal submissions for misconduct. *Research Ethics*, *21*(1). https://doi.org/10.1177/17470161241254052

Huang, S.-C., & Le, T.-H. (2021). Generative Adversarial Network. In *Principles and Labs for Deep Learning* (pp. 255–281). https://doi.org/10.1016/b978-0-323-90198-7.00011-2

Hutson, J. (2024). Rethinking Plagiarism in the Era of Generative AI. *Journal of Intelligent Communication*, *4*(1), 20–31. https://doi.org/10.54963/jic.v4i1.220

Inam, M., Sheikh, S., Minhas, A. M. K., Vaughan, E. M., Krittanawong, C., Samad, Z., Lavie, C. J., Khoja, A., D'Cruze, M., M., Slipczuk, L., Alarakhiya, F., Naseem, A., Haider, A. H., & Virani, S. S. (2024). A review of top cardiology and cardiovascular medicine journal guidelines regarding the use of generative artificial intelligence tools in scientific writing. *Current Problems in Cardiology*, *49*(3), 102387. https://doi.org/https://doi.org/10.1016/j.cpcardiol.2024.102387

Indri Hapsari, D. R., Pratama, A., Hidayah, N. P., & Anggraeny, I. (2024). The Legality of Intellectual Property by Artificial Intelligence in Indonesia. *Kne Social Sciences*, *9*(1), 749–759. https://doi.org/10.18502/kss.v8i21.14791

Iskender, A. (2023). Holy or Unholy? Interview with Open AI's ChatGPT. *European Journal of Tourism Research*, *34*. https://doi.org/10.54055/ejtr.v34i.3169

Jaiswal, R., Singh, A., Rathore, S., Verma, A., Saxena, P., Mishra, M., &. M. (2023). Role of Intellectual Property Theories in Addressing Anomalies Created by the Intersection of Artificial Intelligence and Intellectual Property Rights: An Analysis. *International Journal of Membrane Science and Technology*, *10*(4), 2560–2566. https://doi.org/10.15379/ijmst.v10i4.3657

Jalal, A. (2020). Research Productivity in Higher Education Environment. *Journal of Higher Education Service Science and Management. 2020*, *3*(1). https://www.joherd.co/journals/index.php

Janib, J., Rasdi, R. M., Omar, Z., Alias, S. N., Zaremohzzabieh, Z., & Ahrari, S. (2021). The Relationship between Workload and Performance of Research University Academics in Malaysia: The Mediating Effects of Career Commitment and Job Satisfaction. *Asian Journal of University Education*, *17*(2), 85–99. https://doi.org/10.24191/AJUE.V17I2.13394

Joosten, J., Bilgram, V., Hahn, A., & Totzek, D. (2024). Comparing the Ideation Quality of Humans with Generative Artificial Intelligence. *Ieee Engineering Management Review*, *52*(2), 153–164. https://doi.org/10.1109/emr.2024.3353338

Latifah, S., Muth'im, A., & Nasrullah, N. (2024). The Use of QuillBot in Academic Writing. *Journey: Journal of English Language and Pedagogy*, 7(1), 110–121. https://doi.org/10.33503/journey.v7i1.4047

Lemos, A. L. M. (2024). Digital errors, failures, and disruptions in generative AI hallucinations: Communication typology, premises, and epistemology. *MATRIZes*, *18*(1), 75–91. https://doi.org/10.11606/issn.1982-8160.v18i1p75-91

Liu, H., Azam, M., Bin Naeem, S., & Faiola, A. (2023). An Overview of the Capabilities of ChatGPT for Medical Writing and Its Implications for Academic Integrity. *Health Information & Libraries Journal*, *40*(4), 440–446. https://doi.org/10.1111/hir.12509

Lund, B. D., Wang, T., Reddy Mannuru, N., Nie, B., Shimray, S., & Wang, Z. (2023). ChatGPT and a New Academic Reality: AI-Written Research Papers and the Ethics of the Large Language Models in Scholarly Publishing. *Journal of the Association for Information Science and Technology*, *74*(5), 570–581.

Ma, L., & Zhao, D. (2024). Prospects and Ethical Considerations of Generative Artificial Intelligence in Higher Education. *SHS Web of Conferences*, *187*, 03030. https://doi.org/10.1051/shsconf/202418703030

Malik, A. R., Pratiwi, Y., Andajani, K., Numertayasa, I. W., Suharti, S., Darwis, A., & Marzuki. (2023). Exploring Artificial Intelligence in Academic Essay: Higher Education Student's Perspective. *International Journal of Educational Research Open*, *5*. https://doi.org/10.1016/j.ijedro.2023.100296

Manduchi, L., Pandey, K., Bamler, R., Cotterell, R., Däubener, S., Fellenz, S., Fischer, A., Gärtner, T., Kirchler, M., Kloft, M., Li, Y., Lippert, C., de Melo, G., Nalisnick, E., Ommer, B., Ranganath, R., Rudolph, M., Ullrich, K., Broeck, G. Van den, … Fortuin, V. (2024). *On the Challenges and Opportunities in Generative AI*. http://arxiv.org/abs/2403.00025

Mollaki, V. (2024). Death of a reviewer or death of peer review integrity? the challenges of using AI tools in peer reviewing and the need to go beyond publishing policies. *Research Ethics*, *20*(2), 239–250. https://doi.org/10.1177/17470161231224552

Mondal, S., Mondal, H., Marndi, G., & Behera, J. (2023). ChatGPT for Teachers: Practical Examples for Utilizing Artificial Intelligence for Educational Purposes. *Indian Journal of Vascular and Endovascular Surgery*, *10*(3), 200–205. https://doi.org/10.4103/ijves.ijves_37_23

Nicholls, H., Nicholls, M., Tekin, S., Lamb, D., & Billings, J. (2022). The impact of working in academia on researchers' mental health and well-being: A systematic review and qualitative metasynthesis. *PLoS ONE*, *17*(5). https://doi.org/10.1371/journal.pone.0268890

Pal, J. K., & Sarkar, S. (2020). Evaluation of institutional research productivity. *DESIDOC Journal of Library and Information Technology*, *40*(1), 406–417. https://doi.org/10.14429/djlit.40.01.14804

Patón-Romero, J. D., Vinuesa, R., Jaccheri, L., Baldassarre, & Teresa, M. (2022). State of Gender Equality in and by Artificial Intelligence. *Iadis*

*International Journal on Computer Science and Information Systems*, *17*(2). https://doi.org/10.33965/ijcsis_2022170203

Platt, M., & Platt, D. (2023). Effectiveness of Generative Artificial Intelligence for Scientific Content Analysis. *17th IEEE International Conference on Application of Information and Communication Technologies, AICT 2023 - Proceedings*. https://doi.org/10.1109/AICT59525.2023.10313167

Pu, Z., Shi, C. L., Jeon, C. O., Fu, J., Liu, S. J., Lan, C., Yao, Y., Liu, Y. X., & Jia, B. (2024). ChatGPT and generative AI are revolutionizing the scientific community: A Janus-faced conundrum. *IMeta*, *3*(2). https://doi.org/10.1002/imt2.178

QuillBot. (2024). *QuillBot* [Web application interface]. QuillBot. https://quillbot.com

Rahman, M., Terano, H. J. R., Rahman, N., Salamzadeh, A., & Rahaman, S. (2023). ChatGPT and Academic Research: A Review and Recommendations Based on Practical Examples. *Journal of Education, Management and Development Studies*, *3*(1), 1–12. https://doi.org/10.52631/jemds.v3i1.175

Rodriguez Schon, V., & Colombi, C. (2024). I Asked Chatgpt What the Next Trend Would Be. *Fashion Highlight*, *2*, 72–78. https://doi.org/10.36253/fh-2501

Salah, M., Abdelfattah, F., & Halbusi, H. Al. (2023). Debate: Peer reviews at the crossroads— 'To AI or not to AI?' In *Public Money and Management* (Vol. 43, Issue 8, pp. 781–782). Routledge. https://doi.org/10.1080/09540962.2023.2264032

Satyam, & Geetha, P. (2023). Comprehensive Overview of the Opportunities and Challenges in AI. *International Conference on Sustainable Computing and Smart Systems, ICSCSS 2023 - Proceedings*, 420–423. https://doi.org/10.1109/ICSCSS57650.2023.10169722

Schmidt, L., Piazza, A., & Wiedenhöft, C. (2023). "Augmented Brainstorming with AI"- Research Approach for Identifying Design Criteria for Improved Collaborative Idea Generation Between Humans and AI. *Frontiers in Artificial Intelligence and Applications*, *368*, 410–412. https://doi.org/10.3233/FAIA230113

Shi, H., Xu, Z., Wang, H., Qin, W., Wang, W., Wang, Y., Wang, Z., Ebrahimi, S., & Wang, H. (2024). *Continual Learning of Large Language Models: A Comprehensive Survey*. http://arxiv.org/abs/2404.16789

Silva, J. A. T. da, & Nazarovets, S. (2022). The Role of Publons in the Context of Open Peer Review. *Publishing Research Quarterly*, *38*(4), 760–781. https://doi.org/10.1007/s12109-022-09914-0

Spennemann, D. H. R. (2023). ChatGPT and the Generation of Digitally Born "Knowledge": How Does a Generative AI Language Model Interpret Cultural Heritage Values? *Knowledge*, *3*(3), 480–512. https://doi.org/10.3390/knowledge3030032

Sun, Y., Jang, E., Ma, F., & Wang, T. (2024). *Generative AI in the Wild: Prospects, Challenges, and Strategies*. 1–16. https://doi.org/10.1145/3613904.3642160

Sysoieva, S., & Sokolova, I. (2020). Academic Staff Development Programme to Enhance Research Competence: A Case Study. *Education: Modern Discourses*, 78–87. https://doi.org/10.37472/2617-3107-2020-3-07

Tang, A., Li, K. K., Kwok, K. O., Cao, L., Luong, S., & Tam, W. (2024). The importance of transparency: Declaring the use of generative artificial intelligence (AI) in academic writing. In *Journal of Nursing Scholarship* (Vol. 56, Issue 2, pp. 314–318). https://doi.org/10.1111/jnu.12938

Tao, Y., Viberg, O., Baker, R. S., & Kizilcec, R. F. (2023). Cultural Bias and Cultural Alignment of Large Language Models. *PNAS Nexus*, *3*(9), 346. http://arxiv.org/abs/2311.14096

Watermeyer, R., Phipps, L., L., Lanclos, D., & Knight, C. (2023). Generative AI and the Automating of Academia. *Postdigital Science and Education*, *6*, 446–466. https://doi.org/10.1007/s42438-023-00440-6

Wicherts, J. M. (2016). Peer Review Quality and Transparency of the Peer-Review Process in Open Access and Subscription Journals. *Plos One*, *11*(1), e0147913. https://doi.org/10.1371/journal.pone.0147913

Woodruff, A., Shelby, R., Kelley, P. G., Rousso-Schindler, S., Smith-Loud, J., & Wilcox, L. (2024). *How Knowledge Workers Think Generative AI Will (Not) Transform Their Industries*. 1–26. https://doi.org/10.1145/3613904.3642700

Woods, H. B., Brumberg, J., Kaltenbrunner, W., Pinfield, S., & Waltman, L. (2022). Innovations in Peer Review in Scholarly Publishing: A Meta-Summary. *Wellcome Open Research*, *7*, 82. https://doi.org/10.12688/wellcomeopenres.17715.1

Xie, Q., Schenck, E. J., Yang, H. S., Chen, Y., Peng, Y., & Wang, F. (2023). *Faithful AI in Medicine: A Systematic Review with Large Language Models and Beyond*. https://doi.org/10.21203/rs.3.rs-3661764/v1

Ye, F., Liu, G., Wu, X., & Wu, L. (2024). AltDiffusion: A Multilingual Text-to-Image Diffusion Model. *Proceedings of the Aaai Conference on Artificial Intelligence*, *38*(7), 6648–6656. https://doi.org/10.1609/aaai.v38i7.28487

Yilong Su, N. (2024). A Correlation Study of Automated Writing Evaluation System (Grammarly) and Chinese EFL Learners' Writing Self-Efficacy in Their Self-Regulated Learning. *Journal of Electronic Systems, 20*(3), 1874–1895. https://doi.org/10.52783/jes.3904

Zerka, F., Urovi, V., Vaidyanathan, A., Barakat, S., Walsh, S., Gabrani-Juma, H., Miraglio, B., Woodruff, H. C., Dumontier, M., & Lambin, P. (2020). Blockchain for Privacy Preserving and Trustworthy Distributed Machine Learning in Multicentric Medical Imaging (C-DistriM). *Ieee Access*, *8*, 183939–183951. https://doi.org/10.1109/access.2020.3029445

Zhong, H., Chang, J., Zhang, Y., Wu, T., Chamikara, M. A. P., Pathmabandu, C., & Xue, M. (2023). Copyright Protection and Accountability of Generative AI: Attack, Watermarking and Attribution. *WWW '23 Companion: Companion Proceedings of the ACM Web Conference 2023*, 94–98. https://doi.org/10.1145/3543873.3587321

Zlateva, P., Steshina, L., Petukhov, I., & Velev, D. (2024). A Conceptual Framework for Solving Ethical Issues in Generative Artificial Intelligence. *Frontiers in Artificial Intelligence and Applications*, *381*, 110–119. https://doi.org/10.3233/FAIA231182

# The Impact of a Reflective Professional Development Program on Omani Teachers' Utilisation and Attitude Towards Artificial Intelligence Tools

*Shams Salim Al Zakwani*

**ABSTRACT**
The educational landscape in Oman is rapidly evolving with technologies such as artificial intelligence offering transformative potential through personalized learning and data-driven insights. However, teachers face such barriers as lack of support and inadequate skills, hindering the integration of these technologies. This study aimed to design, develop, and implement a professional development program for teachers on AI tools for education. It also sought to determine the program's impact on participant teachers' utilization and attitudes towards AI tools. A descriptive analytical design is utilized, employing quantitative and qualitative data. Research tools, including a questionnaire and semi-structured interviews, were validated and used to collect data to answer the research questions. The sample comprised 35 Omani teachers from a Muscat school who actively participated in the program. The findings revealed that teachers use AI tools for enhancing student engagement, improving efficiency, saving time, and promoting collaboration. While most teachers exhibited positive attitudes, time constraints, lack of training and tech challenges hindered effective utilization. In light of the findings, future research could focus on long-term impact studies, action research with teachers as active participants, and assessment tools to measure professional development impact on AI utilization and attitudes. Future programs could integrate theoretical frameworks like the Community of Inquiry, emphasize sustainability, and provide authentic learning experiences for teachers.

## Introduction

AI is an expeditiously growing field of computer science and software engineering that intends to develop systems and machines that perform actions traditionally requiring human intelligence. As articulated by Abbass (2021), AI can be defined as "The automation of cognition" (p. 95). Going beyond the usual definition, Abbass (2021) has also defined AI as a combination of social and cognitive aspects that allow machines to seamlessly perform tasks involving cognitive processes and engage with other entities in society. This involves the exchange of messages characterised by high information content and concise representation. This definition does not consider AI as merely a technology or a product but also as a sociocognitive process. Nowadays, tools developed using AI can be used as efficient assistants to automate tasks, enhance the process of decision-making, optimise workflow, and augment human capabilities across various industries (Aktay, 2022).

In the context of education, AI technologies are powerful and particularly suitable for the advancement of educational goals. AI tools open doors for enhancing teaching and learning through processing large amounts of data, managing knowledge, smart diagnostic systems, educational platforms, etc. (Zmyzgova et al., 2020). Furthermore, Taneri (2020) also supports the notion that AI tools can be integrated into education to assess teachers' performance, career-guiding students, provide high-quality education for students with disabilities, provide personalised learning, conduct automated assessments, etc. However, despite the necessity of AI in education, the implementation of AI faces limitations attributed to many factors, such as financial constraints, technological illiteracy, and, most importantly, teachers' resistance to new technologies (Ali, 2023). Undoubtedly, the effectiveness and impact of AI in education depend on teachers' willingness and readiness to integrate technology into the classroom. That is because teachers are the individuals standing at the helm, and their attitudes towards using AI are fundamental determinants of the success of AI integration in education (Dimitriadou & Lanitis, 2023). Teachers naturally play a vital role in shaping the present and future of educational systems. Their attitudes and capabilities are crucial in successfully utilising AI tools in their classrooms. Dimitriadou & Lanitis (2023) claim that teachers require appropriate training and professional development programs to successfully integrate new technologies into their classrooms, especially AI technologies.

Teachers' professional development programs hold perennial significance across societies and have always been considered the main source of educational change in well-organised communities (Oghly, 2023). That is because professional development programs provide an opportunity for continuous growth and improvement in pedagogical and teaching practices. From the viewpoint of Oghly (2023), professional development programs are crucial as they provide room for change and an opportunity to enhance knowledge and skills. As a result, professional development programs are considered a significant element in improving educational systems and consequently improving students' outcomes. Furthermore, professional development programs for teachers provide an opportunity for change and knowledge enhancement, which aligns with Oman Vision 2040, assuring teachers play a crucial role in fostering adaptability, innovation, and student-centred learning. Citing Al-Harthi et al. (2022), Oman's Vision 2040 primarily focuses on enhancing educational outcomes to become a developed country.

The educational landscape in Oman has been going through an expeditious transformation, especially with the emergence of AI. The literature and research on AI are extensive, as it can transform education through personalized learning, data-driven insights, and various other innovative educational tools. However, despite the potential of technology, like AI, to revolutionise teaching and learning, teachers find themselves exploring uncharted terrain as they lack the essential skills and the readiness to integrate these technologies into their teaching practices.

A study by Al-Senaidi et al. (2009) investigated the challenges faced by Omani educators in integrating information and communication technologies in education in Oman. The study revealed that the key barriers and challenges faced by educators when it comes to adopting technology in education include lack of institutional support, lack of confidence, and disbelief and scepticism about the benefits of utilizing technology in education. Moreover, a study conducted by Ranjbaran et al. (2023) investigated Omani ELT teachers' perceptions and behavioral intentions to use technology. The study utilized qualitative interviews, which revealed that teachers are willing to use technology in their teaching, but their inability to use these technologies and the lack of skills were issues of concern. This serious gap hinders the possibility of taking full advantage of AI's full potential and affects the quality of education delivered to students. This highlights the urgent need for implementing a professional development program for teachers in integrating emerging technologies such as AI into education. As outlined by Al Jabri et al. (2018), development measures should primarily focus on teachers as they are considered an essential factor affecting students' learning outcomes.

Al Jabri et al. (2018) assert that there are many effective ways to improve the quality of education in Oman, one of which is modernising teachers' preparation and systemising teachers' professional development programs. Furthermore, Al Belushi (2013) explored professional development activities and their usefulness for Omani teachers in Al Batinah Region in Oman. The findings revealed that some teachers are not satisfied with the lack of professional development opportunities provided at their schools, as well as the lack of relevancy of the training sessions provided. Besides, Al-Badi &

Khan (2022) reported that teachers perceived the importance of professional development programs in AI and believe that they are essential to enhance teaching and learning. Al-Badi & Khan (2022) highlighted that teachers see AI as a powerful tool that can enhance the teaching and learning process by providing personalised learning materials and courses specifically designed to individual learners' needs and preferences. This study, therefore, aimed to design, develop, and implement a professional development program for teachers on AI tools. It also aimed to determine the impact of the professional development program on the participant teachers' utilization and attitudes towards the AI tools.

## Literature Review

Examining the literature on the effectiveness of teacher training programs, it becomes evident that several studies have explored the effectiveness of teachers' reflective professional development programs and revealed a positive impact on participants. Agwu (2020) examined the impact of a teachers' professional development program on science lecturers' knowledge and use of modern technologies in teaching in Nigeria. The participants in the study consisted of 457 science lecturers. A stratified random sampling technique was used to obtain the sample of the study, which included 125 science lecturers. Agwu (2020) used a questionnaire with a five-point Likert scale to assess the impact of the professional development program on science lecturers' knowledge and use of modern technologies in teaching. The study's main finding is a significant increase in lecturers' knowledge and understanding of basic skills in utilising new technologies. Moreover, there was a slight increase in lecturers' utilisation of these new technologies after the professional development program.

Similarly, a study by Hotze et al., (2020) utilized a design-based approach to develop a professional development program for preparing language and science teachers to teach language-oriented science education to primary school students in the Netherlands. The study used a mixed methods design to assess the impact of the program on participants' knowledge and teaching practices. The program consisted of eight online modules, an interactive webinar, and two face-to-face meetings. The study involved 16 participants (5 science teachers, 9 language teachers, and 2 researchers) who completed pre- and post-study questionnaires and participated in interviews. In line with Agwu (2020)'s findings, Hotze et al. (2020)'s results revealed that the program improved participants' knowledge of language-oriented science education, their ability to apply language-based science teaching in their own practice, and their ability to teach language-oriented science education to students. The design of the program was evaluated positively by participants, who appreciated its user-friendliness.

Likewise, Ningsih (2023) conducted quantitative research using a descriptive approach to examine the relationship between Indonesian teachers' participation in professional development programs and their teaching behaviour. The study included 101 teachers from various schools who had engaged in professional development programs. The research aimed to explore the extent of teachers' participation in professional development programs and the relationship between professional development programs and their teaching behaviour. The study concluded that professional development programs are essential for teachers' professional development and positively affect their teaching behaviour.

In a similar manner, a study by Retallick and Mithani (2003) aimed to measure the effectiveness of a teachers' training program on two schools in Pakistan. The study utilised an action research methodology, which allowed for a detailed exploration of how the professional development program training sessions affected teachers and managers of schools in their efforts towards school reform. To achieve that, the researchers made four visits to each school after conducting the professional development program to investigate changes in reflective practices, mentoring, and the implementation of new strategies in teaching. In addition, the researchers gained insights, through the interviews, into how the participant teachers redefined their roles as leaders and managers in their schools. The findings of the study highlighted those teachers shifted from an authoritarian leadership style to more collaborative and reflective practices. Another impact of the professional development program was an increase in the implementation of strategies like reflective writing workshops and mentoring programs. Retallick and Mithani (2003) emphasized the significance of continuous professional development programs in enhancing the knowledge and skills of teachers.

Additionally, similar findings were obtained from a study by Mastour and Faqiri (2024), which utilized a mixed-methods approach to assess teachers' attitudes, experiences, and challenges in professional development programs in Afghanistan. The study aimed to investigate teachers' and educators' perspectives on the professional development programs offered to in-service teachers. To achieve that, the study employed qualitative interviews and quantitative questionnaires specifically designed to address the research objectives. The researchers interviewed 12 experienced teachers and employed thematic analysis in addition to distributing 36-item questionnaires to 75 teachers. The findings of the study revealed a positive attitude towards teachers' professional development programs, as teachers showed appreciation for the effectiveness of professional development programs in developing teachers' teaching methods and utilising and updating educational materials. Additionally, the study also revealed obstacles and challenges faced by teachers in professional development programs in Afghanistan. These challenges include the short duration of programs, lack of interactive activities, and resistance from experienced teachers towards integrating new teaching strategies. To address these challenges, the study emphasised the significance of employing interactive strategies, age-appropriate teaching methods, and practical activities to further enhance the effectiveness of professional development programs.

Likewise, a study by Qablan (2021) investigated the impact of a STEM professional development program on science teachers in Jordan. The study utilized quantitative surveys and qualitative interviews to assess the effect of professional development on participant teachers' content knowledge and abilities. The study sample consists of 20 middle school teachers from private schools in Amman, Jordan. The findings of the study revealed that the STEM professional development program had a positive impact on participating science teachers. The quantitative survey showed that a significant number of participants (89%) had enhanced their knowledge and abilities to teach science through the STEM approach. The participating teachers found the professional development program's activities beneficial in developing STEM learning projects, and they also reported that they are becoming more capable of addressing challenges in the classroom. Moreover, participating teachers expressed a high level of satisfaction with the professional development program content, design, and delivery. About (95%) of participants reported that the professional development program was well organized, and (90%) believed that the learning objectives were met. Furthermore, interviews with participant teachers showed that they faced challenges and obstacles that hindered the effective implementation of STEM strategies in the classroom. These challenges include the lack of resources and technologies, difficulties in managing changes in students' expectations and attitudes, and limited time for planning collaboration with other teachers. To sum up, the results of Qablan's (2021) study highlighted the positive outcomes of the professional development program in enhancing participant teachers' readiness to integrate STEM education.

Contrary to previous researchers' findings, a study by Perera et al. (2020) utilized design-based research to design and develop a professional development program for teachers on the use of Interactive Touch Screens in Sri Lanka schools. The study involved quantitative and qualitative approaches, with a sample consisting of 31 teachers from the Colombo district. The findings revealed that teachers lacked instructional strategies to integrate Interactive Touch Screens in instruction, despite being trained on Interactive Touch Screens. The study addressed TPACK (Technological Pedagogical Content Knowledge) requirements for effective integration of technology in instruction. The professional development program (two-day workshop) implemented in the first cycle of the study covered TPK, TCK, TPACK, and Interactive Touch Screens-based instructional strategies related to different subjects. Perera et al. (2020) suggest that there is a need for increased time allocation, more hands-on experience, and separate professional development programs for teachers.

In a similar manner, a study by Cameron et al. (2023) focused on investigating the impact of a professional development program on teachers' attitudes towards educational technology. The study utilised a questionnaire to assess teachers' attitudes before and after the professional development intervention. According to Cameron et al. (2023), this longitudinal approach allows for tracking changes in attitudes over the duration of the intervention. In addition to attitude, the utilised questionnaire assessed other variables like teachers' efficacy and satisfaction with the professional development program. The findings of the study by Cameron et al. (2023) show a decline in teachers' attitudes towards educational technology after completing the professional development program compared to their attitudes before the intervention. Cameron et al. (2023) proposed a few external factors that might have caused this decline, including challenges caused by the COVID-19 pandemic, national curriculum reforms, and teachers' high expectations of the program. Furthermore, Cameron et al. (2023) suggested that teachers' confidence and prior experience in integrating technology are significant factors to consider when designing teachers' professional development programs.

Additionally, numerous studies have concentrated on assessing teachers' professional development programs to identify key success factors. Bragg et al. (2021) conducted a systematic review of 11 experimental and observational studies that evaluate online professional development programs for teachers. The study aimed to identify effective practices and design elements of online professional development programs that improve content knowledge, pedagogical content knowledge, beliefs about teaching, self-efficacy, and instructional practices of teachers. According to Bragg et al. (2021), the review revealed that successful online professional development programs for teachers should focus on learner support, further acquisition or development of pedagogical content knowledge, engagement, flexibility, individual difference, practical learning activities, reflection, relevance, and application of knowledge and skills.

Additionally, a study by Pimenta et al. (2023) investigated the sustainability of professional development programs for in-service mathematics teachers to integrate technology into their teaching practices. The study utilized a mixed-methods research with qualitative and quantitative data from document analysis and a questionnaire answered by 138 of the 240 initial participants. The aim was to understand if the programs are sustainable and if teachers' years of service influence their sustainability. The results suggested that, although teachers reveal high levels of satisfaction with the effectiveness of the programs, many do not propose tasks for students to use technology in learning, which compromises the sustainability of the programs. The teachers' length of service is not critical for the sustainability of the programs. Overall, the study found that programs can have a significant impact on pedagogical practices both in the short and long term, but the sustainability may depend on how the teachers use technology in their classrooms.

The empirical studies reviewed offer valuable information into the effectiveness of teachers' professional development programs, focusing on diverse aspects of pedagogy and technology integration. Synthesising these findings provides an understanding of the factors influencing the design and implementation of professional development programs, which is necessary in shaping the proposed research. Firstly, studies such as Agwu (2020),

Hotze et al. (2020), and Perera et al. (2020) focus on the importance of professional development programs that address specific needs and challenges faced by teachers. These studies highlight the significance of utilising instructional strategies, such as design-based approaches and TPACK frameworks, to enhance teachers' knowledge and skills in utilizing modern technologies effectively.

Moreover, insights from Bragg et al. (2021), Pimenta et al. (2023), and Ningsih (2023) emphasize the importance of ongoing support, learner-centred approaches, and the alignment of professional development programs with teachers' needs. These findings highlight the need for an approach that goes beyond knowledge acquisition to foster sustainable changes in teaching practices and attitudes towards technology integration. Additionally, studies by Retallick and Mithani (2003), Cameron et al. (2023), and Mastour and Faqiri (2024) focused on the complexities of professional development implementation, including challenges related to program duration, engagement, and resistance to change. These insights underscore the importance of considering contextual factors, providing ongoing support and fostering a collaborative learning environment to maximize the effectiveness of professional development programs.

Furthermore, research by Qablan (2021) highlights the positive impact of professional development programs on enhancing teachers' content knowledge and instructional abilities. These findings highlight the potential of targeted programs to address specific areas of professional growth and facilitate the integration of innovative teaching approaches in the classroom.

In light of these findings, the reviewed research informs the design of this study by emphasizing the importance of an approach that addresses teachers' knowledge gaps, instructional needs, and contextual challenges. This study aims to develop a comprehensive professional development program tailored to the specific needs of teachers in Oman. Moreover, the findings of the reviewed studies provide a theoretical framework and practical guidance for addressing the research questions related to the effectiveness and sustainability of professional development programs in enhancing teachers' proficiency with modern technologies in teaching. Overall, understanding these findings inform the rationale, methodology, and potential outcomes of the study, facilitating an understanding of the complexities involved in designing and implementing effective professional development programs for teachers.

## Methodology

### Research Design

The research adopted a descriptive analytical design to capture a comprehensive understanding of the teachers' engagement with AI tools and their attitudinal changes after participating in the PDP. This design is ideal for addressing the dual objectives of utilization and attitude assessment, offering robust insights into both measurable impacts and nuanced participant experiences. The research procedure unfolds in three stages:

### Analysis and Identification of the Research Problem

This stage involved a thorough needs analysis to determine the baseline competencies and challenges faced by teachers regarding AI tools. Teachers' technological proficiency and pedagogical needs were assessed to identify specific gaps.

### Design and Development of the Professional Development Program

This stage entailed the creation of a tailored PDP based on the findings from the needs analysis. The PDP included modules designed to enhance participants' knowledge and practical skills in integrating AI tools like ChatGPT, QuizGPT, Adobe Express, and others into classroom practices. Emphasizing active learning, the program incorporated workshops, collaborative sessions, and hands-on activities, ensuring alignment with both the Technological Pedagogical Content Knowledge (TPACK) framework and the ADDIE instructional design model. Program content addressed practical applications of AI in lesson planning, student assessment, and resource creation.

### Evaluation and Refinement

This stage involved iterative testing and refinement of the PDP based on participant feedback and observed outcomes. Pilot implementations allowed for adjustments to content, delivery methods, and supporting materials to ensure effectiveness and relevance.

The study targeted a purposive sample of 35 Omani teachers from a school in Muscat, representing a diverse range of experience levels. These participants were chosen for their potential to benefit from the program and their willingness to engage in the study. Two primary instruments were used:

### Questionnaire

The questionnaire was designed to measure participants' utilization of AI tools and their attitudes before and after the PDP. The questionnaire included Likert-scale items aligned with theoretical constructs like TPACK and the Technology Acceptance Model (TAM).

### Semi-structured Interviews

Semi-structured interviews were conducted to gather in-depth qualitative insights into teachers' experiences, challenges, and perspectives regarding AI integration.

The validity and reliability of these instruments were ensured through expert review, pilot testing, and iterative refinement. The questionnaire's alignment with theoretical frameworks strengthened its construct validity, while the interview protocol underwent similar scrutiny for consistency and depth.

Moreover, ethical protocols were rigorously followed. Participants provided informed consent, and their anonymity and data confidentiality were guaranteed throughout the study. Ethical approval was obtained to align the research with institutional guidelines. In addition, quantitative data from the questionnaires were analyzed using descriptive and inferential statistical techniques to identify patterns and measure changes in AI utilization and attitudes. Qualitative data from interviews underwent thematic analysis, providing rich narratives that complement the numerical findings. Together, these methods ensured a holistic understanding of the PDP's impact.

Reflective practices were integrated into the professional development program as a key strategy to support teachers in their journey of adopting AI tools. This process was implemented through a variety of structured activities designed to help teachers critically assess and improve their practices. One core activity was maintaining reflective journals, where teachers recorded their daily experiences with AI tools, highlighting what worked well and identifying challenges. Each journal entry was guided by specific prompts to focus their reflections on areas like lesson delivery, student engagement, and learning outcomes.

Regular reflective workshops were another essential component of the program. Held every two weeks, these workshops created a space for teachers to share their experiences, discuss strategies, and learn from one another. Facilitators guided these sessions to ensure discussions remained practical and centered on actionable takeaways. The workshops also included case studies of AI tool usage, which teachers analyzed in light of their own experiences, sparking deeper insights into their practices.

In addition to group sessions, teachers benefited from individual coaching. During one-on-one meetings, the facilitators reviewed their journals and provided personalized feedback to address specific challenges. Another effective method was the use of video recordings, where teachers reviewed footage of their lessons involving AI tools. This activity allowed them to observe and reflect on their teaching behaviors, how students responded, and the overall impact of the tools on the learning process.

Through these methods, reflective practice became a continuous cycle of learning and improvement. Teachers noted that this approach made them more aware of their teaching strategies and helped them adapt to challenges with confidence and creativity. Over time, this reflective process not only deepened their understanding of integrating AI tools but also empowered them to take ownership of their professional growth. By embedding reflection into the program, the intervention encouraged a sustainable and adaptive approach to using AI in classrooms, ensuring its long-term impact on teaching and learning.

## Findings

### The Impact of Reflective Professional Development Intervention on Omani Teachers' Utilization of AI Tools

The results of this study aim to assess the impact of a professional development program on the utilization of AI (AI) tools by Omani teachers. The program was designed to enhance teachers' knowledge and skills in using AI tools effectively within their classrooms, which is vital for improving educational practices and student outcomes in an increasingly technological world. The data collected from the 35 teachers who participated in the program provides valuable insights into the levels of AI tool adoption and the factors influencing their use.

The findings from the questionnaire reveal the diverse ways in which AI tools are utilized in education, with a particular focus on tools like ChatGPT, Adobe Express, and QuizGPT. However, the analysis also highlights significant variations in proficiency levels among the participants. Table 8.1 presents the descriptive statistics for the dimensions assessed by the questionnaire, which included knowledge of AI tools, the importance of AI integration, the challenges of using AI, attitudes towards AI, and proficiency in using various AI tools.

**Table 8.1:** Descriptive Statistics for the Questionnaire Dimensions

| # | Questionnaire Dimension/ Section | N | Mean | Standard Deviation | Level |
|---|---|---|---|---|---|
| 1 | Level of knowledge and skills related to the use of artificial intelligence applications in education | 35 | 3.05 | 0.69 | Moderate |
| 2 | Importance of integrating artificial intelligence applications in education | 35 | 3.84 | 0.82 | High |
| 3 | Challenges of using artificial intelligence applications in education | 35 | 4.05 | 0.69 | High |
| 4 | Application of knowledge and skills in the classroom | 35 | 3.05 | 0.72 | Moderate |
| 5 | Attitudes toward using and adopting artificial intelligence applications in education | 35 | 3.84 | 0.82 | High |
| 6 | Professional development program evaluation and participant experience | 35 | 3.54 | 0.85 | High |
| 7 | Proficiency in utilizing artificial intelligence tools | 35 | 2.53 | 1.10 | Low |

The majority of the teachers reported a moderate level of proficiency in AI tool utilisation, with a mean score of 2.53 for proficiency, indicating that while there was some success in increasing teachers' familiarity with AI tools, their practical implementation remained limited. Teachers showed moderate knowledge and skills (mean = 3.05) in integrating AI tools into their pedagogical practices. This moderate knowledge was consistent across participants, with a relatively low standard deviation of 0.69, suggesting that while teachers had an understanding of AI tools, their practical application varied significantly depending on their exposure and experience.

Despite the moderate proficiency levels, there was a high level of recognition of the importance of AI in education (mean = 3.84). Teachers acknowledged that AI could improve teaching effectiveness, facilitate better communication with students, and increase student engagement. For instance, several teachers reported using AI tools to enhance interaction and engagement in lessons, save time, and provide immediate feedback on assignments. This positive attitude towards AI in education reflects the potential of these tools to transform teaching practices, although the challenge remains to enhance teachers' technical proficiency to more fully integrate AI tools.

However, the study also identified several barriers hindering the effective utilization of AI tools. The most significant challenge was time constraints, with 58.33% of teachers citing this as a major obstacle to integrating AI tools in their classrooms. Other challenges included technological difficulties such as inadequate infrastructure, especially the lack of reliable internet connections and insufficient hardware (41.66%), as well as a lack of sufficient training and professional development (41.66%). These barriers highlight the need for continuous support and the development of training programs that not only introduce AI tools but also provide ongoing guidance on overcoming these obstacles.

To further understand the impact of the professional development program, the content analysis of the interview data reveals that ChatGPT was the most commonly utilized tool, followed by Adobe Express and Canva. Teachers reported that ChatGPT significantly enhanced their lessons, especially in language teaching, by providing dynamic and interactive learning experiences. However, some teachers reported lower proficiency levels with other tools such as Narakeet and QuizGPT, which had mean scores of 2.23 and 2.46, respectively, suggesting that more focused training on these specific tools might be necessary.

Furthermore, the study's findings point to a strong positive correlation between the teachers' perceptions of AI's role in education and their willingness to adopt these technologies in their teaching. The majority of teachers (mean = 4.03) expressed a willingness to share their experiences with colleagues, indicating a supportive community-building aspect to AI tool integration. This peer support can play a critical role in overcoming the barriers to AI adoption, as teachers are likely to be influenced by the experiences and success stories of their peers.

In conclusion, while the professional development program positively influenced Omani teachers' utilisation of AI tools, there are clear areas for improvement. The program successfully enhanced teachers' attitudes towards AI tools, but there is still a need for further training to improve proficiency levels. Future professional development programs should focus on providing more hands-on experience, addressing the identified barriers such as time constraints and technological challenges, and offering ongoing support to ensure sustained AI tool integration in the classroom. These changes could significantly boost the impact of AI tools in Omani educational settings.

## The Impact of Reflective Professional Development Intervention on Omani Teachers' Attitudes Towards the Utilization of AI Tools

The professional development program had a notable impact on Omani teachers' attitudes toward the utilization of AI (AI) tools, demonstrating that the intervention effectively shaped teachers' beliefs and perceptions regarding AI in educational settings. The mean score for teachers' attitudes towards AI integration was 3.84, indicating generally positive perceptions of AI tools in education. This is further supported by the standard deviation of 0.82, which reflects a moderate variation in individual attitudes across participants. The teachers recognized the potential of AI tools to enhance their teaching practices, particularly in areas such as tracking student performance, improving communication with students, and boosting lesson effectiveness. The data show that teachers believe AI can significantly contribute to the educational process, especially in increasing students' motivation (mean = 3.94) and enhancing the effectiveness of teaching methods (mean = 3.83), with the highest scores for these items reflecting the strong belief in the benefits AI brings to the classroom environment.

The results from the questionnaire also highlighted that the teachers enjoyed using AI tools in their teaching (mean = 3.66), which is a strong indicator of the positive attitude fostered by the professional development program. Despite these positive attitudes, variability in individual responses was observed, as evidenced by the range of standard deviations for each statement (e.g., 0.86 for communication and 1.01 for effectiveness). This variation points to differences in how teachers apply AI tools based on their personal experiences and previous exposure to technology. Nonetheless, it is clear that the program contributed to improving teachers' willingness to adopt AI tools, as evidenced by the high mean score of 4.03 for teachers' recommendations to colleagues about using AI tools, suggesting that they were not only confident in the tools' efficacy but were also motivated to share their positive experiences.

In addition, the teachers widely agreed that AI technologies would enhance classroom performance, with statements such as "I believe that the use of AI technologies will contribute to tracking students' performance" (mean = 3.80) and "I recommend my fellow teachers to experience AI technologies in education" (mean = 4.03). These results demonstrate that the professional development program had a lasting impact on teachers' perceptions of AI tools, as from then on, they viewed them as essential to their pedagogical practices.

Moreover, the content analysis of interview data reflected similar positive views. Many teachers expressed enthusiasm about the potential of AI tools to improve both their teaching efficiency and their students' learning experiences. However, despite the positive reception, challenges persist, particularly with regard to the varying proficiency levels in using these tools. As noted earlier in the chapter, while some teachers were confident in integrating AI into their practices, others still felt uncertain or lacked the necessary technical skills to fully leverage these technologies. The feedback from teachers underscored the importance of continued professional development to further solidify these positive attitudes and help them overcome technical barriers.

An essential aspect of the program was fostering a supportive community for teachers, as indicated by the willingness of participants to share their experiences with colleagues. This peer support system emerged as a key factor in overcoming resistance to AI adoption. The collaborative environment created by the program helped reduce the initial apprehension about AI, encouraging teachers to explore and experiment with these tools in their classrooms.

In conclusion, the professional development program successfully shaped Omani teachers' attitudes toward the utilization of AI tools, enhancing their perceptions of AI's value in education. Teachers generally viewed AI as a useful tool for improving both teaching efficiency and student engagement, with an overwhelming majority willing to recommend AI tools to their colleagues. However, the study also highlighted that there are areas for further improvement, particularly in terms of increasing teachers' proficiency and confidence in using these tools. Future professional development programs should build on these positive attitudes by offering more targeted, hands-on training and ongoing support to address the specific challenges teachers face in integrating AI tools into their classrooms.

## Discussion

The results of the study demonstrate both similarities and differences when compared to previous empirical studies in the literature. Studies by Agwu (2020) and Retallick & Mithani (2003), for instance, reveal a significant improvement in teachers' knowledge of new technologies, a result that aligns closely with this study's observations of Omani teachers' enhanced utilization following the professional development program. Similarly, the results reported by Hotze et al. (2020) regarding the positive impact on participants' knowledge and teaching practices are similar to the improvements in Omani teachers' utilisation of AI tools investigated in this study. However, unlike the study by Cameron et al. (2023), which reported a decrease in teachers' attitudes toward educational technology after a professional development program, Omani teachers showed positive attitudes toward utilizing AI tools in education. This contrast may be attributed to contextual and environmental factors, such as the specific focus on AI and the tailored approach of the professional development program in the Omani context.

Additionally, Perera et al. (2020) highlight challenges in effectively integrating technology into teaching, focusing on the importance of addressing instructional strategies and providing specific experience and aspects that this study's professional development program on AI tools seeks to address. Additionally, Bragg et al. (2021) stress the importance of learner support and practical activities, principles that correspond with the design elements of this study's professional development program on AI tools. Pimenta et al. (2023) emphasize the need for sustained support in technology integration, a concern that this study's professional development program aimed to address through ongoing assistance for classroom implementation. Ningsih's (2023) findings regarding the positive relationship between professional development and teaching behaviour are consistent with this study's observations. Mastour and Faqiri (2024) identify challenges faced by teachers in professional development programs, emphasizing the importance of interactive strategies and practical activities, which this study's professional development program on AI tools sought to integrate to minimize these obstacles. Lastly, Qablan's (2021) study underscores positive outcomes in content knowledge and abilities, which align closely with this study's findings.

Moreover, the findings suggest that while this professional development intervention in Oman has positively influenced teachers' attitudes and utilization levels of AI tools, there are still areas for improvement, particularly in enhancing teachers' practical skills and proficiency levels across all tools. Therefore, future iterations of the professional development program could consider incorporating more in-depth training sessions, providing ongoing support, and addressing contextual barriers to ensure sustained effectiveness and impact.

What is more, the findings of this study revealed an improvement in teachers' proficiency and comfort levels with modern technologies. This enhancement suggests a deeper acceptance and integration of technology within their instructional practices, aligning closely with the foundational principles of the Technology Acceptance Model (TAM). Furthermore, the professional development program emphasized the importance of integrating technology with pedagogical strategies, resulting in significant advancements in teachers' Technological Pedagogical Content Knowledge (TPACK). Moreover, the findings revealed alignment with various ISTE Standards, particularly those focusing on technology integration and pedagogical competence. The observed increase in teachers' positive attitude and proficiency in leveraging technology for instructional purposes signifies progress toward meeting the criteria set by the International Society for Technology in Education (ISTE) Standards, ensuring that teachers are adequately equipped to employ technology for enhancing student learning experiences.

## Conclusion

In conclusion, Omani teachers currently exhibit a moderate level of knowledge and skills related to the utilization of AI tools in education. What is more, teachers show an understanding of the basic concepts and terminology of AI, yet they also showed variations in their confidence levels and practical experience with AI tools and applications. Some teachers have a moderate level of proficiency, yet other teachers struggle with technical problems, lack of training, and limited experience in integrating AI tools into their teaching.

Omani teachers recognize the importance of integrating AI tools in education and the potential of these tools in enhancing teaching effectiveness, student engagement, and communication between teachers and students. This recognition reveals a positive attitude toward the adoption and utilization of AI tools and technologies in educational settings. Omani teachers show willingness to share their experience of utilization of AI tools with their colleagues. This indicates a supportive and collaborative professional development environment that encourages innovation and sharing of knowledge. The teachers expressed beliefs in these tools' abilities to enhance teaching and outcomes of learning, as well as improving students' engagement and tracking their performance, in addition to encouraging collaboration between students. Although Omani teachers acknowledge the importance of more fully integrating AI tools in education, they face many challenges in effectively utilizing these tools in their pedagogical practices. These challenges include time constraints, lack of training, technological barriers, and uncertainties regarding the benefits of AI integration.

The teachers positively evaluated the professional development program, which indicated satisfaction with the delivery method and the overall experience. Moreover, some teachers appreciated the face-to-face approach while other participants expressed a preference for future professional development program sessions to be conducted online and asynchronously. This preference indicates a need for flexibility in professional development delivery methods to suit teachers' different learning preferences and busy schedules. Even though the teachers evaluated the professional development program positively and reported satisfaction with its content, many of the teachers still displayed moderate confidence levels in their ability to utilise AI tools into the classroom. This indicates that even though the professional development program was successful in providing the fundamental knowledge, there is still room for improvement in building teachers' confidence in practical utilization by adding extra practical sessions and different instructional strategies.

Ultimately, this study has provided valuable insights into the process of designing and developing a professional development program that focuses on AI tools in education, as well as insights on the level of utilization and attitudes toward AI tools among Omani teachers. While the findings highlight obstacles and areas for improvement in utilizing AI tools, they also address the potential of AI tools to improve pedagogical and learning achievements. It is necessary to address the identified challenges and implementing the recommendations by teachers and policymakers to take advantage of AI's full potential to transform education in Oman.

## References

Abbass, H. (2021). What is artificial intelligence?. *IEEE Transactions on Artificial Intelligence, 2*(2), 94–95.

Agwu, U. D. (2020). Impact Of Teacher Professional Development Programmes On Science Lecturers' Knowledge And Use Of Modern Technologies In Teaching in Tertiary Institutions. *Journal of the Nigerian Academy of Education, 16*(1), 111–128.

Aktay, S. (2022). The usability of images generated by artificial intelligence (AI) in education. *International Technology and Education Journal, 6*(2), 51–62.

Al-Badi, A., & Khan, A. (2022). Perceptions of learners and instructors towards artificial intelligence in personalized learning. *Procedia Computer Science, 201*, 445–451.

Al-Belushi, H. (2013). English Teachers Perceptions of the Usefulness of Professional Development Activities in Some Omani Schools. *INTED2013 Proceedings* (pp. 2561–2569). IATED.

Al-Harthi, A. S., Hammad, W., Al-Seyabi, F., Al-Najjar, N., Al-Balushi, S., & Emam, M. (2022). Evaluating the effectiveness of teacher education in Oman: a multiple case study of multiple stakeholders. *Quality Assurance in Education, 30*(4), 477–494.

Ali, A. (2023). *Assessing Artificial Intelligence Readiness of Faculty in Higher Education: Comparative Case Study of Egypt* [Doctoral dissertation, The American University in Cairo].

Al-Jabri, M. J. H., Silvennoinen, H., & Griffiths, D. (2018). Teachers' Professional Development in Oman: Challenges, Efforts and Solutions. *International Journal of Learning, Teaching and Educational Research, 17*(5), 82–103.

Al-Senaidi, S., Lin, L., & Poirot, J. (2009). Barriers to adopting technology for teaching and learning in Oman. *Computers & Education, 53*(3), 575–590.

Bragg, L. A., Walsh, C., & Heyeres, M. (2021). Successful design and delivery of online professional development for teachers: A systematic review of the literature. *Computers & Education, 166*, 104–158.

Cameron, D. L., Matre, M. E., & Canrinus, E. T. (2023). Influences of a Professional Development Program on Teachers' Attitudes Towards Educational Technology and Digital Learning Resources for Inclusion. In P. Escudeiro, N. Escudeiro, & O. Bernardes (Eds.), *Handbook of Research on Implementing Inclusive Educational Models and Technologies for Equity and Diversity* (pp. 218–235). IGI Global Scientific Publishing. https://doi.org/10.4018/979-8-3693-0453-2.ch011

Dimitriadou, E., & Lanitis, A. (2023). A critical evaluation, challenges, and future perspectives of using artificial intelligence and emerging technologies in smart classrooms. *Smart Learning Environments, 10*(1), 1–26.

Hotze, A., Gijsel, M., Vervoort, M., Peters, S., & Post, A. (2020). Preparing teacher educators for language-oriented science education: Design and impact of a professional development program. *EDULEARN20 Proceedings*, pp. 636–643. IATED.

Mastour, Q., & Faqiri, F. (2024). Teachers' perceptions, experiences, and challenges in professional development programs in Afghanistan. *Science and Education, 5*(2), 229–236.

Ningsih, S. K. (2023). The Effect of EFL Teachers' Participation in Professional Development Program on The Change of Their Teaching Behaviour. *JETAL: Journal of English Teaching & Applied Linguistics, 5*(1), 38–45.

Oghly, J. S. Z. (2023). A Japanese approach to in-service training and professional development of science and physics teachers in Japan. *American Journal of Public Diplomacy and International Studies, 1*(9), 167–173.

Perera, K. G. S. K., Wijesundara, M., & Siriwardhena, I. (2020). Design of a Framework for Professional Development Programs for Teachers in the Use of Interactive Touch Screen. *SLIIT Journal of Humanities and Sciences, 1*(1), 49–61.

Pimenta, P., Domingos, A., & Costa, M. C. (2023). Sustainability of professional development programmes to teach mathematics using technology. In P. Drijvers, C. Csapodi, H. Palmér, K. Gosztonyi & E. Kónya (Eds.), *Proceedings of the Thirteenth Congress of the European Society for Research in Mathematics Education* (pp. 2760–2767). Alfréd Rényi Institute of Mathematics.

Qablan, A. (2021). Assessing Teachers Education and Professional Development needs to Implement STEM after Participating in an Intensive Summer Professional Development Program: Teacher professional development and STEM. *Journal of STEM Education: Innovations and Research, 22*(2).

Ranjbaran, F., Al-Abri, A., & Al-Hashmi, S. (2023). Exploring ELT teachers' behavioral intention to continue using technology in the post-COVID-19 era: A case study of Oman. In *Handbook of CALL Teacher Education and Professional Development: Voices from Under-Represented Contexts* (pp. 387–405). Springer Nature. https://doi.org/10.1007/978-981-99-0514-0_23

Retallick, J., & Mithani, S. (2003). The impact of a professional development program: A study from Pakistan. *Journal of In-service Education, 29*(3), 405–422.

Taneri, G. U. (2020). Artificial Intelligence & Higher Education: Towards Customized Teaching and Learning, and Skills for an AI World of Work. *Research & Occasional Paper Series: CSHE, 6*, 1–12.

Zmyzgova, T. R., Polyakova, E. N., & Karpov, E. K. (2020, May). Digital transformation of education and artificial intelligence. *Proceedings of the 2nd International Scientific and Practical Conference "Modern Management Trends and the Digital Economy: from Regional Development to Global Economic Growth" (MTDE 2020)* (pp. 824–829). Atlantis Press.

PART IV

# Reflective Practice for Student Support

# Integrating Technology in English Language Teaching: Challenges and Opportunities

*Ahmed Al Rahbi, Iman Al-Khalidi, Salwa Al Anqoodi and Iman Al Hajri*

**ABSTRACT**
Technology plays an increasingly important role in higher education institutions, offering opportunities to enhance student academic support. This chapter reports the results of a study into how technology can enhance student academic support in English Language Teaching in higher education institutions in Oman, specifically at the University of Nizwa. The objectives are to identify the current technological tools used for student academic support in UoN; to explore the challenges and benefits of UoN encounter in implementing technology-based support systems; and to propose recommendations for maximising the potential of technology-based support systems for English Language Teaching. The challenges and opportunities of integrating such technologies into English Language Teaching are investigated. The study also provides recommendations on expanding the utilisation of various technological tools in enhancing learner's learning progress. The research involves a mixed-method approach, including a critical literature review, surveys, and mini-structured interviews with stakeholders such as students, academic staff, and administrators. The findings of this research deliver insights for HEIs in Oman and similar contexts which aim to optimise English Language Teaching through technology, enhancing student success and learning outcomes.

## Introduction

Technology is playing an increasingly important role in higher education institutions, offering opportunities to enhance student academic support (Al-Ammary, 2012; Al-Khalidi, 2021a). In the field of education, educators, instructors, and administrators worldwide have identified the use of technology as a common, easily available, and easy-to-use teaching aid. In the field of English language teaching, technology provides several benefits related to methodology, assessment, materials, and all aspects of the curriculum (Al-Khalidi, et al., 2022; Al-Khalidi, et al., 2023). The role of technology is further underscored by the diversity of its usability, which makes it easy to integrate into lesson-planning activities. Therefore, the roles and the benefits of technology have been varied, and the application areas have been diverse (Ashour, 2019).

Teaching English as a second language in Oman has been aided by the use of technology platforms based on many empirical research studies. For example, instructors at the University of Nizwa (UoN), where the current study takes place, have applied interactive learning platforms that allow them to give assessments and have them automatically graded. The learner appreciates immediate feedback that further improves their success in learner-paced learning. Additionally, English teachers in Oman have used chat platforms like WhatsApp to enhance their communication with the learners further. Developing quality lessons is largely founded and supported by technology tools and platforms. It is, therefore, vital that the development of effective teaching and learning of the English language is supported through communications tools, video tools, and websites that allow diverse learning methodologies, and varied learning assessments.

Despite the immense benefit of using technology in the classroom to conduct and manage engaging classes, technology still has some of its flaws that create several challenges in its use. Thus, many teachers making use of technology as an integrated part of the lessons must be aware of the possibilities of distractions that can be common among learners using technology. Additionally, teachers need to be overly aware and skilled in the ways to operate technology devices. It is, therefore, important that early preparations and deliberate measures are put in place to ensure that technology use in the classrooms is safe and aids learning. On the same note, teachers must realize that technology itself is not a learning platform, but rather, it must be viewed as a learning aid. Thus, using technology as a leading learning tool challenges the value and quality of the lesson delivery. Teachers must always ensure that they remain vigilant and only use technology platforms as models to aid learning, not to control the class learning process.

In addition to the challenges above, technology remains a major tool for creating a social divide. It is always expensive to make effective use of technology in the learning platform because technology is normally expensive, and not everyone can afford it (Fishman et al., 2016). As a result, the insistence on the use of technology may be applied to the disadvantage of other learners who cannot get access to evaluable internet or the right devices to pursue learning needs. This means that the challenges associated with the use of technology in teaching and learning the English language are always personalized. Nonetheless, instructors must be well informed about the technology access needs of every learner. Moreover, technology platforms require technical support and skills. Learners and instructors without the skills may not effectively run and attend classes through the platform.

This makes it even more challenging to seamlessly conduct classes. The need for additional skills, support, or manpower frustrates the effective implementation of teaching and learning through technology.

Research on educational technology has recently presented a plethora of studies that have been conducted to investigate the role of technology in English language teaching. However, in the context where the study takes place, there is a lack of studies that have been carried out to investigate the technological tools and platforms that are mostly effective for teaching the Foundation Program (FP) at UoN, their benefits, and challenges. Therefore, this study seeks to address this gap by reviewing the literature and utilizing a survey questionnaire to collect data. It is the seriousness of this issue where challenges in integrating technology in teaching and learning of English need to be addressed. That has motivated the researchers in the context of UoN to conduct the current study to investigate the technology platforms and apps that are integrated into English language teaching.

This study specifically aims to identify the current technological tools that are used for student academic support in the FP at UoN; explore the benefits of technology tools and platforms used in teaching English at the FP in UoN; investigate the challenges that the teachers at UoN face when implementing technology-based support systems; and propose certain recommendations for maximizing the potential of technology-based support systems for student learning.

Based on the objectives above, the study is shaped and guided by the following questions:

- What are the current technological tools used for student academic support in the FP at UoN?
- What are the benefits of implementing technology-based support systems in the FP at UoN?
- What are the challenges that teachers encounter in the FP at UoN when implementing technology tools and platforms in teaching English?
- How can technology-based support systems be used for students learning EFL?

The significance of this study lies in the findings that are anticipated to deliver insights for the Foundation Program at the University of Nizwa in Oman and similar contexts which aim to optimize student academic support through technology and enhance their learning outcomes.

## Literature Review

### Introduction

Various research studies have been conducted to investigate the role of technology in the classroom. To the teachers of English as a second language, the use of technology and the relevance it carries in the classroom cannot be overemphasized. The benefits that technology platforms vary according to learners, teachers, and overall learning needs. Moreover, the skill set of learners and teachers using particular technology tools can also enhance or create frustration in the learning processes and outcomes. In the current study, it would be vital to explore the role and benefits, as well as the challenges of using technology in teaching English. This section explores research developed in the area, with a focus on examining the benefits of the use of the applications of technology in the classrooms as well as the challenges.

### Theories of Technology Adoption in Education

There are theories that determine the framework for the adoption of technologies in the education systems and platforms. The theories explain why educational decisions in the inclusion of technology should be applied at any given time. Some of the theories that are particularly relevant to explain the adoption of technology include the Technology Acceptance Model, the Unified Theory of Acceptance and Use of Technology and the Activity Theory. According to Yeou, (2016), the Technology Acceptance Model explores the perceived usefulness of the presented technology platform in the education sector and the perceived ease of use. According to this theory, people will embrace technologies that they consider vital in solving their problems under the concept of perceived usefulness. Moreover, people will be more interested in using technologies that they consider easy to use. This explains why portals and other technology solutions are easy to navigate.

Another theory that defines the acceptance of technology in the education systems is the Unified Theory of Acceptance and Use of Technology (Sarfaraz, 2017). According to the theory, technology is adopted in education not only based on its perceived usefulness and ease of use but also based on the performance expectancy of the adopted technology, the effort expectancy and the social influence. Technology is also adopted in the education systems based on the facilitating conditions that remain vitally important on a case-by-case basis. This theory is useful for the current study because it highlights the extended need for technological solutions and reasons for adoption. When applied effectively, the use of technology would be vital in drawing the maximum benefits possible from the teaching perspective, and in examining the values it can add to the educational platforms. Lastly, Activity Theory also examines how technology would be useful in mediating human activities in education systems. It explores the social context of education including examining the rules, objects, and communal attitude in making use of technology solutions.

## Opportunities in Technology Integration in ELT

There are many attempts to integrate technology into language teaching and the success of this integration should consider two important factors: namely interactivity and engagement. Language needs to be used and practiced through attractive and stimulating educational tools such as language learning apps, online games, and video platforms allow students to actively participate in their learning. Spence (2022) states that such tools can achieve diversity of classroom activities, promote student-centred learning and allow interactive language practice. According to Wu & Lee (2022) mobile apps allow learners to engage with language outside the classroom and support both formal and informal learning contexts.

Al-Habsi, Al-Busaidi, and Al-Issa (2021) emphasise how technology can help teachers in Oman to meet various learning needs and support a model of differentiated instruction. One of the language teaching principles is to consider the typical classroom context that comes with different students' learning styles, their different knowledge levels and their different needs. Therefore, technology can assist to achieve these goals through customizing target instructions. Through teaching apps, technology can offer adaptive tasks and activities that facilitate students' learning and allow the teachers to fill the gaps in students' knowledge. This attempt to personalize learning is particularly crucial in ELT because students often display a wide range of proficiency levels in one setting. Furthermore, it also allows high performing students to enhance their learning and take it to even higher levels without disrupting the general learning pace of other students.

Connecting students to real-world contexts can be facilitated through the use of technology, which offers access to authentic language resources that are considered essential in developing students' language skills. Dudeney and Hockly (2012) argue that this flexibility has revolutionized how language skills are taught, providing students with exposure to diverse dialects, accents, and cultural contexts. Additionally, technology contributes to the development of multi-media as a key strategy to support textbooks with available and regularly updated content, such as videos or news that discuss real-life issues, making language learning more dynamic (Mayer, 2014; Al-Khalidi, 2021b). It also facilitates the practical use of language, connecting it to everyday matters.

## Benefits of Integrating Technology in Classrooms

Technology has brought about various benefits to educational systems. According to Guangul (2020), technology can bridge the gaps in education and ensures sustained practices. According to Ammade et al. (2018) integrated technology in the classroom is important in fostering effective communication between the learner and the teacher. The communication model is important for developing a proper understanding of learning needs, hence creating a complete educational system that fosters knowledge acquisition for learners. Additionally, educators can make use of social media platforms like WhatsApp to ensure that learning takes place (Ammade et al., 2018; Al-Khalidi and Khouni 2021c). As an example, in Indonesia, platforms like WhatsApp are used by educators to share learning materials, and learners in turn can share their completed homework materials. This has contributed to more engaging classes and course delivery processes. Similar sentiments are shared by Gunuç and Babacan (2017), who, in their research report, attest that technology can be used to promote the targeted use of English materials in classrooms, such as for reading and writing, similar to a case reported by Al-Habsi, Al-Busaidi, and Al-Issa, (2021) in Oman. In these research models, teachers could use technology to improve comprehension, pronunciation, and even spelling. Applications were also noted in technology assisted-reading and writing practices, with all these varied uses collectively contributing to improved knowledge acquisition in the subject.

Teachers and English language instructors in Pakistan have used technology to transform the attitudes of learners (Abbasi, Ibrahim, & Ali, 2022). By incorporating technology, they have made learning activities engaging and enjoyable. In some cases, quizzes and platforms such as Kahoot have facilitated collaborative and fun-based learning. Furthermore, learners have realized that continued learning through technology makes the process of learning more engaging and relevant.

In Oman, students have been using learning platforms like Moodle, which have proven to be vital tools for organizing educational content into structure classrooms and courses (Jose & Zainol Abidin, 2015). Access to Moodle is provided through university approval and authentication system. As a result, these technological tools not only enhance learning experiences but also allow administrators to organize content and manage access effectively (Rintaningrum, 2023). Additionally, they can improve the management of learning materials such as homework, assignments, and assessments, which can be tracked through using the platform's calendar feature. Moodle structures learning content to reflect a classroom setup, including subject courses, modules, topics, and necessary notes, with different teachers assigned to conduct lessons.

## Challenges of Integrating Technology in Classrooms

Despite the effective uses of technology in the area of English language teaching, it also has presented some glaring flaws and challenges. According to Ramorola (2013), the primary challenge instructors face in implementing technology in the classroom lies in integrating it effectively into lesson plans. Ideally, technology should serve as a tool to support learning as an instructional material. However, owing to its ease of use and efficiency, many teachers often rely on technology platforms as the primary learning materials. Teachers often end up relinquishing control entirely to technology (Christopoulos & Sprangers, 2021). When technology takes the lead in learning rather than serving as a learning aid, it undermines the value of quality instructional methods. This challenges the value of effective application of technology in the learning process and learning needs. Furthermore, Wu and Lee (2022) refer to the lack of devices, such as mobile-assisted language tools, and other socio-economic factors that negatively impacts learning experiences. As a result, a national strategy or policy should be established to invest in and support the integration of technology in education at all levels, maximizing its benefits and improving outcomes within educational systems.

Teachers have also been experiencing different kinds of barriers, ranging from low skills to apathy when handling lessons integrated with technology. It is reported that in some cases, teachers have been inconsistent when posting information on Moodle. As such, learners feel at a loss when they check the Moodle platform and find that homework has not been posted or the previous grades have not been assessed by the teacher (Khodabandelou, et al., 2016). Inconsistencies in the use of the technology platforms discourage learners from actively participating in the learning process. Training and upskilling of teachers to effectively use learning platforms is important (Khodabandelou, et al., 2016). At the same time, teachers and educators who have not used technology platforms and systems before must be encouraged to embrace the same towards improving the overall performance of technology tools in the classroom setup. In some cases, collective training of teachers through workshops would go a long way in ensuring that teachers are adequately equipped to make good use of technology when handling their technology-aided classrooms.

According to Nkengbeza, Mbuzi, and Chainda (2022), many teachers experience challenges related to integrating technology into schools. These challenges include limited access to technology platforms, teachers' persistent resistance to change, and time constraints that hinder the exploration of technology solutions. Additionally, the study's a correlational and cross-sectional analysis reveals a lack of training and technical support as additional barriers to technology implementation, further complicating teachers' efforts to use technology and media effectively in their classrooms (Nkengbeza, Mbuzi, and Chainda, 2022). Though there have been many challenges that have been realized in the implementation of technology in schools, Ramanair (2016) indicates that it is not all gloom and doom. Teachers, instructors, school administrators, and all the stakeholders can take advantage of the challenges and transform them into opportunities. The idea is that there is a need to investigate technology integration in tertiary-level English language programs through the lens of Activity Theory and come up with solutions that can entrench effective applications and adoption into schools.

Another challenge that faces educational programs in the current technological era is qualifying teachers who can be proficient in using digital tools. Therefore, teacher training programs should be one of the pillars of teacher education. Teachers need to be educated and ready to use constantly developing applications to support their teaching methodologies. Doe and Smith (2022) assert that teachers' confidence and skills in using technology directly impact their willingness to adopt it in the classroom. In this respect, Al-Habsi et al. (2021) emphasize the importance of building communities of practice, where teachers collaborate, share experiences, and support each other in integrating new tools. Professional local and international gatherings can be an impactful way in updating the educational field of the available e-tools that can be used, particularly in teaching English. The lack of these digital resources, on the other hand, can impact the learning process and further slowdown the integration of technology in teaching English.

Over-reliance on digital tools constitutes another challenge of technology. To address this issue, teachers are always advised to devise a 'Plan B' when they prepare their digital lessons in order to deal with the unexpected and unforeseen situations caused by technological and non-technological factors. Spence (2022) suggests a balanced approach of learning using "blended learning" and combine traditional methods with digital tools to create an inclusive learning environment. Pentucci et al (2023) support designing Learning Ecosystems that have two levels: micro and macro (Gutierrez, 2008, cited in Pentucci et al, 2003). The former describes micro level as "adaptive, transformative, dynamic, supporting and directing practices." (Pentucci et al, 2003, p.4). Whereas they define macro level as "the ecosystem is the networks of interactions between training agents either formal, informal and no formal one is participating in an intentional and designed way to the training path." (Pentucci et al, 2003, p.4). Teachers might encounter a challenge of striking this balance of learning methods to maximize learning outcomes without overwhelming students with digital content.

Data privacy and security is a global concern with people using technology and it is further complicated in the educational field because of the limited experience of users whether teachers or students. Students' personal information and learning data are often collected by educational apps and platforms, which could lead to data breaches or misuse. Wu and Lee (2022) caution that student data needs to be secured and protected when they use these educational apps and platforms through privacy policies to ensure a risk-free learning environment.

It is also possible to identify a few challenges with the learning needs especially for the learners taking English as a second language. Learners with low skills in technology and with low skills in English will find double problems when attempting to learn the English language through technology platforms (Abbasi, Ibrahim, & Ali, 2022). These challenges may hinder their commitment and ability to understand the learning tools and learning needs. In such cases, technology can lead to demoralized learners. There have been more challenges reported by researchers investigating the possible effectiveness of integrated technology in classrooms. Some learners have expressed a general preference for traditional learning methods and tools (Salehi & Salehi, 2012). For instance, they still prefer to attend in-class lessons where teachers guide the learning process in person and notes are taken. Assessments that are done in real-life cases tend to hold more value than those done through virtual online media. To such learners, it is important, therefore, to explore the learning materials through the traditional classroom setup. Some learners have also expressed frustrations with technology systems that they indicate are harder to navigate. It is important, therefore, to realize that effective development of technology tools would be an ideal way to enhance learning processes. Moreover, it is important to explore technology learning models that would be simpler to navigate with simple interfaces (Poudel, 2022).

## Strategies for Effective Technology Integration

Based on the above discussed challenges that might occur when using technology in education, here are some proposed ways to overcome these challenges to maximize the benefits of using technology in classroom teaching.

Through teacher training programs, teachers will be equipped with the skills that help them to use the technology effectively in their teaching. Training should focus on two important areas namely technical skills and pedagogical strategies. Doe and Smith (2022) suggest that teachers who have effective training in those areas are more capable of using digital tools to enhance learning in their classrooms. Since technology is evolving and continuously changing, training programs need to be flexible and adaptive in nature to allow teachers to continuously update their skills.

Collaborative learning is not only associated with students learning context but can also be used in teachers' communities. Teachers need to be encouraged to build a culture of collaborative networks and sharing practices to learn from each other about challenges and how they overcome these challenges. It should be part of their professional growth. In fact, many Higher Education Institutions (HEIs) in Oman promoted this approach and host professional conferences or seminars for this purpose. Al-Habsi et al. (2021) demonstrate the success of this approach in Oman to overcome challenges associated with technology. This approach not only builds teachers' confidence in using technology but also encourages reflective practice and shared knowledge.

Blended learning approaches are new to the educational systems around the world but took precedent during and after the pandemic. Many national and international systems adopted this learning approach where balanced synchronous and asynchronous learning took place to maximize the benefits of technology while minimizing its drawbacks. Spence (2022) supports adopting a blended learning model. Teachers can integrate technology and select what can help to achieve specific learning outcomes. For instance, digital tools can be used in synchronous face-to-face learning tasks, allowing students to experience both interactive and direct instruction.

## Research Design

This study aims to identify the technological tools that are currently used for student academic support in the FP at UoN and to explore their challenges and benefits. Based on these objectives, this study uses a questionnaire survey shaped and guided by the quantitative and qualitative approach to collect data from a group of teachers at the foundation program in the UoN. The researchers chose a survey questionnaire, which is a technique whose primary goal is to describe a population's "attitudes, opinions, behaviors, experiences, or other characteristics" (Creswell, 2016, p.112).

### Methods of Data Collection

The method of data collection used in this study is a questionnaire survey. The survey consists of four sections that are designed in line with the four research questions and objectives. Each section consists of a set of items or questions to generate the data qualitatively and quantitatively. Participants are required to mark options that match their classroom practices from the video conferencing tools, social media platforms, frequency of using these tools and their perceived learning effectiveness. To collect qualitative data, the survey includes a set of open-ended questions to allow participants to share their expertise and opinions towards the investigated subject. Google Form was used as a digital software for designing the survey and storing and analyzing the data statistically.

### Sample

The sample of this study consists of over 100 teachers who teach English in the Foundation Program at UoN. The foundation program is a one-year pre-degree program that includes courses for students who did not meet the entry requirements in English, Mathematics, Digital Literacy and Study Skills. The teachers have been involved in this study due to their experience in technology integration as part of the EFL curriculum employed in this context. The investigation of technology platforms, their benefits and challenges, and the provision of recommendations from the perspectives of this sample can reveal significant insights into the investigated topic (Creswell, 2007; Dorney, 2011; Punch, 2009).

### Data Analysis

The quantitative data relating to first and second research questions were generated quantitatively using Google Forms as a Web-based management tool. Google spreadsheet analyzed the data automatically and displayed the results in a format with several charts as graphical representation. Regarding the quantitative data, a set of open-ended questions were set up in the third and fourth sections according to research questions three and four, respectively. Following the models of Miles and Huberman (1994) and Miles et al. (2013), the data that were generated from open-ended questions went through the qualitative analysis process including data reduction, data display, and conclusion drawing/verification. This process includes focussing on answers that address the questions, decide on the coding scheme and categories that will be presented in tables and graphs, and finally summarize the conclusions from the available data analysis.

## Findings

The findings obtained from the data are presented in two parts based on the research questions. The first part presents the findings obtained from the quantitative data while the second part presents the findings obtained from the qualitative data. For the purpose of clarification and illustration, diagrams and charts with items and percentages are attached along with the discussion.

## Quantitative Findings

This section outlines the findings that provide answers to the research questions 1 and 2 that assisted in exploring the tools used in teaching English in the foundation program and the benefits of the tools. Thus, this section is organized into two parts in terms of research questions one and two.

## Technological Tools Used for Student Academic Support in the FP at UoN

The obtained data assisted in exploring the technological tools and platforms that are mostly used in classes at the UoN. The answers are related to first research question: "What are the current technological tools used for student academic support in the FP at UoN?"

The data analysis shows that three main categories of online platforms are used for teaching English at UoN. They include video conferencing tools, social media platforms, and educational software. Overall, Table 9.1 shows that the highest percentages were assigned to the educational applications or software in both cycles, Cycle1 (C 1) and Cycle 2 (C 2). The Foundation Program (FP) at UoN is adopting a cycle system where a semester of sixteen weeks is divided into two cycles that each consists of eight weeks of teaching followed by a final assessment of students' achievement. This assessment will qualify them to stay or move to the next level. However, C1 teachers voted equally for the video conferencing tools and educational apps.

**Table 9.1:** Technological Tools Used for Student Academic Support in the FP at UoN

| Technological tools | C1 | C2 |
|---|---|---|
| Video conferencing | 74.7% | 39.7% |
| Social media platforms | 35% | 22.4% |
| Educational software | 74.7% | 77.6% |

Overall, the most commonly used platform among the teachers, based on the results above, is Educational Apps or Software (such as Kahoot). This indicates that these types of tools are highly favored for teaching purposes.

Table 9.1 shows that the respondents in C1 voted for the video conferencing tools and educational software apps, giving them a high percentage (74%) in comparison to the social media platform, which scored a less percentage (36%). However, in C2, the educational apps received the highest score (77.6%). The second rank was given to video conferencing (39%), in comparison to the social media platform that received the lowest score (22.4%).

To explore further details about the types of online tools and platforms in each category, the questionnaire survey generated several responses. In both cycles, C1 and C2, Google Meet is the most commonly used platform, with occasional mentions of Zoom and YouTube. The reliance on Google Meet may be driven by its ease of use, institutional support, or preference among instructors. Based on the responses in C1, there follows an analysis of the video conferencing tools used by respondents.

The majority of the respondents use Google Meet as their primary video conferencing tool. Many teachers indicate that they only use it when required for online classes, suggesting that it is generally employed when physical classes are not possible. A few respondents mention using Zoom, sometimes alongside Google Meet. However, it appears that Zoom is less commonly used, possibly due to institutional restrictions or preferences. A small number of responses mention using YouTube, not as a live conferencing tool, but to supplement classes with educational videos. A handful of respondents include tools like Kahoot, Mentimeter, and Wordwall, but these are likely for interactive learning rather than video conferencing. Some respondents indicated that they do not use video conferencing tools, either because their classes are face-to-face, or they do not find it necessary.

Table 9.2 provides a visual representation of the video conferencing tool usage among instructors. Google Meet is the primary tool used by about (50%) of respondents, followed by Zoom, which served as a secondary option and used by (10%) who either prefer it or use it alongside Google Meet. The third rate was given to face-to-face classes, accounting for 25%, where instructors do not use video conferencing tools as they teach in-person. The less used tools are Situational Use Only (10%), representing those who use video conferencing in specific cases, such as bad weather, and institutional requirements (5%), reflecting cases where the platform is prescribed by the institution.

**Table 9.2:** Video Conferencing Tools Used Among Teachers

| Video conferencing tool usage among instructors | Percentage |
|---|---|
| Google Meet | 50% |
| Zoom | 10% |
| Face to Face | 25% |
| Situational Use only | 10% |
| Institutionally required | 5% |

The respondents were asked to specify the categories of social media that are mostly used by them for English language teaching. The results show that WhatsApp is the most frequently mentioned platform, suggesting that it is widely used by participants as a preferred social media or communication tool.

According to Table 9.3, WhatsApp scored the highest percentage (65%) and (40%) in C1 and C2, respectively. In comparison, other platforms such as Email, Google Classroom, and YouTube are mentioned as occasionally receiving lower percentages (10%), (5%), and (3%) respectively. A few responses also indicate the use of Instagram and Twitter. A significant portion of the responses indicated no use of social media, with answers like "None," "N/A," and "No social media only emails." This suggests that a subset of participants prefer not to use social media for communication in this context. According to the category "Multiple Platform Usage," the results show that some participants listed more than one platform, such as WhatsApp and Instagram or WhatsApp and YouTube, indicating a preference for varied platforms depending on their needs.

**Table 9.3:** Social Media Platform Usage Distribution

| Social Media Platform Usage Distribution | Percentage |
|---|---|
| WhatsApp | 65% |
| None | 15% |
| Email | 10% |
| Google classroom | 5% |
| Youtube | 3% |
| Others | 2% |

The findings also show that there was a big variation in the use of educational apps between Cl and C2 – see Table 9.4. Kahoot is overwhelmingly popular, receiving the highest rate (65%) and (45%) by the majority of respondents in both cycles, respectively. It appears to be a go-to tool for interactive quizzes and classroom engagement. Other tools got the second rate in both Cycles (12%) and (16%), respectively, followed by Padlet, which got the third rate (12%) whereas in C2, it got a lower rate (8%). Mentimeter received (10%) of the responses in both C1 and C2. YouTube also received a low rate (8%) and (6%) in both C1 and C2. However, there was a variation in the percentages of using Bamboozle as only (6%) in C1 voted for it compared to (15%) in C2.

**Table 9.4:** Benefits of Implementing Technology-Based Support Systems in the FP at UoN

| App | C1 | C2 |
|---|---|---|
| Kahoot | 65% | 45% |
| Padlet | 12% | 8% |
| Mentimeter | 10% | 10% |
| Wordwall | 10% | 6% |
| YouTube | 8% | 15% |
| Moodle | 7% | – |
| Baamboozle | 6% | – |
| Others | 12% | 16% |

This section provides answers to the second research question "What are the benefits of implementing technology-based support systems in the FP at UoN?" The data shows that the respondents gave high rates to all technology platforms, Cambridge One, Presentation Plus, and Moodle.

According to Cambridge One, Table 9.5 illustrates that Cambridge One is mostly used for out-of-class activities. Around half of the respondents (47. 1%) in C1 and (50%) in C2 voted for out-of-class activities. The second rate (46%) and (43.1%) were assigned to the Both equally option. The third rate (4.6%) and (5%) in C1 and C2, respectively, was given to the "In-class activities" Option. However, the option "I never use Cambridge One" was less rated in both classes.

**Table 9.5:** Cambridge One Activities Usage

| Cambridge One Activities Usage | C1 | C2 |
|---|---|---|
| In-class activities | 4.6% | 6.9% |
| Out-of-class activities | 47.1% | 50% |
| Both equally | 46% | 43.1% |
| I have never used Cambridge One | 1.1% | 0% |
| Homework primarily | 1.1% | 0% |

Table 9.6 represents whether teachers are aware of the Cambridge One Platform is use out of class or not. It illustrates that most of the participants (78.2%) and (84.5%) in C1 and C2, respectively chose "Yes" indicating that students use it regularly. In comparison, fewer participants chose "Yes, my students use it occasionally." However, those who were "not sure" were very few (5%).

**Table 9.6:** Teachers' Awareness of Cambridge One Usage

| Teachers' Awareness of Cambridge One Usage | C1 | C2 |
|---|---|---|
| Yes, my students use it regularly | 78.2% | 84.5% |
| Yes, my students use it occasionally | 18.4% | 13.8% |
| No, students do not use it outside the classroom | 1.1% | 0% |
| Not sure | 2.3% | 1.7% |

According to the effectiveness of Cambridge One, Table 9.7 reveals that more than half of the respondents (37.9%) and (44.8) voted for its effectiveness in both C1 and C2, respectively. The second rate was given to the "Extreme Effectiveness" option (25.3%) and (27.6%) in both. Those who were neutral were around a quarter (27.6%) in C1 and less than a quarter (19%) in C2. In contrast, those who didn't vote for the effectiveness of Cambridge One were very few (5.7%) and (6.9%) in C1 and C2, respectively.

**Table 9.7:** Effectiveness of Cambridge One

| Effectiveness of Cambridge One Usage | C1 | C2 |
|---|---|---|
| Effective | 37.9% | 44.8% |
| Extreme effective | 25.3% | 27.6% |
| Not effective | 5.7% | 6.9% |
| Neutral | 27.6% | 19% |

According to the use of Presentation Plus, Table 9.8 displays that most participants (66.7%) and (75.7%) in C1 and C2, respectively, use it regularly in the classroom. Around a quarter of the participants (31%) and (22.4%) reported that they occasionally use it in the classroom, while those who voted for the "No use" were very few (5%) in both classes.

**Table 9.8:** The Use of Presentation Plus

| Presentation Plus Usage | C1 | C2 |
|---|---|---|
| Yes, regularly | 66.7% | 75.7% |
| Yes, occasionally | 31% | 22.4% |
| No | 5% | 5% |

Regarding the effectiveness of Presentation Plus in enhancing English language instruction in Table 9.9, the results indicate that more than half of the responses were assigned to the options of "Effective" and "Extremely Effective" in both cycles. The "Extremely Effective" received the highest rate (46%) and (56.9 %) in C1 and C2, respectively, followed by the "Effective" option, which received (25.3%) and (29.3) of the responses. Those who remained neutral were (27.6%) in C1 and (10.3%) in C2. In contrast, the responses to the less effective were only (1.1%) in C1 and (3.4%) in C2.

**Table 9.9:** Effectiveness of Presentation Plus

| Effectiveness of Presentation Plus Usage | C1 | C2 |
|---|---|---|
| Effective | 25.3% | 29.3% |
| Extreme effective | 46% | 56.9% |
| Not effective | 1.1% | 3.4% |
| Neutral | 27.6% | 10.3% |

As depicted in Table 9.10, the usefulness of Presentation Plus received a high rate as more than half of the responses (44.8%) and (50%) were assigned to the "Extremely Useful" option in C1 and C2, respectively. In C1, the second rate (32.2%) was given to the "Not Sure" option, while in C2, the second rate (24%) was given to the "Useful" option and those who remained neutral were (20%). However, those who disagreed on the usefulness were very few (4.6%) in C1 and (3.4%) in C2.

**Table 9.10:** The Usefulness of Presentation Plus in enhancing English language instruction

| Usefulness of Presentation Plus in enhancing English language instruction | C1 | C2 |
|---|---|---|
| Extremely useful | 44.8% | 50% |
| Not sure | 32.2% | 24% |
| Not effective | 4.6% | 3.4% |
| Neutral | 20% | 20% |

With regard to the usage of Moodle, as shown in Table 9.11, the results show that in C1, the highest rate was assigned to the out-of-class activities (59.8%), followed by both equally (39.1%), then in-class activities (14%). However, the "Other" and "I never use Moodle" options were given a lower rate (4.6%) and (3.4%), respectively. Likewise, C1, Table 11 shows that "Out of class activities" got the highest rate (65.5%) in comparison to the second-rated option "Both equally" (32.8%) and "In class option" (6.9%). The "I never use Moodle" option was given the lowest rate (1.7%).

**Table 9.11:** The Usage of Moodle

| Usage of Moodle | C1 | C2 |
|---|---|---|
| In-class activities | 14.9% | 6.9% |
| Out-of-class activities | 59.8% | 65.5% |
| Both equally | 39.1% | 32.8% |
| I never used Moodle | 4.6% | 1.7% |
| Other | 0% | 3.4% |

Concerning the effectiveness of Moodle in enhancing English language proficiency, the Likert scale in Table 9.12 displays that most of the responses were between "Agree" and "Strongly Agree" in both classes. In C1, 36.8% of instructors reported their agreement and 24.1% strong agreement in comparison to only 4.6% and 6.9% who reported their strong disagreement and agreement, respectively. Similarly, C2 responses were between "Agree" and "Strong Agree" (44.6%) and (25.9%), respectively, while only (3.4%) and (8.6%) expressed their strong agreement and disagreement. The percentages of neutral responses were (27.6%) in C1 and (17.2%) in C2.

**Table 9.12:** The Effectiveness of Moodle in Enhancing English Language Proficiency

| Effectiveness of Moodle in Enhancing English Language Proficiency | C1 | C2 |
|---|---|---|
| Agree | 36.8% | 44.6% |
| Strongly agree | 24.1% | 25.9% |
| disagree | 4.6% | 3.4% |
| Strongly disagree | 9.9% | 8.6% |

When the participants were asked about the role of Moodle in student engagement, the analysed data shows that in C1, they were between agree (29.9%) and strongly agree (28.7%) in contrast to those who expressed their disagreement (8%) and strong disagreement (5.7%). Around a quarter of the participants remained neutral. However, C2 results showed a variation in responses. Table 9.13 shows that (50%) of the participants reported their agreement, and (15.5%) reported their strong agreement in comparison to (15.5%) and (3.4%) who reported their disagreement and strong disagreement, respectively. Around (15.5%) remained neutral.

**Table 9.13:** The Role of Moodle in Student Engagement

| Role of Moodle in Student Engagement | C1 | C2 |
|---|---|---|
| Agree | 29.9% | 50% |
| Strongly agree | 28.7% | 15.5% |
| Disagree | 8% | 15.5% |
| Strongly disagree | 5.7% | 3.4% |
| Neutral | 27.6% | 15.5% |

## Qualitative Findings

This section presents the qualitative data that were collected from the open-ended questions. The findings are organized into two categories; the first category concerns the challenges, and the second one concerns the recommendations according to the third and fourth research questions.

## The Challenges of Implementing Technology-based Support Systems in the FP at UoN

The participants from both cycles (1 and 2) reported several challenges they face with the current platforms. They are listed below with a brief description of every challenge.

- Inconsistent Uploading on Moodle: Multiple responses pointed out that Moodle materials are not consistently uploaded, affecting students' ability to prepare and engage. This inconsistency caused issues with assessment and hindered proper learning progression.
- Technical Issues: Teachers faced technical difficulties, such as poor internet connectivity, non-functional projectors, or outdated classroom technological equipment, which disrupted the use of online platforms.
- Low Student Motivation and Access Issues: Some teachers highlighted that students struggle with or show low motivation for using Moodle and other platforms. Additionally, students often lack access to reliable internet or personal devices, limiting their participation.
- Frustration with Platform Complexity: Teachers found that using multiple platforms could cause more confusion than benefit, likening it to inefficient transportation systems
- Sharing Answers: Several responses indicate that students share answers on Moodle and Cambridge One, reducing the effectiveness of these platforms for genuine learning.
- Overwhelming: There are concerns that the heavy reliance on online platforms can feel overwhelming for students and may become a burden rather than a support for learning.
- Issues with University Infrastructure: Such as weak networks and outdated projectors, were noted as barriers to effectively using digital tools.

## Recommendations for Improving Technology Employment in EFL Teaching

The findings provide a set of recommendations that are outlined below.
Recommendations for Support and Training

- Teachers suggest that additional workshops and professional development would help them utilize these platforms more effectively.
- Some teachers highlight the importance of accessibility, clear communication, and technology literacy to maximize the effectiveness of online platforms.

Suggestions for Improvement:

- Platform Consolidation: Several respondents suggested simplifying the digital setup by focusing on a single platform rather than multiple tools. This would help avoid confusion and streamline students' experiences.
- Training for Teachers: Teachers expressed a need for professional development to maximize the use of online tools effectively. Training would help both new and seasoned teachers integrate digital resources into their teaching practices.
- Enhanced Classroom Infrastructure: Improving the technological infrastructure in classrooms, such as providing stable internet and functional projectors, was a common suggestion to support digital learning.
- Quality Control and Accountability: Some responses suggested stricter adherence to guidelines for platform usage, emphasizing the need for consistent implementation and follow-up to ensure a smooth learning process.
- Some respondents feel that Moodle and Cambridge One need improvements. Concerns about Moodle include inconsistent upload times for exercises and its high weight in assessment relative to Cambridge One.
- Several comments suggest that Cambridge One could be enhanced to prevent students from sharing answers and that it should display student names alphabetically for easier management.
- Teachers mentioned that there are additional tools (e.g., Socrative, Nearpod) that could be integrated to further engage students.

## Discussion of Findings

This study has revealed that the teachers in UoN use various technology platforms and technical tools. However, "Educational Apps" emerged as the most prominent tool. This finding indicates that e-learning tools such as Kahoot,

Mentimeter, Padlet, Wordwall, and the like are excellent choices for English language teaching in the context where the study takes place. The result of the study aligns with previous studies on educational technology (such as Li, et al., 2024; Noordan & Younis, 2022; Ahmed et al., 2022; Al-Khalidi, 2022) that highlight the importance of educational apps in enhancing English language teaching via providing a positive environment in the classroom and increasing students' motivation.

Regarding the benefits of implementing technology-based support systems in the FP at UoN, the main findings reveal the significant role of three categories, "Cambridge One, Moodle, and Presentation Plus," in supporting English language pedagogy. Overall, the teachers expressed their agreement regarding the use of these platforms. Perhaps the most attractive benefit of these platforms is the out-of-class activities, followed by the in-class activities. Although the findings suggest that the highest percentage was given to out-of-class activities, the indication is still positive. This implies that the benefits of these platforms are restricted not only to the in-class activities but also to the out-of-class activities. This benefit might lead to the conclusion of a similar study that was conducted by Al-Khalidi (2020) in an EFL context. In her study on classroom flipping (2020) Al-Khalidi pointed out that technology out of the classroom "serves as the driving force towards helping students, particularly the less linguistically proficient ones, to overcome issues of lack of engagement, motivation, and academic achievement" (p.10). Al-Khalidi's study also suggests that using technology platforms out of class help "empower low English proficiency students through the potential of reviewing and practicing prior to class" (p. 10).

The benefit of technology for supporting inside-classroom activities aligns with the literature on information and communication technology (ICT). The latter confirms the contribution of technology in encouraging motivation, engagement, and interaction, which is crucial for creating a dynamic-student-centered learning environment (Richards, 2005; Brown & Lee, 2014).

Among the important findings emerging from the qualitative data is the one that is related to the challenges of technology, such as inconsistent uploading on Moodle, technical issues, frustration, and complexity, sharing answers, and so on. This implies that such challenges would result in academic issues such as academic dishonesty, plagiarism, delays in resolving technical issues, and the like. Some teachers, for instance, lack the necessary skills or confidence to integrate technology effectively into the classroom. Thus, it is necessary for teachers and the management to take into consideration how to handle technology issues. In response to this issue, the fourth category of findings provides a set of recommendations that need to be taken into consideration when dealing with technology issues. In this regard, Al-Khalidi et al. (2022) conducted a study in a similar EFL context in which she pointed out that:

> Nowadays, technology is considered as an integral rather than a supplementary aspect of high-quality education within the area of TESOL. Accordingly, English language teachers need to be equipped with effective ways to integrate technology into instructional practices not only for enhancing academic outcomes but for confronting the challenges of dealing with the digital native students as well. (p. 106)

## Conclusion

This research study aimed to identify the technological tools and platforms that are currently employed in the FP at UoN. Additionally, the study sought to explore the benefits of technology and challenges that face teachers when using technology tools, platforms, and apps. Through utilizing a survey questionnaire, the study came up with several findings that indicate a significant reliance on the employment of technology in teaching English. The findings also indicate a high level of satisfaction with the integration of technology in English teaching. However, the findings explore several challenges that need to be taken into consideration when using technology in this context.

The study has contributed to the previous studies and literature on the integration of technology into the EFL classroom by providing a synthesis of theoretical and practical views that both confirmed the usefulness, effectiveness, and importance of using technology tools and platforms in the context where the study takes place. Furthermore, the study provides a set of recommendations that are of value to the stakeholders in the context of the study when designing materials, activities, assessment, and other aspects of curriculum development.

This study faced several limitations related to the sample, context, and objectives that may affect the generalizability of the findings. To address the limitations, further research is required to broaden the sample size, diversify the contexts, and expand the objectives to enhance the generalizability and depth of the findings.

## References

Abbasi, W. T., Ibrahim, A. H., & Ali, F. B. (2022). Perceptions about English as second language teachers' technology-based English language teaching in Pakistan: Attitudes, uses of technology and challenges. *Proceedings of International Conference on Emerging Technologies and Intelligent Systems: ICETIS 2021 (Volume 1)* (pp. 314–325). Springer.

Abel Jr, A. (2020). The phenomenon of learning at a distance through emergency remote teaching amidst the pandemic crisis. *Asian Journal of Distance Education, 15*(1), 127–143.

Ahmad, A., Mukhaiyar, M., & Atmazaki, A. (2022). Exploring Digital Tools for Teaching Essay Writing Course in Higher Education: Padlet, Kahoot, YouTube, Essay Bot, Grammarly. *International Journal of Interactive Mobile Technologies, 16*(13), 200–209.

Al-Ammary, J. (2012). Educational technology: A way to enhance student achievement at the University of Bahrain. *Procedia – Social and Behavioral Sciences, 55*, 248–257. doi: https://doi.org/10.1016/j.sbspro.2012.09.501

Al-Habsi, T., Al-Busaidi, S., & Al-Issa, A. (2021). Integrating technology in English language teaching through a community of practice in the Sultanate of Oman: implications for policy implementation. *Educational Research for Policy and Practice, 21*(1), 43–68.

Alkhalidi, I. (2020). Developing a flipped learning model for teaching EAP students struggling with multi-level challenges in a college context. *International Journal of Applied Linguistics and English Literature, 9*(6), 1–12.

Al-Khalidi, I. (2021a). Examining teachers' beliefs on developing a digital pedagogical framework based on the SAMR Model for undergraduate English language learning. *International Journal of English Language Education*, 9(1), 106- 125. https://doi.org/10.5296/ijele.v9i1.18306.

Al-Khalidi (2021b). How to make learning effectiveness with Mayer's multimedia instructional model? *International Journal of Science: Basic and Applied Research, 60*(4), 123–139.

Al-Khalidi, I., & Khouni, O. (2021c). Investigating the effectiveness of social media platforms (SMPs) in English language teaching and learning from EFL students' perspectives. *Journal of Applied Linguistics and Language Research, 8*(4), 46–64.

Al-Khalidi, I. M. A. N., Al Hinai, O. M. A. I. M. A., & Al Sabah, M. A. R. I. A. M. (2022). Think, Pair, and share while Using Plotagon: A Digital App for Replacing the Classroom Boredom and Demotivation with Engagement and Motivation. *International Journal of English Language Education, 10*(1), 1–20.

Al-Khalidi, I., Al-Shukaili, D. K. D., Sulaiman, M. M. S. B. A., Al Hinai, O., & Alsabah, M. (2023). Investigating The Integration of a Workplace English Digital Course into the Curriculum of the University of Technology and Applied Sciences in Oman. *Journal of Namibian Studies: History Politics Culture, 33*, 345–374.

Ammade, S., Mahmud, M., Jabu, B., & Tahmir, S. (2018). Integrating technology in English language teaching: global experiences and lessons for Indonesia. *International Journal of English Linguistics, 8*(6), 107.

Anene, J. N., Imam, H., & Odumuh, T. (2014). Problem and prospect e-learning in Nigerian universities. *International Journal of Technology and Inclusive Education (IJTIE), 3*(2), 320–327.

Ashour, S. (2019). How technology has shaped university students' perceptions and expectations around higher education: An exploratory study of the United Arab Emirates. *Studies in Higher Education, 34*(12), 2513–2525. doi: https://doi.org/10.1080/03075079.2019.1617683

Brown, H.D., and Lee, H. (2014). *Teaching by principles: An interactive approach to language pedagogy*. Pearson.

Creswell, J. W. (2007). *Qualitative inquiry and research de- sign: Choosing among five traditions*. Sage.

Christopoulos, A., & Sprangers, P. (2021). Integration of educational technology during the Covid-19 pandemic: An analysis of teacher and student receptions. *Cogent Education, 8*(1), 1964690.

Dornyei, Z. (2011). *Research methods in applied linguistics*. Oxford University Press.

Erdogdu, F., & Erdogdu, E. (2015). The impact of access to ICT, student background and school/home environment on the academic success of students in Turkey: An international comparative analysis. *Computers & Education, 82*, 26–49.

Fishman, B., Dede, C., & Means, B. (2016). Teaching and technology: New tools for new times. *Handbook of Research on Teaching, 5*, 1269–1334.

Guangul, F. M., Suhail, A. H., Khalit, M. I., & Khidhir, B. A. (2020). Challenges of remote assessment in higher education in the context of COVID-19: a case study of Middle East College. *Educational Assessment, Evaluation and Accountability, 32*, 519–535.

Gunuç, S., & Babacan, N. (2017). Technology integration in English language teaching and learning. *The Journal of Teaching English for Specific and Academic Purposes, 5*(2), 349–358.

Jose, J., & Zainol Abidin, M. J. (2015). Application of information and communication technology tools for English language teaching in an Omani context. *Arab World English Journal (AWEJ) Special Issue on CALL No. 2*. https://ssrn.com/abstract=2843977

Khodabandelou, R., That, J. E. M., Ken, T. Y., Kewen, Z., Yan, Z., & Ning, T. Y. (2016). Exploring the Main Barriers of Technology Integration in the English Language Teaching Classroom: A Qualitative Study. *International Journal of Education and Literacy Studies, 4*(1), 53–58.

Li, Y., Chen, D., & Deng, X. (2024). The impact of digital educational games on student's motivation for learning: The mediating effect of learning engagement and the moderating effect of the digital environment. *PLOS ONE, 19*(1), 1–21. https://doi.org/10.1371/journal.pone.0294350.

Mayer, R. E. (2014). Multimedia instruction. Multimedia Instruction. In J. Spector, M. Merrill, J. Elen, & M. Bishop (Eds), *Handbook of Research on Educational Communications and Technology* (pp. 385–399). Springer. https://doi.org/10.1007/978-1-4614-3185-5_31

Nkengbeza, D., Mbuzi, D., & Chainda, A. M. (2022). Challenges faced by primary school English teachers in integrating media technology in the teaching and learning of English. *Creative Education, 13*(4), 1139–1153.

Noordan, M. N. H. B., & Yunus, M. M. (2022). Using digital comprehension to improve reading comprehension skills among young learners. *International Journal of Academic Research in Progressive Education and Development, 11*(2), 727–748. https://doi.org/10.6007/IJARPED/v11- i2/11555

Poudel, A. P. (2022). Information and Communication Technology in English Language Teaching: Some Opportunities and Challenges. *Journal of Comparative and International Higher Education, 14*(4), 103–116.

Ramanair, J. (2016). Turning challenges into opportunities: Investigating technology integration in tertiary level English language programs through the lens of activity theory. In D. S. P. Gedera & P. J. Williams (Eds.), *Activity Theory in Education* (pp. 121–138). SensePublishers. https://doi.org/10.1007/978-94-6300-387-2_8

Ramorola, M. Z. (2013). The challenge of effective technology integration into teaching and learning. *Africa Education Review, 10*(4), 654–670.

Richards, J. C. (2005). *Communicative Language Teaching Today*. Singapore: SEAMEO Regional Language Centre.

Rintaningrum, R. (2023). Technology integration in English language teaching and learning: Benefits and challenges. *Cogent Education*, *10*(1). https://doi.org/10.1080/2331186X.2022.2164690

Roschelle, J. M., Pea, R. D., Hoadley, C. M., Gordin, D. N., & Means, B. M. (2000). Changing how and what children learn in school with computer-based technologies. *The Future of children*, *10*(2), 76–101.

Salehi, H., & Salehi, Z. (2012). Integration of ICT in language teaching: Challenges and barriers. *3rd International Conference on e-Education, e-Business, e-Management and e-Learning IPEDR Vol. 27* (pp. 215–219). IACSIT Press.

Sarfaraz, J. (2017). Unified theory of acceptance and use of technology (UTAUT) model-mobile banking. *Journal of Internet Banking and Commerce, 22*(3), 1–20.

Srite, M., & Karahanna, E. (2006). The Role of Espoused National Cultural Values in Technology Acceptance. *MIS Q., 30, 679–704*.

Tashkandi, A. N., & Al-Jabri, I. M. (2015). Cloud computing adoption by higher education institutions in Saudi Arabia: an exploratory study. *Cluster Computing, 18*, 1527–1537.

Yeou, M. (2016). An investigation of students' acceptance of Moodle in a blended learning setting using technology acceptance model. *Journal of Educational Technology Systems, 44*(3), 300–318.

# Enhancing L2 Learners' Awareness of Teacher's Corrective Feedback in Language Classrooms through Reflective Journal Writing

*Ehsan Rassaei*

**ABSTRACT**
This chapter draws on a study that investigated the effect of reflective journal writing on enhancing EFL learners' perceptions of an implicit form of Corrective Feedback (CF) known as recasts. The participants included 50 EFL learners who were enrolled in two intact classrooms. Participants in one EFL class were instructed to compose reflective journals at the end of the regular English classes where they received recasts for their errors. The participants in the other class received recasts for their errors but were not asked to engage in reflective journal writing. Following four treatment sessions over two weeks, the participants' awareness of recasts was explored using stimulated recall interviews. The findings revealed that learners who were engaged in reflective journal writing had significantly more accurate perceptions of recasts compared to learners who did not practice reflective journaling. The findings suggest that reflective journal writing can help L2 learners become more aware of CF they receive in language classroom and notice the mismatches between their erroneous utterances and the target-like forms.

## Introduction

One important aspect of classroom interaction in L2 language classrooms is feedback which is provided by language teachers in response to learners' errors. In recent years, researchers have looked at corrective feedback (CF) from different perspectives and provided evidence for the efficacy of CF for L2 development (e.g., Fu & Li, 2023; Nassaji, 2020; Rassaei, 2023, 2024). Two major perspectives from which CF has been investigated in recent years are the cognitive/interactionist and the sociocultural perspective. In addition to these two major approaches, there were other SLA theories that impacted the way SLA researchers studied and operationalized CF. While various L2 acquisition perspectives endorse the importance of different forms of CF for L2 development, the role of learners' noticing and attention has been underscored when evaluating the efficacy of CF. More specifically, it is believed that the efficacy of CF is predicated on learners' perceptions or awareness of the feedback provided on their errors. The accuracy of learners' perceptions of CF is often considered as a measure for evaluating the extent to which learners have noticed CF.

## CF and L2 Development

An increasing number of studies in L2 acquisition have explored the potential benefits of various CF forms for L2 development (e.g., Ellis, et al., 2006; Nassaji, 2020; Rassaei, 2024; Sheen, 2008). These studies have established that CF is in general effective for promoting L2 development, but its effectiveness might be moderated by a range of factors. Different forms of CF are identified based on various dimensions such as input providing vs. output triggering, and also implicit vs. explicit dimension (Loewen & Nabei, 2007). With regard to its input providing aspect, CF provides L2 learners with target-like forms and allows them to compare their own language production with the target norms. With respect to its output triggering function, CF can push learners to modify their language use, encouraging them to produce more accurate utterances.

Moreover, different forms of CF can be depicted on a continuum ranging from implicit to explicit. The distinction between explicit and implicit CF has significant implications for how learners process and respond to feedback and therefore for the effectiveness of CF. Explicit forms of CF, such as metalinguistic explanations, are more noticeable to learners and can capture learners' attention more effectively (Lyster & Ranta, 1997; Sheen, 2007). Therefore, learners are more likely to notice the mismatches between their incorrect and the target-like form. In contrast, implicit CF such as recasts, do not explicitly signal the error and therefore their corrective function may not be recognized by L2 learners in language classrooms.

As a commonly used implicit form of feedback, recasts occur when an instructor reformulates a learner's erroneous utterance in a correct form. Despite their frequent use in language classrooms, studies in various contexts indicated that learners often fail to notice or correctly interpret recasts, which can diminish their effectiveness (e.g., Lyster & Ranta 1997; Mackey et al., 2000). This limitation arises because the implicit nature of recasts makes them less salient, and they fail to overtly signal that an error has been made. As a result, learners may miss the corrective intent and instead interpret them as negotiation of meaning strategies.

The cognitive/interactionist perspective on SLA offers valuable insights into how CF, including recasts, facilitates language learning. This approach views language acquisition as a process driven by meaningful interaction, where cognitive mechanisms like noticing and awareness are pivotal. A central concept in this perspective is the Noticing Hypothesis (Schmidt, 1993), which states that for input to become intake, it must first be noticed by L2 learners. In this view, learners' awareness and the act of noticing specific language features or errors are crucial for effective language learning. CF, therefore, has the greatest impact when learners notice the feedback and correctly perceive why it has been provided.

Because recasts are among the most frequently used forms of CF in language classroom, a topic that merits attention is how to increase learners' awareness and the correct perceptions of recasts and as a result increase their effectiveness. One such strategy that can potentially enhance learners' awareness of recasts is to engage learners in reflective practices, which encourage them to actively think about and analyze the feedback they receive. Reflective journaling in language classrooms, in particular, holds promise as a tool for enhancing language awareness. By prompting learners to document and reflect on their classroom experiences, reflective journaling can make recasts more salient and help learners internalize the linguistic corrections provided.

This chapter explores the potential of reflective journaling as a means to increase learners' awareness and noticing of recasts, drawing on the cognitive/interactionist perspective to explain how enhanced reflection can bridge the gap between implicit feedback and successful language learning.

## Journal Writing and Learners' Reflection

While there is a considerable amount of research highlighting the potential benefits of reflective learning and teaching across various areas of education (e.g., Thorpe, 2004; Kingkaew et al., 2023; Xie, Ke, & Sharma, 2008), studies focusing on the role of reflective learning and teaching in L2 acquisition appear to be less prevalent. Nonetheless, as the recognition of the role of reflective teaching and learning in L2 acquisition research continues to grow, some L2 researchers and practitioners have explored ways to incorporate reflective practices into L2 classrooms (e.g., Abednia, et al., 2013; Lo, 2010; Shin, 2003). Raelin (2001) describes reflection as "the practice of periodically stepping back to ponder the meaning to self and to others in one's immediate environment about what has recently transpired" (p. 1). Through reflective learning, individuals may be able to make sense of their past experiences, potentially being enabled to gain more from future learning opportunities

(Daudelin, 1997). Thorpe (2004) suggests that reflection allows individuals to consider their past experiences, which may help them address questions about what they have done and the reasons behind their actions. Reflective learning can be promoted in language classrooms using different techniques. One common approach to fostering reflective learning is for learners to document their classroom experiences in a reflective journal, where they regularly document their thoughts and reflections on their classroom experiences. As noted by Richards and Farrell (2005), journal writing "serves as a means of generating questions and hypotheses about teaching and the learning process" (p. 70). In this way reflecting journal writing can be considered as a means of enhancing L2 learners' awareness in language classrooms.

Despite the theoretical arguments in favor of the role of reflective journal writing in enhancing learners' noticing of L2 features and language learning, the empirical studies examining the interplay between reflective journal writing and L2 form-focused instruction continues to be limited. More specifically, further research is needed to better understand how reflective journal writing can moderate learners' attention to language features during classroom interaction. In particular, it is interesting to know if combining journal writing with implicit forms of CF can enhance learners' perceptions and noting of such feedback forms. Among various forms of CF, as noted earlier, recasts are sometimes criticized as being implicit and therefore not salient enough to L2 learners in language classrooms. Therefore, exploring various ways of enhancing noticeability of recasts merits attention.

## The Study

As noted above, the goal of the study is to investigate how learners' awareness of recasts, which are considered as implicit forms of CF, can be enhanced through reflective journal writing. To this end the following research question guides the present study: Does reflective journal writing enhance EFL learners' awareness of recasts in response to their errors during classroom interaction?

## Participants

The participants were students at a language teaching institute in Iran. The sample consisted of 36 females and 14 males, ranging in age from 18 to 25.

All participants had completed an average of 20 months of English instruction and were either university graduates or currently enrolled in university. Additionally, two female EFL teachers, who possessed native-like proficiency in both spoken and written English, were recruited to serve as instructors during the treatment sessions and as interviewers for the stimulated recall sessions. Although intact classes were used in this study, the regular teachers were replaced by these guest instructors, as they were considered more experienced and qualified to deliver the treatment and provide corrective feedback.

## Target Forms

The study focused on two functions of the English article system as its target structures. Specifically, the definite article "the," used to refer to someone or something previously mentioned, and the indefinite article "a," used for first mentions. Articles were selected as the target forms following an interview with the EFL teachers who taught the participant classes. During the stimulated recall interviews, the teachers highlighted that articles were among the linguistic forms their learners found particularly challenging.

## Data Collection Procedure

The four intact classes in this study were identified in terms of one of the following conditions:

- recasts/reflective (n=26),
- recasts/non-reflective (n=24),

Over two weeks, participants took part in four treatment sessions. Additionally, a preparatory session was conducted for the reflective group prior to the first treatment session, where they were introduced to the concept of reflective learning through journal writing and received instructions on how to reflect on their learning experiences. During the treatment sessions, learners in both groups were engaged in storytelling tasks and received recasts exclusively for errors related to the target forms. At the end of each session, participants in the journal writing group reflected on their learning experiences by writing in journals. Participants of the non-reflective condition performed the same storytelling activities and received recasts for their errors, but they were not asked to do reflective journal writing at the end of each session.

Each storytelling task followed a structured procedure. Learners were divided into groups of three, with each group receiving a story accompanied by 10 sequenced pictures. They collaboratively read and practiced retelling the story for 10 minutes in preparation for a retelling activity without the aid of the text. Groups were then called upon individually to present their story to the class, with each learner narrating two sentences. During each treatment session, the teacher corrected article-related errors using recasts, while errors in other structures were ignored. Each treatment session involved a unique story for each group. In the first three storytelling sessions, participants practiced and presented one story per session. However, during the fourth session (day 13), which involved videotaping learners' interactions in the recast groups for stimulated recall interviews, each group practiced and presented two stories. On average, it took approximately 13 minutes for each group to present a story. Post-tests were conducted the day after the final treatment session, followed by stimulated recall interviews the next day.

## Learners' Reflection

As noted above, the learners were classified into two groups, namely reflective and non-reflective, with the reflective groups engaging in activities designed to promote reflective learning. Prior to the first treatment session, reflective learners participated in a 45-minute instructional session conducted by a teacher. This session introduced them to the concept of reflective learning, journal writing, and strategies for becoming effective reflective learners. The purpose of journal writing was explained as a self-dialogue process, not meant for evaluation or approval, and learners were shown a sample journal by the researcher. The specific purpose of journal writing to enhance the noticeability of recasts was not disclosed to maintain the study's integrity. Reflective learners then practiced journal writing based on their experiences in this preparatory session.

Throughout the study, the reflective groups completed journal writing in five sessions, including the preparatory session and the four treatment sessions. After each treatment session, following a 15-minute break, they spent 30 minutes responding to reflective questions provided to guide their writing.

In the second, third, and fourth treatment sessions, learners reviewed and reflected on their previous journal entries for 10 minutes before answering new reflective questions. To make the process easier, learners were allowed to write their answers in Farsi, their native language. This approach followed Holly's (1984) framework of journal writing as a two-stage cyclical process: reflecting while writing and later reconsidering journal entries. The specific reflective questions are provided below:

1. What did you learn in this session?
2. What caught your attention during class activities?
3. What aspects of the class were most interesting to you?
4. What are some examples of what you have learnt in this session?
5. What difficulties or problems did you experience during the class time?
6. Which activity was most beneficial to you?
7. What are your expectations of a language learning classroom in general?

## Measuring Learners' Perceptions of Recasts

To examine the effects of journal writing on learners' interpretations of recasts, stimulated recall interviews were conducted on the final day of the study for the recast groups. During each interview, learners watched a videotape of their storytelling presentations from the last treatment session, which included errors they had received recasts for. After each instance of corrective feedback, the video was paused, and the learner was asked to verbalize their thoughts at the moment of receiving the feedback. Prior to viewing these feedback episodes, each learner was given a set of instructions on how to reflect and articulate their thoughts during the process.

In order to reduce the obviousness of the study's purpose, one non-recast episode was included for every three recast episodes. To support their verbal reflections, learners were permitted to pause the video whenever they wished to re-watch a part that they found necessary. Additionally, to ease the process of verbalizing their thoughts, the interviews were conducted in the learners' first language (L1). The entire session was videotaped for subsequent analysis.

## Analysis

Learners' perceptions of recasts following the stimulated recall interviews were transcribed and analyzed using the following framework:

1. Noticed: learners' perceptions were coded as noticed if a learner could identify the source of error for which he/she received feedback.
2. Partially noticed: learners' perceptions were coded as partially noticed if the learner could acknowledge making an error for which he/she received feedback but was unable to identify the grammatical source of the error.
3. Not noticed: learners' perceptions were coded as "not noticed" if the learner was unable to identify teacher's recasts following his/her errors as CF.

## Results

Table 10.1 indicates learners' perceptions of recasts for both reflective and non-reflective groups.

**Table 10.1:** Learners' Perceptions of Recasts

| | Noticed as CF | | Partially noticed | | Not noticed | |
|---|---|---|---|---|---|---|
| Type | Count | % | Count | % | Count | % |
| Reflective | 30 | 35.7 | 45 | 53.6 | 9 | 10.7 |
| Non-reflective | 15 | 19.7 | 32 | 42.1 | 29 | 38.2 |

The results presented in Table 10.1 reveal a notable difference in learners' awareness of recasts across the two conditions. In the reflective group, 35.7% of learners clearly noticed the recasts as corrective feedback, and 53.6% partially noticed them. Only 10.7% failed to notice the feedback. Conversely, in the non-reflective group, just 19.7% noticed the recasts, 42.1% partially noticed them, and a significant 38.2% did not notice them at all. A chi-square test of independence was conducted to examine whether this difference between reflective and non-reflective learners was statistically significant in terms of their perceptions of recasts. The results revealed a significant association between instructional condition and learners' perception of recasts, $\chi^2$ (2) = 17.36, $p < .001$. This suggests that the reflective condition had a meaningful impact on learners' ability to notice and interpret recasts as CF.

Overall, these findings highlight the potential benefits of incorporating reflective activities, such as journal writing, into language instructions to enhance learners' awareness of recasts.

## Discussion and Conclusion

The main aim of the present study was to investigate the effects of learners' reflective practice through reflective journal writing on L2 learners' perceptions of recasts. The findings indicated that learners who were engaged in reflective journaling during the treatment sessions were more capable of identifying recasts as CF. Learners in the reflective condition, who engaged in journal writing, were more likely to notice or partially notice recasts compared to those in the non-reflective condition. The statistically significant difference between the two groups ($p < .001$) suggests that structured reflection plays a crucial role in helping learners recognize implicit feedback. These results support the view that noticing can be facilitated through pedagogical interventions and particularly reflective practices that promote conscious attention to feedback.

An important issue to discuss with regard to the role of reflective journal writing in enhancing learners' awareness of recasts is how learners' reflections through journal writing can improve the accuracy of their perceptions of recasts. The value of journal writing in enhancing learners' awareness of CF may be associated with its ability to encourage reflective thinking, which, in turn, enhances learners' self-awareness regarding their learning processes. By fostering reflection, journal writing helps learners become more attuned to various aspects of classroom instruction. As Andrusyszyn and Davie (1997) pointed out, "journal writing can engage an individual in conversation with the self, promoting the development of introspective awareness" (p. 7). Research across different educational fields also provides evidence that writing, especially journal writing, facilitates understanding, deeper cognitive processing, and improved learning outcomes (e.g., Berthold, Nückles, & Renkl, 2007; Hancock, 1992; Wong, Kuperis, Jamieson, Keller, & Cull-Hewitt, 2002). Thus, the findings of the present study provide further evidence that journal writing can be utilized as an awareness raising tool in language classrooms.

Regarding the role of journal writing in enhancing learners' awareness and noticing in language learning, the results of the present study are especially significant given that due to their implicit nature, recasts are often considered as a less noticeable form of feedback compared to other forms of CF. Some studies also indicated that in general recasts are less effective than more explicit forms of feedback on the grounds that they are less noticeable to L2 learners (e.g., Rassaei, 2023, 2024, Sheen, 2008). However, despite this limitation, recasts are also considered efficient in language classrooms because they correct learners' errors without disrupting communication. As noted above, one concern with the use of recasts is that since they are reformulations of learners' errors, they may be misinterpreted by learners as non-corrective and interactional comments. Therefore, teachers might be looking for how to increase the noticeability of recasts.

According to the findings of the present study, reflective journal writing can be an effective tool for increasing learners' awareness of classroom interactions and in particular recasts. One important implication of the present study for language teachers is that reflective journal writing can be considered as an effective tool for increasing learners' noticing and awareness of specific language features as well as different aspects of classroom interactions such as CF. While the present study investigated the effects of reflective journal writing on learners' perceptions of recasts, one suggestion for further research is to examine the effects of journal writing on learners' perceptions of written feedback. Replicating the present study with other modalities of CF such as written feedback can shed further light on the role of journal writing in enhancing L2 learners' perceptions of CF and other aspects of classroom interaction.

## References

Abednia, A., Hovassapian, A., Teimournezhad, S., & Ghanbari, N. (2013). Reflective journal writing: Exploring in-service EFL teachers' perceptions. *System*, *41*(3), 503–514.

Berthold, K., Nückles, M., & Renkl, A. (2007). Do learning protocols support learning strategies and outcomes? The role of cognitive and metacognitive prompts. *Learning and Instruction*, *17*(5), 564–577.

Daudelin, M. W. (1997). Learning from experience through reflection. *Organizational Dynamics, 24*(3), 36–48.

Ellis, R., Loewen, S., & Erlam, R. (2006). Implicit and explicit corrective feedback and the acquisition of L2 grammar. *Studies in Second Language Acquisition*, *28*, 339–368.

Fu, M., & Li, S. (2020). The effects of immediate and delayed corrective feedback on L2 development. *Studies in Second Language Acquisition*, *44*, 2–34.

Hancock, M. R. (1992). Literature response journals: Insights beyond the printed page. *Language Arts, 69*(1), 36–42.

Holly, M. L. (1984). *Keeping a personal-professional journal*. Deakin University Press.

Kingkaew, C., Theeramunkong, T., Supnithi, T., Chatpreecha, P., Morita, K., Tanaka, K., & Ikeda, M. (2023). A Learning Environment to Promote Awareness of the Experiential Learning Processes with Reflective Writing Support. *Education Sciences*, *13*(1), 64. https://doi.org/10.3390/educsci13010064.

Lo, Y. F. (2010). Implementing reflective portfolios for promoting autonomous learning among EFL college students in Taiwan. *Language Teaching Research, 14*(1), 77–95.

Loewen, S., & Nabei, T. (2007). Measuring the effects of oral corrective feedback on L2 knowledge. In A. Mackey (Ed.), *Conversational interaction in second language acquisition: A collection of empirical studies* (pp. 361–376). Oxford University Press.

Lyster, R., & Ranta, L. (1997). Corrective feedback and learner uptake: Negotiation of form in communicative classrooms. *Studies in second language acquisition*, *19*(1), 37–66.

Mackey, A., Gass, S., & McDonough, K. (2000). How do learners perceive interactional feedback?. *Studies in Second Language Acquisition, 22*(4), 471–497.

Nassaji, H. (2020). Assessing the effectiveness of interactional feedback for L2 acquisition: Issues and challenges. *Language Teaching*, *53*(1), 3–28.

Rassaei, E. (2023). The interplay between corrective feedback timing and foreign language anxiety in L2 development. *Language Teaching Research*, *0*(0). https://doi.org/10.1177/13621688231195141 Rassaei, E. (2024).

The effects of recasts on L2 grammar: A meta-analysis. *The Language Learning Journal*, *52*(1), 16–36.

Raelin, J. A. (2001). Public reflection as the basis of learning. *Management Learning*, *32*(1), 11–30.

Richards, J. C., & Farrell, T. S. C. (2005). *Professional development for language teachers*. Cambridge University Press.

Schmidt, R. (1993). Awareness and second language acquisition. *Annual Review of Applied Linguistics*, *13*, 206–226.

Sheen, Y. (2007). The effects of corrective feedback, language aptitude, and learner attitudes on the acquisition of English articles. In A. Mackey (Ed.), *Conversational interaction in second language acquisition* (pp. 301–322). Oxford University Press.

Sheen, Y. (2008). Recasts, language anxiety, modified output, and L2 learning. *Language Learning*, *58*, 835–874.

Shin, S. J. (2003). The reflective L2 writing teacher. *ELT Journal*, *57*(1), 3–10.

Thorpe, K. (2004). Reflective learning journals: From concept to practice. *Reflective Practice*, *5*(3), 327–343.

Wong, B. Y., Kuperis, S., Jamieson, D., Keller, L., & Cull-Hewitt, R. (2002). Effects of guided journal writing on students' story understanding. *The Journal of Educational Research*, *95*, 179–191.

Xie, Y., Ke, F., & Sharma, P. (2008). The effect of peer feedback for blogging on college students' reflective learning processes. *The Internet and Higher Education*, *11*(1), 18–25.

# Afterword: Reflective Practice and Beyond

*Peter I. De Costa*

Fifteen years ago, when I first started teaching graduate students in California at the Middlebury Institute of International Studies at Monterey, one of the courses assigned to me was a pedagogical methods course. And while I did not have an official course textbook, I found myself drawing heavily on Kumaravadivelu's (2003) book, *Beyond methods: Macrostrategies for language teaching*. This book espoused a *postmethod* stance, that as radical as it may seem, is one that believes that teachers should not be bound to a set of cookie cutter pedagogical practices, in particular practices imported from the West and applied in non-Western educational contexts without question. Depending on how you frame it, my general sentiment has always been that we should eschew scripted curricula where teachers fail to customize their instruction and tailor it according to local student needs. One way to ensure that teachers "construct their own personal theory of learning" (Kumaravadivelu, 2003, p. 17), and correspondingly design their own instruction is through having them engage in reflective practice. On this topic, Farrell (2025) rightly observed that:

> [W]hen teachers engage in reflective practice, they have the opportunity to examine their relations with students, their values, their abilities, and their successes and failures in a realistic context. Teachers who engage in reflective practice can develop a deeper understanding of their teaching, assess their professional growth, develop more informed decision-making skills, and become proactive and confident in their teaching. (p.2)

In the above quote, Farrell addresses *what* reflective practice entails (e.g., an examination of teacher selves) and the benefits of participating in such an important endeavor (e.g., to gain a deeper understanding of their teaching). In that same chapter, Farrell goes on to explain *how* to engage in reflective practice and *when* to do this. With respect to the former, he provides several valuable pointers, suggesting among other things that they write teaching journals, find critical friends, join teacher reflection groups, conduct classroom observations, and carry out action research. And drawing on the work of the iconic educational reformer, John Dewey, Farrell underscores that reflective practice is a constant process, which should span the entirety of one's professional teaching career (Dewey, 1933).

Crucially, the aforementioned essential concerns of the *what*, *why*, *when* and *how* of reflective practice are well addressed in this volume edited by Peter Mitchell and Saleh Al-Busaidi. By bringing together scholars from across Oman, the contributors to this book demonstrate how reflective practice in the Sultanate can be elevated to a new level within their higher education context. For example, as to *what* reflective practice is, Mitchell (Chapter 1) explains that it involves an exploration of the relationship between teachers' beliefs, knowledge and actions. As to *why* should we incorporate reflective practice into our pedagogical repertoires, we are reminded that it can help support students (e.g., Chapter 9 by Al Rahbi and colleagues), and thus enhance their learning. The chapters in this volume also do an excellent job in showing us *how* to execute reflective practice successfully. In alignment with Farrell's recommendations stated earlier, such success can be achieved through carrying classroom observations (e.g., Chapter 5 by Al Hasani), keeping reflective journals (e.g., Chapter 3 by Elsayed and Chapter 10 by Rassaei), and peer mentoring (e.g., Chapter 3 by Elsayed and Chapter 4 by Poole). Crucially, we are alerted to the value of harnessing technology in general (e.g., Chapter 5 by Al Hasani and Chapter 9 by Al Rahbi and colleagues) and AI in particular (e.g., Chapter 7 by Salah El Din and Chapter 8 by Al Zakwani) to facilitate reflective practices. Equally important to note is that these reflective practices need to be carried out in conversation with prevailing standards, such as the local Omani Interstate Teacher Assessment and Support Consortium (InTASC) standards (Chapter 2 by Al-Rawahi and Al-Balushi) and the International Society for Technology in Education (ISTE) standards (Chapter 8 by Al Zakwani). As to *when* exactly such reflection should occur, Mitchell (Chapter 1) informs us that it should take place prior to teaching (reflection-for-action), during teaching (reflection-in-action) and after teaching (reflection-on-action).

Notably, we are encouraged by the contributing authors to adopt a structured approach when it comes to embarking on reflective teaching practices, with a long-term view to develop a culture of reflective practice that involves different stakeholders such as administrators (Siddique in Chapter 6), as well as academic staff and legislators (Salah El Din in Chapter 7). Put simply, reflective practice is a collaborative enterprise. Indeed, this book is a valuable addition to the extensive body of work on teaching reflective practices (e.g., Eickoff & De Costa, 2018; Ustuk & De Costa, 2020), to which I have also had the privilege of contributing. In my more recent scholarship, I have started to move away from the notion of reflection to that of reflexivity, inspired in part by the work of Julian Edge (2011) and other critical teacher educators. One primary difference between reflection and reflexivity is that the latter also emphasizes the importance of taking into consideration sociopolitical inequities during the self-evaluation and self-reflective process. I provide one brief example next. In Kennedy and De Costa (2023), I report on how my co-author, Laura Kennedy (my former doctoral student at the time) negotiated the tensions between being a student teacher educator (Kennedy) and a faculty teacher educator (me) as we developed a course for master's students. We also factored in the graduate student-professor power dynamics between us as well as working with colleagues who assisted with setting up practicum possibilities for our students. By focusing on the political dimensions of our complex arrangement, we were able to highlight the collaborative nature of engaging in reflexivity. In other words, the reflection enterprise needs to take issues of power into account.

Returning to this volume, a reflective (or my preferred term *reflexive*) practitioner would need to go beyond investigating the relationship between teachers' beliefs, knowledge, and action. Rather than focusing only on beliefs and knowledge, teachers' identities and emotions also need to be taken into careful consideration (for an elaboration, see De Costa, 2025; De Costa & Nazari, 2024; De Costa & Uysal, 2025) because identity and emotion are often sites of political struggle. That is, teachers often have to deal with a slew of politically-inflected problems such as power inequalities at the work place, unequal access to pedagogical resources, or having to comply with externally imposed standards that they are expected to meet. Circling back to the Omani higher education context, one way to develop reflexivity would be to have teachers problematize the Interstate Teacher Assessment and Support Consortium (InTASC) standards described by Al-Rawahi and Al-Balushi in Chapter 2 and have them think about the ideologies – and by extension the potential inequities – that may be embedded within such standards. In short, a thoughtful evaluation of teachers' professional identity and the emotional tensions that may stem from sociopolitical factors may help address larger issues within education such as teacher burnout, and thus enhance the value and significance of reflection.

Almost a century ago, the educational visionary John Dewey (Dewey, 1933) argued that three essential attitudes were central to developing a reflective disposition. These attitudes were: *wholeheartedness* (i.e., that practitioners continually reflect and seek professional development throughout their career), *open-mindedness* (i.e., that practitioners not be afraid to heed the evidence they obtained from their systematic reflections and admit that they could be wrong), and *responsibility* (i.e., practitioners consider the consequences of their actions on their students' learning, their school, and the community in which they teach). Admittedly, these attitudes still ring true today. And they remain important now more than ever, especially at a time when education systems across the globe are facing a rise in the use of AI and emergent neo-nationalism. But as we enter the second quarter of the 21st century, teacher education needs to do more than just develop reflective practitioners. We need to cultivate reflexive practitioners who are committed to enhancing their instruction on both a cognitive and sociopolitical level.

## References

De Costa, P. I. (2025). Pedagogizing Identity: Why it Matters, and Where do we go from Here? *RELC Journal*, *56*(1), 214–218. https://doi.org/10.1177/0033688225132118

De Costa, P. & Nazari, M. (2024). Emotion as pedagogy: why the emotion labor of L2 educators matters. *International Review of Applied Linguistics in Language Teaching*, *62*(3), 1159–1168. https://doi.org/10.1515/iral-2024-0218

De Costa, P. I., & Uysal, H. (2025). An interview with Peter De Costa on language teacher emotions and identities. *TESOL Journal*. https://doi.org/10.1002/tesj.70041

Dewey, J. (1933). *How we think*. University of Wisconsin Press.

Edge, J. (2011). *The reflexive teacher educator in TESOL*. Routledge.

Eickoff, L., & De Costa, P. I. (2018). Collaborative teaching reflection: Insights on a globalized partnership. *ELT Journal*, *72*(2), 121–130.

Farrell, T. S. (2025). Reflective practice for language teachers. In H. Nassaji (Ed.), *The TESOL encyclopedia of English language teaching* (pp. 1–8). John Wiley & Sons, Inc.

Kennedy, L. M., & De Costa, P. I. (2023). Reflexivity, emerging expertise, and mi[s-step]s: A collaborative self-study of two TESOL teacher educators. In. S. Cansoli & S. Ganassin (Eds.), *Reflexivity in applied linguistics: Opportunities, challenges, and suggestions* (pp. 153–170). Routledge.

Kumaravadivelu, B. (2003). *Beyond methods: Macrostrategies for language teaching*. Yale University Press.

Ustuk, O., & De Costa, P. I. (2020). Reflection as meta-action: Lesson study and EFL teacher professional development. *TESOL Journal*. https://doi.org/10.1002/tesj.531

# Contributors

**Salwa Al Anqoodi** is a TESOL instructor and supervisor of the Language Enhancement Center (ANJIZ) at the University of Nizwa. Her interests in research include e-learning, computer-assisted language learning programs, language acquisition, motivation, social networking learning, foreign languages, and qualitative research. She is also an active researcher and peer reviewer for The Research Council in Oman, helping to expand knowledge in the field of TESOL.

**Sulaiman M. Al-Balushi** is Professor of Science Education, Quality Assurance Director, and former Dean of the College of Education at Sultan Qaboos University. He is a recipient of the Royal Order of Commendation (Research Field), Oman (2024), Hamdan-ALECSO Award for Distinguished Educational Research-2024, and Abdul Hameed Shoman Award for Arab Researchers in 2019, as well as several other national and international awards. He is a member of the Board of Directors of the Omani Academic Accreditation Authority, Quality Assurance of Education (OAAAQA), and serves on the editorial boards of several refereed educational journals. He earned his PhD from the University of Iowa (USA) and has published numerous papers in refereed journals. He has headed several funded research projects and contributed to the authorship of numerous refereed books, and book chapters.

**Saleh Al-Busaidi** is Dean and Professor of English as a Foreign Language at the College of Education, Sultan Qaboos University (SQU), Sultanate of Oman. He received his BA in TEFL at Sultan Qaboos University, his MA in TEFL at the University of Exeter, and his PhD in curriculum studies at the University of Illinois at Urbana-Champaign. He previously served as Director of the Language Centre at SQU (2010 – 2016). He has also chaired and taken part in many committees and project teams in and outside SQU. Dr. Al-Busaidi has also served on several audit and accreditation review panels, and participated in many national and international conferences and symposia. He has published many journal articles and book chapters on a range of topics. His main research interests are learner autonomy, material development, study/academic skills, academic readiness and language acquisition.

**Iman Al Hajri** serves as Quality Management Officer at the Foundation Institute, University of Nizwa. She earned her bachelor's degree from the University of Nizwa and pursued further studies in Applied Linguistics at the University of Vienna. She is currently pursuing her MA in TESOL at the University of Nizwa. She has extensive experience in teaching English as a Foreign Language at university level and has also coordinated and taught TOEFL preparation courses. In addition, she has contributed to the development of assessment and supplementary English language materials for the Foundation Institute. In her current role, Iman develops teacher professional development and support sessions. Her research currently focuses on mentoring programs and teacher development.

**Sulaiman Al Hasani** is Deputy Dean (Academic Affairs and Resources) at the Global College of Engineering and Technology. He received a BEng (Hons) degree in Electrical and Computer Systems Engineering and a PhD in Electrical and Electronics Engineering from Monash University and received a postgraduate certificate in academic practice from the University of the West of England. His research interests and activities are in areas such as signal processing, compressive sensing, deep learning, and robotics, and an increasing interest and dedication to leadership in higher education to address aspects of quality education, accessibility, and inclusivity within higher education.

**Iman Al-Khalidi** is Professor at the University of Technology and Applied Sciences, Sultanate of Oman. She also lectures at the University of Toronto. Iman holds a PhD in Teaching English to Speakers of Other Languages from the University of Exeter, UK. She holds a bachelor's degree in English language and Linguistics and a master's in applied linguistics from the University of Baghdad. Iman also completed a diploma in Instructional Design from Seneca College in Toronto and a postgraduate degree in TESL from Humber College in Toronto and TESL Canada from the Canadian Center for Language and Cultural Studies. She holds certificates in teaching business English, IELTS, and teaching effectiveness. She has participated in numerous research projects on course design, instructional design, and digital pedagogy. She has given several invited/plenary talks at international conferences.

**Ahmed Al Rahbi** is Director of the Foundation Institute at the University of Nizwa. He holds a BA in TESOL from the University of Leeds, an MA in TESL from Northern Arizona University, and a PhD in Educational Innovation and Lifelong learning from the University of Deusto. He is also an external reviewer for Foundation Programs at the Oman Authority for Academic Accreditation and Quality Assurance of Education (OAAAQA) and an Academic Supervisor of M.A. theses. His research interests focus on Applied Linguistics and Teacher Education.

**Sharifa S. Al-Rawahi** is a Senior Professional Development Program Evaluation Specialist at the Ministry of Education in the Sultanate of Oman, holding a PhD in Education with a specialization in Science Curricula and Teaching Methods from Sultan Qaboos University. She also holds a master's degree in education from Sultan Qaboos University, a Professional Diploma in Communication and Information Technology in Education (ICTE) from the University of Jordan in collaboration with Al-Faisal Academy and Ohio University (USA), and a bachelor's degree in education, specializing in Physics/Chemistry, from the College of Education in Rustaq. She has published different research papers and participated in several local and international educational conferences.

**Shams Salim Al Zakwani** is a Digital Content Specialist in the Specialized Institute for the Professional Training of Teachers at the Ministry of Education, Sultanate of Oman. With a bachelor's degree in physics education and a master's in instructional and learning technologies at Sultan Qaboos University, Shams is deeply passionate about leveraging technology to enhance education. Shams focuses on pioneering AI-driven solutions and pedagogical innovations for educational advancement. Her fervor lies in bridging the gap between traditional teaching methods and modern digital approaches, particularly in designing professional development programs tailored for educators and crafting engaging digital educational content.

**Peter I. De Costa** is Professor in the Department of Linguistics, Languages & Cultures and the Department of Teacher Education at Michigan State University, where he directs the master's in TESOL program in the College of Arts & Letters. He is also the English as a Second Language (ESL) graduate director in the College of Education. As a critical applied linguist, his research areas include emotions, identity, ideology and ethics in language learning, language teaching, and language policy. His work has appeared in *AILA Review*, *Applied Linguistics Review*, *International Journal of Applied Linguistics*, *Language Learning*, *Language Policy*, *Language Teaching*, *Linguistics and Education*, *Research in the Teaching of English*, *System*, *TESOL Quarterly*, and *The Modern Language Journal*. He recently guest edited special journal issues that focus on language teacher emotions. He is the co-editor of *TESOL Quarterly* and the Immediate Past President of the American Association for Applied Linguistics.

**Mohamed Salah El Din** is Senior Lecturer in the Faculty of Information Technology at Majan University College. He has a master's in international transport & logistics from the Arab Academy for Science, Technology and Maritime Transport (AAST), and extensive industry experience in shipping and logistics. Certified by the Association for Supply Chain Management (ASCM) and having taken several courses on AI and digital transformation, Mohamed adds industry validation and cutting-edge knowledge to his research. Mohamed's accomplishments include securing multiple research grants, and winning several research competitions. He has published on AI adoption in management, including a groundbreaking book on using ChatGPT in academia, and is currently co-editing a book on the broader scope of AI use in higher education.

**Mohamed Abdelraouf Attia Elsayed** is Associate Professor of Foundations and Educational Administration in the College of Education at Sultan Qaboos University. He earned his BA with distinction in English and obtained an MA and a doctorate in foundations of education with distinction from Al-Azher University. Mohamed has diverse experience in teaching, intercultural communication, and teacher education at undergraduate and postgraduate levels. He has supervised more than 65 theses. His research interests focus on methods and ethics of academic research, contemporary technologies and their applications in education and research, sustainable development, identity, cultural diversity and citizenship, and contemporary trends in teacher education and the internationalization of programs.

**Peter Mitchell** is Head of the Faculty of English Language Studies and Associate Professor at Majan University College. He earned his BA with distinction in liberal arts from Durham University. He holds a master's with distinction in teacher education from the University of Oxford and a doctorate in language education from the University of Derby. He is a Fellow of the UK's Royal Society of Arts and Chartered Institute of Linguists, and Senior Fellow of the Higher Education Academy (Advance HE). He has consulted leaders of educational institutions in various countries and is an external reviewer for the Ministry of Higher Education, Research & Innovation and Oman Authority for Academic Accreditation and Quality Assurance of Education. His research focuses on teacher education and institutional development.

**Brian Poole** is a Visiting Expert in Teaching Quality and former Associate Dean (Teaching, Research & Innovation) at Majan University College. He received his doctorate in education from the University of Bath. His teaching and thesis supervision have been mainly in applied linguistics, although he has also published papers on various aspects of higher education, including quality assurance and doctoral education. He has presented conference papers in a range of countries, including Greece, Turkey, Thailand, Singapore, Kazakhstan, Ukraine, Serbia and Oman. He is an external reviewer for the Oman Authority for Academic Accreditation and Quality Assurance of Education, and an external examiner for Durham University.

**Ehsan Rassaei** is Professor of Applied Linguistics and Director of Studies for the MA in Applied Linguistics at Majan University College. He has published in top international journals such as System, Computer Assisted Language Learning, Language Teaching Research, Modern Language Journal, and Computer Assisted Language Learning. His areas of interest include corrective feedback in language classrooms, dynamic assessment, vocabulary teaching and computer-mediated language learning. He is particularly interested in investigating the application of different forms of technology to language teaching.

**Mohammed Siddique** is Head of Registry Systems and Examinations at Majan University College. He has coordinated and developed many real-time large-scale applications in IT companies using both Microsoft and Java platforms with the latest technologies on several domains. He is a Senior Fellow of the UK's Higher Education Academy, and has a doctorate and master's in computer applications, bachelor's in computer science and many certifications.

**Higher Education Research and Policy (HERP)**

Edited by Marek Kwiek

Vol. 1 Marek Kwiek / Andrzej Kurkiewicz (eds.): The Modernisation of European Universities. Cross-National Academic Perspectives. 2012.

Vol. 2 Marek Kwiek / Peter Maassen (Eds.): National Higher Education Reforms in a European Context. Comparative Reflections on Poland and Norway. 2012.

Vol. 3 Marek Kwiek: Knowledge Production in European Universities. States, Markets, and Academic Entrepreneurialism. 2013.

Vol. 4 Pavel Zgaga / Ulrich Teichler / John Brennan (eds.): The Globalisation Challenge for European Higher Education. Convergence and Diversity, Centres and Peripheries. Second Revised Edition. 2016.

Vol. 5 Jelena Branković / Maja Kovačević / Peter Maassen / Bjørn Stensaker / Martina Vukasović (eds.): The Re-Institutionalization of Higher Education in the Western Balkans. The Interplay between European Ideas, Domestic Policies, and Institutional Practices. 2014.

Vol. 6 Hamish Coates (ed.): Higher Education Learning Outcomes Assessment. International Perspectives. 2014.

Vol. 7 Gabriella Pusztai: Pathways to Success in Higher Education. Rethinking the Social Capital Theory in the Light of Institutional Diversity. 2015.

Vol. 8 Pavel Zgaga / Ulrich Teichler / Hans G. Schuetze / Andrä Wolter (eds.): Higher Education Reform: Looking Back – Looking Forward. 2016. 2nd Revised Edition 2019.

Vol. 9 Ahoud Al-Asfour: Higher Education Privatization in Kuwait. A Study in the Processes of Policy Production. 2019.

Vol. 10 Marta Kowalczuk-Walędziak: Building a Research-Rich Teaching Profession. The Promises and Challenges of Doctoral Studies as a Form of Teacher Professional Development. 2021.

Vol. 11 Gabriella Pusztai and Klára Kovács (eds.): Well-Being of Academic Staff in Rapidly Changing Higher Education. A Focus on Central and Eastern Europe. 2025.

Vol. 12 Peter Mitchell and Saleh Al-Busaidi (eds.): Reflective Practice for Elevating Higher Education: Voices from Oman. 2026.

**www.peterlang.com**

www.ingramcontent.com/pod-product-compliance
Ingram Content Group UK Ltd.
Pitfield, Milton Keynes, MK11 3LW, UK
UKHW041827100926
8556IPUK00002B/60

9 783631 926413